My Adventures in Marketing

Marketing

The Autobiography of Philip Kotler

by Philip Kotler

MY ADVENTURES IN MARKETING

ISBN# 978-0-9905767-6-1

Cover photograph: Paul Cohan

Published by IDEA BITE PRESS
www.ideabitepress.com
Printed in the United States of America

About Philip Kotler

"There's only one name in marketing: Phil Kotler. His latest may be his best–a summa that captures the best of his insights, as original today as when he first took pen in hand, forty years ago."

Tom Peters, author of *In Search of Excellence*

"What Peter Drucker is to management, Philip Kotler is to marketing. Kotler's ideas are endlessly interesting, relevant, and ahead of the times."

Al Ries, author of *The Fall of Advertising and the Rise of PR*

"An unrivalled opportunity to spend quality time with one of the leading marketing thinkers in the world."

Leonard L. Berry, Texas A&M University

"An amazing guide to marketing excellence, with original and powerful advice…from one of the greatest minds in marketing today."

Kevin J. Clancy, Chairman and CEO, Copernicus

"A masterful job by the master thinker about marketing…The latest thinking on all the enduring issues of how to find, win, and keep customers."

George S. Day, Wharton School, U. of Pennsylvania

"Everyone says we need really new products, but Kotler actually gives the reader effective and practical concepts and tools to create them based on thinking across rather than within markets."

Glen L. Urban, Sloan School, M.I.T.

"To many marketing students and marketing practitioners around the world, 'marketing' and 'Kotler' are two synonymous concepts…No other single individual has influenced the marketing field more than Philip Kotler."

Torger Reve, Wil Wilhelmsen Chair in Strategy and Professor of Marketing, BI Norwegian School of Management

---

"Philip Kotler is again leading the way in strategic marketing with timely insight into a transformational period. Marketing 3.0 makes a compelling case for the competitive benefits of tapping into the human spirit to engage consumers."

Dennis Dunlap, past CEO, American Marketing Association

"Phil Kotler is the reigning sage of marketing, with vast knowledge, penetrating insight, and a fabulous ability to synthesize a complex topic into truthful simplicity. A master teacher, Kotler continues to shape the minds of marketing leaders around the world–and through his writing, he can shape your mind, too."

Jim Collins, author of *Good to Great*

"With Phil Kotler's many years of studying marketing, no one is better equipped at spotting marketing sins."

Jack Trout, President, Trout & Partners Ltd.

"For more than three decades, Philip Kotler has been the authority on marketing for business grad students around the world. Kotler has done more than probably anyone else to cement marketing's reputation as a serious business discipline."

Howard Rothman, Amazon.com.

"Philip Kotler's (1971) book, *Marketing Decision Marking: A Model-Building Approach*, initiated me into marketing modeling research. Given that there was hardly any marketing modeling literature in the 1970s, I found Kotler's book exhilarating, and even now, I read it before writing any modeling article."

Vijay Mahajan, holder of the John P. Harbin Centennial Chair in Business at McCombs School of Business, University of Texas at Austin.

"In the 1960s, Philip Kotler, with his definitive *Principles of Marketing*, gathered insights from economics, social science, and analytics and applied them to the marketing practice. At the time, the ideas he espoused seemed really odd and new and not everyone agreed with his concepts. In time, every single one of his ideas became standard operating procedure for the marketing profession. And his concepts stood the test of time for forty or so years.

Jon Wuebben, *Future Marketing: Winning in the Prosumer Age*, 2017

"First, he (Philip Kotler) has done more than any other writer or scholar to promote the importance of marketing, transforming it from a peripheral activity, bolted on to the more "important" work of production. Second, he continued a trend started by Peter Drucker, shifting emphasis away from price and distribution to a greater focus on meeting customers' needs and on the benefits received from a product or service. Third, he has broadened the concept of marketing from mere selling to a more general process of communication and exchange, and has shown how marketing can be extended and applied to charities, arts organizations, political parties and many other non-commercial situations."
Financial Times, 2003

TABLE OF CONTENTS

ABOUT THIS BOOK

In early 2013, I received an invitation from the Nikkei newspaper in Japan to write 30 columns (each between 600-800 words) to be published during the month of December, 2013, one a day.

In addition, I was told that Nikkei has been inviting different people to do this over many years, people who made outstanding contributions, such as great business founders, including Konosuke Matsushita (Panasonic), Akio Morita (Sony), my revered Peter Drucker, and Tony Blair.

I have been a writer of books and articles but not a columnist. I think of a columnist as someone like Thomas Friedman, David Brooks or Paul Krugman who agree to deliver to the *New York Times* two columns a week as long as they work for the newspaper. I am impressed with their ability to deliver an interesting column every three or four days.

Needless to say, I was intrigued with the invitation. I agreed without hesitation. I got carried away and ended up writing 54 columns, leaving it to Nikkei to decide which 30 to publish. To make sure that the other columns wouldn't be lost to history, Nikkei and I agreed to publish the columns in Japanese in a book after December 2013. Nikkei agreed that I would have rights to publish an English edition of my columns and to sell foreign translation rights anywhere outside of Japan.

When I looked back at the columns, it dawned on me that the best title of this book would be *My Adventures in Marketing*. Why? Because it was my view of the world – seeing the world through marketing eyes.

Marketing is about identifying and meeting human and social needs. One of the shortest definitions of marketing is "**meeting needs profitably**." The American Marketing Association offers the following definition: *"Marketing is the activity, set of institutions, and processes for creating, communicating, delivering and exchanging offerings that have value for customers, clients, partners, and society at large."*

Marketing management is therefore *the art and science of choosing target markets and getting, keeping and growing customers through creating, delivering and communicating superior customer value.*

A **marketer** is someone who seeks a response – **attention, a purchase, a vote, a donation** – from another party, called the **prospect**. There are many things that can be marketed. They include not only *goods and services,* but also *events, experiences, persons, places, properties, organizations, information, ideas* and *causes.*

I shared in these columns pieces of my history and family, my friendships, prized experiences, and my ideas on poverty, peace, religion, nations, city planning, museums, performing arts, innovation, wealth generation, competition, corruption, government regulation, economic theory, marketing science, corporate social responsibility, social marketing, transformation, disruption, nonprofit organizations, collecting, branding, business purpose, and happiness.

Of late my thoughts have turned towards the state of our **Capitalism** and our **Democracy**. Is Capitalism working for the many or the few? Are we turning from a Democracy into a Plutocracy? Is our Capitalism "eating" our Democracy? As a trained economist and social scientist, I have been researching these questions lately. In 2015, I published *Confronting Capitalism* and in 2016 I published *Democracy in Decline.* The 2016 election of Donald Trump as President is raising a great number of new questions. We owe it to our children and grandchildren to leave them a world that, if not better, is at least as good as the one we enjoyed. I am deeply troubled that we may not have that choice any more.

Philip Kotler
phil@philkotler.com

1. LOOKING BACK

I have been in the marketing field as a professor, consultant, and author for 50 years. I have thoroughly enjoyed marketing. It is a branch of applied economics and I hopefully have made contributions to this field. I have published over 60 books on different aspects of marketing and I have introduced ideas including social marketing, demarketing, place marketing and atmospherics that have enriched the field. In recognition, I have received 20 honorary degrees and several other awards.

If you are asked the question, "What is 'marketing'?" what comes to your mind? I am sure that it is 'selling.' It is using advertising, direct mail, sales promotion and publicity to get things sold. Yet these activities are only a tiny portion of marketing. Marketing in principle should help producers decide what products to make, how to price them, how to distribute them, and, of course, how to promote them (the 4Ps: products, prices, place, and promotion). Marketing is a practical science aimed at improving a company's sales and profits and enhancing people's lives by creating customer value and satisfaction.

Half a century has passed since I entered the field of marketing. I have had opportunities to contribute to the development of marketing science, teaching this subject at several universities, while serving as a consultant to businesses and government agencies in different countries. I reached the age of 85 on May 27, 2016, so I think now it is a good time to reflect on my life and experiences. I am fortunate to be healthy, full of curiosity, and eager to learn and do new things. I feel like I am 60 in my mind and body. I have no desire to retire.

In fact, a number of new projects are now underway. I am interested in bringing together prominent marketing experts who will discuss different ways to "Create a Better World through Marketing." The question is how to promote sound economic growth and social justice and a sustainable planet? How can businesses, government, and nonprofit organizations work together to improve the lives and well-being of the 700 billion people living today and their offspring.

Marketing is a philosophy centered on serving customers and includes a set of skills and activities to solve economic and social problems. Almost everyone is involved in marketing, whether it is a young man courting a young woman, a CEO trying to get a contract, a junior worker trying to get a promotion, and so on. I hope that many readers will have an interest in this field of study.

If you know me even a little bit, you might have heard about the "4Ps" of Product, Price, Place and Promotion. These are key elements in the marketing planning process. My book, *Marketing Management*, describes and applies the 4Ps. *Marketing Management* is the most widely used graduate-level marketing textbook worldwide and it is now in its 15th edition. I have also published 59 other books on a great variety of marketing and other subjects (see appendix listing publications). My research has led to many honors and 20 honorary doctoral degrees. I would like to share my odyssey with you, the reader.

2. MY FAMILY

Let me start with the story of my family. I was born in Chicago, Illinois on May 27, 1931, when the U.S. economy was in the midst of the Great Depression. My father Maurice Kotler was born in Nizhyn Novgorod, Russia. At the age of 17, he left Russia that was in the midst of the Russian Socialist Revolution and he emigrated to the United States, landing on Ellis Island almost penniless. Shortly afterwards, he settled in Chicago with the help of relatives.

My mother Betty Bubar was born in Berdichev, Ukraine. At the age of 12, she emigrated, arriving in Canada at first, but moving to Chicago shortly thereafter. Some years later she met Maurice Kotler, fell in love, and they married. Both of them found jobs. My mother worked as a sales lady in a large department store. My father worked for a laundry, and later worked in and opened a fish store.

My mother gave birth to three children. I am the oldest and my brother Milton Kotler is five years younger and my brother Neil Kotler was ten years younger than I.

Although each of the brothers is a very different person physically and emotionally, we had one thing in common. The three of us chose to pursue academic interests and are committed to make the world a better place for all people.

Chicago, our home town, was struggling with an increasing gap between the rich and the poor and a deteriorating level of public safety. Though we were children, we saw and felt the contradictions in the economic lives of different people. We felt relatively poor even though we had enough in the way of creature comforts.

Milton, Neil, Phil and Maurice and Betty Kotler. Philip by himself

Milton, my middle brother, entered the University of Chicago at age 16. After graduating from college, he remained at the University of Chicago and majored in political science followed by law school. Milton later moved to Washington, D.C., and worked in a liberal and later left-wing research institute called the Institute for Policy Studies. He met many interesting thought leaders, including Hannah Arendt, Paul Goodman, Richard J. Barnett, and David Reisman. Milton published an important book called *Neighborhood Government*, advocating setting up governance structures in neighborhoods to determine what each city neighborhood should be making, exporting, and importing.

Over the years, his political position changed and he eventually became a dedicated conservative. It is not uncommon for persons to convert from radical to conservative at different stages in their lives. Milton also developed a strong entrepreneurial business sense. He set up the Kotler Marketing Group in China in 2004 to take advantage of the new business opportunities opening up in China. His small 50 employee company was recently rated as the No. 1 marketing strategy consultancy in China, outperforming major Western consulting firms including McKinsey. More recently, Milton and I published two books with Wiley,

Market Your Way to Growth: Eight Ways to Win, and *Winning Global Markets: How Businesses Invest and Prosper in the World's Top Cities.*

Milton, Phil, and Neil Kotler

My youngest brother Neil took a different path. He majored in political science at the University of Wisconsin in Madison and he earned a doctorate degree in political science from the University of Chicago. He devoted himself passionately to the study of democracy and early American history. He delved deeply into the way an ideal democratic government would work. He taught in Texas and later took a position at the Smithsonian Institution in Washington, D.C. He focused his research on museums and other nonprofit organizations (NPOs). Neil and I co-authored wrote *Museum Strategy and Marketing: Designing Missions, Building Audiences, Generating Revenue and Resources.* Our book was published in 1998 and some museum people describe it as a "bible" on museum strategy and marketing. We invited Neil's wife Wendy to join us in writing a second edition that we published in 2008. Unfortunately, my brother Neil contracted leukemia and he passed away at age 72. I was very saddened to lose this wonderful and gifted brother at the prime of his life.

We three intellectuals managed to be born into a family of immigrant parents who had little education. We loved our pretty and sweet mother. Our father was a gifted soccer player and he wanted his sons to be athletes. But the three of us had little interest in sports. We relished the life of the mind.

In his later years, my father said to me with a smile on his face, "Never have I been more proud of my sons than now." My brothers and I were almost certain that he had gotten over his disappointment that we had not become athletes.

3. EARLY SCHOOLING, THE GREAT BOOKS & THE UNIVERSITY OF CHICAGO

From my childhood on, every time I heard news about a person who did a wonderful thing, I felt the desire to do a similar thing. When I read an article about astronauts, I wanted to be an astronaut. When I read about Einstein, I wanted to be a scientist and mathematician. When I read the biography of Abraham Lincoln, I wanted to enter the political world. I was similar to Zelig in Director Woody Allen's film "Zelig," who adores people around him and always dreams of becoming a person like them.

Behind the fact that I fantasized about different careers, much influence came from the many books that I read. I was deeply moved by reading Herman Melville's *Moby Dick*, Thomas Mann's *The Magic Mountain*, Dostoyevsky's *Crime and Punishment*. Leo Tolstoy's *War and Peace*, and Henry James, *The Portrait of a Lady*. Reading these and other novels, I dreamed of becoming a novelist and portraying complex characters wrestling with difficult moral dilemmas.

My interest in writing showed up in high school. I wrote articles for the school newspaper. I commented on and criticized the trends of the day. I argued that young people were spending too much time on sports, that there was a shortage of good-quality news and discussion programs on the radio, that many American movies were of little worth. As the head of my high school debate club, I debated with other students over current issues, such as whether workers should be required to join a union or whether the United Nations should have its own army. World War II was over and a new order was being built in those days.

I was also elected editor-in-chief to prepare the annual class album called the "Log."

Phil on far left. The editors included Shel Silverstein, who later displayed his immense talents as a poet, a singer-songwriter and a cartoonist. His gifts were already apparent.

As a high school student, I started to think about my future. Children of Jewish immigrants were often persuaded to think of three careers: a doctor, a lawyer or an engineer. However, I was not attracted to those professions. I decided to become an accountant, because I would learn a lot about economics and the profession was likely to produce a good and steady income.

I sent my college application to DePaul University, a prestigious school in Chicago. DePaul offered me a full scholarship. I planned to get a degree in accounting and law because the combination was highly respected in the business world. However, after one year, I came to think that something was missing. I thought that I should pursue a broader education and not just practical knowledge of accounting and law.

At that time, I learned of the Great Books movement that identified the most important books ever written. The movement's founder was Mortimer Adler who worked closely with Robert Hutchins, the famous President of the University of Chicago.

Robert Maynard Hutchins
University of Chicago

Mortimer Adler
Founder of Great Books

The Great Books introduced readers to the ideas of the world's greatest thinkers. Adler and his staff developed a list of the 100 best classics and led discussion groups to deliberate on the basic issues facing mankind. Because the movement was going on mainly at the University of Chicago, after spending two years at DePaul University, I applied for admission to the University of Chicago and received a scholarship to enter the university's department of economics. I kept reading about the ideas of philosophers such as Plato, Aristotle, Machiavelli, Immanuel Kant, among others. I sharpened my ability to think critically. The Great Books helped me develop a lifelong interest in "building a better society."

Of course, one cannot acquire knowledge of mathematics, economics or engineering from Plato and the other great books. Furthermore, in the Internet Age, students are more interested in entrepreneurship, innovation and technologies. Yet I continue to believe that learning the great ideas of the past can arm people with inspiration and ideas for contributing to a better world. I sometimes feel that it is precisely because of the lack of a strong liberal education that we are currently facing many problems in the world today.

The atmosphere of the University of Chicago was especially stimulating. Its economics department faculty was outstanding. I learned the value of the play of free markets and competition from the professors belonging to the Chicago School of Economics, which included Milton Friedman, Frank Knight and many other eminent economists.

Milton Friedman, University of Chicago

In 1976, two hundred years after Adam Smith published his *Wealth of Nations*, Milton Friedman received Sweden's Nobel Laureate Prize in economics (1976). He became the major exponent of individualism and free markets through his books on *Capitalism and Freedom* (1962) and *Freedom to Choose* (1979).

When I was 14, I read Marx's *The Communist Manifesto*, and I felt that it presented a powerful polemic against capitalism. Because I was brought up in poor circumstances, I felt angry when I heard about the great wealth of the Rockefeller and Carnegie families. "Why is income so poorly distributed?" I was clearly aware from those days that I wanted to help create a more equitable society by making better use of economic theory.

However, I was too young to understand that in the real world, Marx's idea of equality would be subverted by men who wanted power and would organize authoritarian regimes. Listening to the lectures of the great economists at the University of Chicago, my ideas were changing and I became fascinated with capitalist theory.

At the University of Chicago, there were many eminent professors in the broader social sciences. I learned a great deal from University of Chicago professors in psychology, sociology, anthropology, and political science. That I came to know the other social sciences benefited my thinking greatly.

4. FROM THE UNIVERSITY OF CHICAGO TO M.I.T.

In my early 20s, when I received my master's degree in economics from the University of Chicago, the path I should follow became clear. I aimed at becoming a distinguished economist at some leading university.

The next step was to obtain a doctorate. In those days, the universities most advanced in economic studies were Harvard University, the Massachusetts Institute of Technology (M.I.T.) and the University of California, Berkeley, aside from the University of Chicago. I chose to apply to M.I.T. and I received a Westinghouse research scholarship. I was delighted and I headed for Boston, Massachusetts, a city filled with intellectual stimulation.

Here again I was able to study economics under eminent professors. One was Paul Samuelson who wrote numerous research papers and published ten editions of his famous textbook *Economics* that was read all over the world. Samuelson was awarded a Nobel Prize in Economics in 1970. That I met him changed my economic thinking from free market economics to Keynesian economics. I came to think that, in times of recession, the government must play an active role to stimulate the economy even if it increased the country's debt in the short term.

Paul Samuelson, Robert Solow, and Franco Modigliani

MIT's economics faculty also included Franco Modigliani, who made contributions to financial theory, and Robert Solow, who contributed to our theory of the role of innovation and technology in economic growth. Modigliani received a Nobel Prize in Economics in 1985 and Solow received a Nobel Prize in Economics in 1987.

When I finished writing my doctoral dissertation, the last step was to be examined by a department committee. The three members of my committee were Professors Paul Samuelson, Robert Solow and Charles Myers. I remember Samuelson posing the question, "What do you think about Karl Marx's labor theory of value?" I answered, "Value is produced not only by labor but also by capital, and ultimately it is a concept found in buyers' minds out of their consumer experience." When I recall it now, I realize that I said something similar to the concept of value used in marketing. After a half hour of questions, I exited the room and waited outside for a decision. I was naturally nervous.

An anecdote came across my mind. I had heard that when Samuelson took his oral examination at Harvard, he was examined by Professors Joseph Schumpeter and Alvin Hansen. When Samuelson left the examining room, the two professors looked at each other and Schumpeter asked whether they had passed.

Five minutes had passed when Samuelson, Solow and Myers came out and said to me, "Congratulations, Mr. Kotler. You have passed." And they opened a bottle of champagne.

I didn't know it then, but the teachings of these wise men were to echo in my mind for the rest of my days.

5. MEETING NANCY AT A JOLLYUP AND GETTING MARRIED

Everyone should have a best friend and fall in love. My wife, Nancy Kotler, is my best friend and my love, and this feeling has been clearly expressed in the dedication of my book *Marketing Management* from its first edition (in 1967 through the latest 15th edition). "This book is dedicated to my wife and best friend, Nancy," with heartfelt and ineffable thanks and love.

It was a real wonder for me to meet Nancy without the help of a matchmaker or an Internet-based dating service. It happened when I was 23 years old. One day, in my dormitory at MIT, I saw a poster telling of an informal party called a "jollyup," to be held at Radcliffe College, which was Harvard's College for female students.

"What's a jollyup?" I asked an acquaintance of mine. He told me that it was "a party organized by Radcliffe students to meet eligible young men."

I decided to check out the "jollyup" that evening.

The party took place in a dormitory at Radcliffe College. I saw about 30 young women and a greater number of young men at the party. There were Harvard students in jackets, and they looked cool. On the other hand, MIT students mostly wore large calculator wristwatches with some of us having a slide rule in our pocket. We nerds dressed the part.

I looked around and spotted a beautiful woman with black hair and pretty eyes. I approached her and I asked for a dance. "Yes," she said with a smile. While dancing, I said, "You look like Cleopatra." She replied "I am Cleopatra." That's the way love begins.

Nancy Kotler

Before leaving, I asked her out for next week to go sailing on the Charles River that bordered MIT. She agreed. There was only one problem. I had never sailed before. I had a week to read up on sailing a boat. The day finally came, and I went to pick up Nancy. Upon seeing me, she looked surprised, as I wore a pair of black leather shoes, not exactly what real sailors wear. The weather was fine, and the boat glided over the Charles River. Unfortunately, the wind died suddenly, and so our boat could go nowhere. A Coast Guard boat had to tow us in. Nancy, far from being panicked, had a big laugh and appeared to be amused by my ineptness as a sailor.

Nancy and Philip

Our romance that began in 1953 led to our wonderful married life, now 64 years. All thanks to a poster I had seen announcing a jollyup! I have been blessed with a beautiful wife, three daughters and nine grandchildren. My wife not only brought beauty, love and refinement into my life. She also brought along an uncommon sense that shaped my life and career.

Nancy spent two years at Radcliffe. After we married, we moved to Chicago. My parents adored her. Nancy registered at the University of Chicago and found the program to be extremely stimulating with smaller classes and more applied Socratic teaching. She graduated with honors and received a Woodrow Wilson fellowship. She chose to join the English department at Northwestern University and study for a Master's degree. After receiving her Master's, she continued at Northwestern to pursue a Ph.D. She proposed doing a dissertation on Saul Bellows, who won the Nobel Prize in Literature. Her advisor discouraged her, saying that Saul Bellows had not died yet! This discouraged her and other factors led her to drop out of the program.

Later Nancy went on to get a law degree at Loyola University. She worked for an excellent law firm for several years. Her sharp mind helped me navigate many contracts for homes, book contracts, and the like. Besides all this, Nancy bore our three beautiful daughters, Amy, Melissa, and Jessica.

Daughters Amy, Jessica, and Melissa

Marriages take place in different ways around the world. People set great store on whether partners come from the same social class or whether the parents of the bride could provide a sufficient dowry, rather than on the existence of love between the couple. Finding a life partner is also influenced by luck. The marriage market is one of the least efficient in the world. Imperfect as the market is, a variety of new dating services have appeared, making available more information and larger choices for men and women. Though this service did not exist for Nancy and me, we thrived without it.

6. ON TO INDIA WITH NANCY FOR MY PH.D. DISSERTATION

Why did Professor Samuelson ask me questions regarding the labor theory of value during my dissertation examination at MIT? It is because I had developed a keen interest in labor economics during my doctoral studies.

I always had a deep compassion for the working class from where my parents came, and I felt angry because of the extreme gap between the rich and the poor which only seemed to be getting worse. I doubted whether workers are paid fairly for their labor; most were certainly not paid a living wage. I decided to address labor issues as my research area. I also wanted to identify the role of trade unions in redressing income inequality. Management's treatment of labor is an eternal theme. I remember workers at McDonalds protesting that the company was buying another expensive private airplane instead of raising the wages of its workers.

My professor mentor at MIT was Charles A. Myers who was a world authority on labor and industrial economics. Myers was working on a major research project -- funded by the Ford Foundation -- to examine the actual conditions and pay of workers and the role of trade unions in developing countries. He was working on this project with three other major labor economists – Clark Kerr of the University of California at Berkeley, Fred Harbison of the University of Chicago, and John Dunlop of Harvard University.

In Spring 1955, Myers invited me to join his project and go to India to do research there for one year starting in the Fall of 1955. My only concern was how Nancy would react to this plan because we had just married on January 30, 1955.

I immediately discussed the opportunity with her. Nancy was still a student at Radcliffe College and she would be a junior in September. Nancy had already read a number of books on India, including E. M. Forster's *A Passage to India*. She said that she was delighted for us to go to

India. It would be an ideal place for our honeymoon. She applied for a one-year leave of absence from Radcliffe and we left for India.

We flew from Boston to Bombay via London and Karachi and began to experience the wide-open world. I had traveled only once abroad in 1954 where I spent 60 days as a solo tourist seeing 20 European cities, including London, Paris, Rome, Copenhagen, Vienna, Budapest and Cannes.

The journey took us into a completely different and strange part of the world. India was the world's second largest country with over a billion people, and with a great percentage of its people under the age of 20. India contained some of the wealthiest people in the world and yet most of the country's population lived in dire poverty. Nancy and I encountered begging children, people sleeping on the streets, free-roaming cows and the smell of exotic spices wafting in the air. India was a mixture of the culture of the Far East, with its spiritual and religious character, and the culture of the West, brought to India by its occupier, Great Britain. India was a land of yogas, ashrams, Eastern medicine, and multiple Gods and at the same time included many highly Western educated Indians with a good command of mathematics, business, and Western culture. They may be Western educated, comfortable with Western culture, but hold what they consider Indian values in their hearts.

The main theme of my dissertation research was whether paying higher wages to Indian workers would lead to improving their productivity. My hypothesis was that Indian companies would attract more able workers who would live and eat better, keep their children in school, and afford to see a doctor if necessary. I assumed that the workers would spend their higher earnings for food and education and have a better life.

But my hypothesis was not supported by my data. The reality is that when many Indian workers earn higher wages, many would drop out and return to their village and some would waste money on gambling, alcohol and prostitutes. Their wives would try to directly receive their husband's pay and manage it before he spent it all. At that time, I knew little about real life.

After three months in Bombay, Nancy and I moved to Delhi. We met a number of Indian scholars (such as Subbiah Kannapan) as well as other Americans studying the Indian economy (such as Leon V. Hirsch). We met two Americans, Larry and Terry who drove a Volkswagen "beetle" and we enjoyed traveling with them to see the Taj Mahal at Agra and the fabulous city of Jaipur. They joined us in our move to Delhi, India's capital, where we shared a small home with a servant. It was winter and quite cold in Delhi but we enjoyed being with another young couple and living in a house.

We stayed in Delhi for three months and then left for three months in Calcutta. Calcutta had a magnificent city center with monumental British buildings but everywhere else there was tremendous poverty and people sleeping on the streets at night.

Nancy, who enjoyed wearing a sari and meeting many people began to have problems with the food and started to lose weight. She visited doctors who told her that perhaps she should return to the U.S. earlier while I finished my dissertation research. Nancy left India a month before me and her health returned. I continued working on my dissertation and flew back to Boston in August 1956.

Nancy Kotler

Although I failed to prove my hypothesis, my research dissertation contained many new observations. I submitted the dissertation to my committee at MIT and obtained the committee's approval. As a result, I received a doctorate degree in economics and graduated from MIT in September 1956.

I started looking for a teaching position in labor economics, but one thing happened that inspired me to change my area of research.

7. TEACHING AT ROOSEVELT UNIVERSITY AND THEN TO HARVARD FOR HIGHER MATHEMATICS TRAINING

As America moved into the 1960s, many problems had to be faced, particularly the Vietnam War and a mounting concern at home about social problems, such as environmental pollution, racial discrimination and women's rights. The young were changing with the rise of the Beatles, hippie culture and the counter-culture pitted against the established order.

Nancy and I moved to Chicago and I started to look for a teaching position. My first choice was Northwestern University or the University of Chicago, but neither had a vacant position.

While thinking about a few other colleges, I was attracted by Roosevelt University, a college with high ideals established with the support of Eleanor Roosevelt, the wife of Franklin Roosevelt, our 32nd U.S. president. I accepted Roosevelt University's offer of an assistant professorship in the economics department. The department included the eminent Professor Abba Lerner who was described as the "Milton Friedman of the Left." I enjoyed working with Prof. Walter Weisskopf, who brought philosophical and humanistic viewpoint into economics. Weisskopf criticized the then prevailing trend in economics to assume rational maximizing decision making on the part of all consumers, producers and distributors, as if economics could resemble Newtonian physics. Both Weisskopf and Lerner had fled to the U.S., barely escaping the atrocities of the Nazis, and I was emotionally drawn to both of them and their stories.

I enjoyed teaching the students at Roosevelt University. Many were the first generation to go to college in the hope of achieving the American Dream. As they were close to me in age, I developed a warm and friendly relationship with them.

In my second year at Roosevelt, I heard that the Ford Foundation planned to select 50 young professors of economics and send them to Harvard for a year to study higher mathematics. The Ford Foundation wanted to upgrade the teaching of business management by introducing more mathematics and social science. U.S. managers had felt a growing need to use more mathematical analysis in making their decisions on complex issues. I was fortunate to be chosen as one of the fifty promising young scholars. This meant that Nancy and I would move to Boston for a year where her family lived. She was pleased.

The professors selected for the Ford Foundation program came from various fields, including accounting, finance, business strategy, operations, human resources and marketing. I chose to spend more of my time with the professors specializing in marketing, which included Frank Bass, Ed Pessemier, Robert Buzzell, Jerry McCarthy, and Bill Lazer, all of whom later made a strong reputation in the marketing field. I made this choice because I wanted to know how markets and pricing mechanisms really worked. In those days, economic studies had abstractly described and analyzed the setting of prices and outputs in terms of demand and supply. But this had never fully satisfied me.

Frank Bass, Robert Buzzell, William Lazer, Jerry McCarthy

Some readers may think that economics and marketing are different fields of study. But that is not the case.

Marketing is an area of applied economics, which looks into how prices of goods are actually determined as goods move through different stages from producers to wholesalers to retailers. Economists had little to say about marketing channels. They also had little to say on how demand is influenced by advertising, sales-promotion activities, product features, merchandising and other marketing tools. Traditional economists said that those tools simply shift the demand curve upward without adding much analysis or measurement.

My joining the marketing group influenced me in two ways. I started to consider changing my primary research interest from labor economics to market economics. The other was that I became deeply convinced of the vital importance of mathematics in improving the quality of decision making in economics and marketing. I began to think of writing a first book entitled *Marketing Decision Making: A Model-Building Approach*.

Marketing Decision Making:
A Model-Building Approach

8. JOINING THE KELLOGG SCHOOL OF MANAGEMENT, NORTHWESTERN UNIVERSITY

My one year in 1960 studying higher mathematics at Harvard led me to undertake writing a different book than I had planned. The change was partly due to Professor Donald Jacobs of Northwestern University who also attended the Ford Foundation program at Harvard. Don and I became good friends in the program. After returning to Chicago to teach at Roosevelt University, I received a phone call from Don asking me if I would be interested in teaching at Northwestern University in their Graduate School of Management (later renamed the Kellogg School of Management after a major gift came from a member of the Kellogg family, but not from the Kellogg company). I was pleased and Nancy agreed that this would be a good move.

Philip and Don Jacobs

I met Dean Richard Donham and we had a good talk about Northwestern's School of Business. Shortly thereafter I received a phone call from Don Jacobs that I am hired and that I could start teaching in the Fall of 1961. Don added that there was only one decision to be made, namely whether I wanted to teach managerial economics or marketing. He was well aware that I had not formally studied marketing but he said that's an advantage! I would bring a fresh lens into marketing because my training was not in marketing. He said that economics was a well-developed discipline and that the chance of adding much original theory to economics was not as great as the chance of adding much original theory to marketing. He saw marketing as underdeveloped and worth an attack by a well-trained economist. I told Don that I would make a decision after meeting the marketing department faculty at the school.

First I met Professor Stuart Henderson Britt, a fascinating scholar who had written extensively on psychology theory and advertising. Stuart seemed more British than American although he hailed from Fulton, Missouri. He explained the role of advertising by saying "Doing business without advertising is like winking at a girl in the dark. You know what you are doing, but nobody else does." Stuart was also a practical joker. I remember him driving his Rolls Royce with a fake full-sized sculptured figure sitting next to him, who would watch the car when he stopped on errands. I remember coming to a party at his home and pressing the buzzer only to hear a scream come out. It was hard to know what would happen next in his home.

Then I met Harper Boyd, Ralph Westfield, and Richard Clewett. All three had a high reputation in the academic marketing world, having written many Harvard-type teaching cases in marketing strategy and marketing research based on companies they consulted. What was even more interesting is that they all traveled abroad and wrote interesting studies of how marketing is practiced in such countries as Egypt, Turkey, Hungary, and others. I had a strong interest in learning about marketing practice around the world. I also met Sidney Levy who had joined the department a year earlier. Sidney had received his education at the University of Chicago in the social sciences and he had been a member of Social Research applying his skills at analyzing consumer behavior. Sidney made a deep impression on me as a kindred spirit.

Professor Sidney Levy

Needless to say, my experience in meeting these senior members of the marketing department was more than sufficient for me to answer Don's question, that I would put my future into helping shape marketing theory and practice rather than teach economics.

I never regretted this decision. Our marketing department grew largely by recruiting Ph.D.'s who were trained not in marketing but in the social and mathematical sciences. Gerald Zaltman, trained in sociology, joined our department and brought a deep understanding of the diffusion of innovation theory and later on the role of metaphors in consumer decision making.

Philip and Gerald Zaltman

We continued to attract very good scholars.

- Louis Stern from Ohio State University joined our department and brought a deep theoretical and practical understanding of marketing channels and was a superb teacher.
- Alice Tybout and Brian Sternthal came into our department and brought a deep understanding of consumer behavior and advertising theory.
- Mohan Sawhney hailed from Wharton and became our technology and social media expert who advised a multitude of companies on the new media.
- Andy Zoltners and Sinha Prabha applied mathematical thinking to improving sales force decision making and they went on to write three of the best books on sales management.
- Robert Blattberg joined us from the University of Chicago and helped advance retail decision making theory and the measurement of customer lifetime value.
- James Anderson brought a deep understanding of business to business marketing and wrote the major B2B textbook in the area as well as publishing over several highly-praised articles in the *Harvard Business Review*.
- John Sherry and Robert Kuznets, both anthropologists, carried out interesting ethnographic studies of consumer behavior.
- Stanley Stasch did original work in advancing our understanding of customer information systems.
- Dipak Jain joined us later and applied advanced mathematical theory to understanding new product development, and as an instructor, scored a 10 out of 10 on student ratings (and later became our Dean).
- John Hauser joined us from M.I.T. and brought excellent skills in marketing model building.

Kellogg faculty: Louis Stern, Brian Sternthal, Alice Tybout, Mohan Sawhney, Andy Zoltners, Robert Blattberg, James Anderson, Dipak Jain

An earlier photo featuring Phil, John Hauser, Lou Stern and Andy Zoltners

Don Jacobs, Lou Stern, Matt Tuite, Stan Stasch, Phil, Ralph Westfall gather at a reunion (2013)

I had yet to decide whether I should finish my book *Marketing Decision Making: A Model Building Approach*. This book would clearly be my contribution to economic theory as a market economist rather than as a macro-economist or a micro-economist.

Or should I undertake to write a different book proposed to me by Frank Enenbach, a star salesperson at Prentice-Hall (Pearson).

9. DECIDING TO WRITE MARKETING MANAGEMENT

After joining the Kellogg School of Management in 1963, I was visited by Frank Enenbach, an exceptionally talented salesperson from Prentice-Hall. He wanted to publish my first book. I showed him the draft of *Marketing Decision Making: A Model-Building Approach.* He gave me the following advice. "This will be an original contribution to marketing but this should not be your first book. You should first write a textbook with an innovative approach to marketing." The book that I had started to write was at a high-level and not for a broad readership. Frank said: "If you write a superb textbook, you will win a much larger number of readers and you will be rewarded with a larger reputation." His suggestion made sense to me. I was not happy with any of the existing marketing textbooks.

Most marketing textbooks at the time contained detailed descriptions of marketing channels, sales management, advertising and sales promotion, and other matters. Few textbooks presented analytical approaches to marketing decision making; they were light on research findings and methodology; and they failed to place customers at the center of the marketing universe.

For the next two years, I worked on preparing *Marketing Management: Analysis, Planning and Control.* I published this first edition in 1967. Twenty-nine years later, the British newspaper *Financial Times* on December 9, 1996, p. 14 cited *Marketing Management* as one of the 50 greatest business books of all times, with *The Wealth of Nations* by Adam Smith topping the list.

Marketing Management, 1st ed., 1967

In writing *Marketing Management,* I decided to base it on four fundamental disciplines -- social science, economics, organizational behavior and mathematics. In order to illustrate fundamental marketing principles, I filled the book with much empirical information and case studies.   I explained that business organizations can have one of four orientations: production-oriented, sales-oriented, marketing (customer)-oriented and society-oriented. I strongly emphasized that companies should focus on customers and understand their needs, and research their tastes and preferences. I also said that companies should care about how their products and services affect the well-being of citizens.

I had no idea whether this new book would be a total failure or a great success. It turned out to be the latter, but what made me happy more than anything else was that the book helped marketing to be recognized as a legitimate and important business discipline. The book helped boost the image of marketing as a field of study. Frank's premonition was right and the book rapidly became the first choice of universities around the world.

Marketing does not simply consist of distributing coupons, putting out ads, and running sales specials. Its significance lies in building a sound marketing plan based on the four Ps - Product, Price, Place (distribution) and Promotion - and being able to implement and control its execution.

It is characteristic of marketing that new concepts, theories, types of practice and cases keep emerging all the time. I prepared a new edition of *Marketing Management* every three years in response to rapid changes in marketing and in society. Paul Samuelson's famous textbook on economics went through only 10 editions.

After finishing writing the 10th edition of *Marketing Management*, I invited Professor Kevin Keller of Dartmouth, one of the world's leading experts in branding, to join me as co-author. Kevin proved to be an excellent friend and he added many new features to the book. *Marketing Management* is now in the 15th edition and it remains the leading textbook in marketing management.

Kevin Keller, Dartmouth,
co-author of Marketing Management

I finally finished and published in 1970 *Marketing Decision Making*, and it was adopted at some top business schools. In 1983, I invited Professor Gary Lilien of Penn State University to co-author a new edition that we renamed it *Marketing Models*. It became the leading textbook on mathematical methods in marketing. In 1992, we invited Professor K. Sridhar Moorthy to join us as a third co-author and the book went through further editions.

Earlier I had decided to prepare simpler versions of *Marketing Management*. I published *Principles of Marketing* (1980) for use in the most demanding undergraduate business schools. Then I published Marketing: *An Introduction* (1984) for typical business schools teaching marketing.

After writing the first few editions of these two books, I invited one of my best former students, Professor Gary Armstrong of the University of North Carolina, to be my co-author. Gary has done a superior job in keeping these the leading marketing textbooks in undergraduate schools of business.

Gary Armstrong, University of North Carolina

In parallel with writing these two books, I wanted to deal with a new idea on expanding the concept of marketing.

10. OBSERVATIONS ON THE ORIGIN AND EVOLUTION OF MARKETING

The idea of persuading someone to do something goes way back to the Biblical story of Adam and Eve and the snake. The snake convinces Eve to convince Adam to eat the apple although it was forbidden.

Temptation in Eden, Lucas Cranach the Elder (c.1472-1553)

Techniques of persuasion have a long history. In ancient Greece, great orators such as Demosthenes and Pericles brought their silver tongues to influence Athenian policy and strategy. Aristotle presented brilliant theories on how rhetoric and logic could be used in persuasive discourse and this had a profound influence on orators, authors and others engaged in persuasion.

Trading and selling in ancient Athens took place in the "agora," the plaza where people gathered. In the Middle Ages, towns held open market days that served as major events in each community.

Though commercial activity has a long history, and the term "market" was in common use, the word "marketing" itself did not appear in professional literature until around 1905-1910. Several dissatisfied institutionally-oriented economists observed that supply, demand and price were not the only decisive factors influencing the buying and selling of goods. They pointed out that demand is influenced by more than price, particularly by advertising, sales force, and sales promotion. And they pointed out that many institutions are involved in market activities, such as wholesalers, distributors, retailers, jobbers, agents, advertising agencies, market research firms, and public relations firms. The first marketing textbooks appeared in the early 1900s written by economists who wanted to put more reality into how markets actually worked.

Most companies conducted their "selling" activities with a sales department. To improve sales effectiveness, companies would occasionally hire someone to do some market research, or find customer leads, or develop brochures and ads. People with these skills often were added to large sales departments.

The idea of starting a marketing department came later in large consumer firms as they developed different brands and appointed brand managers. Brand managers needed access to marketing researchers, advertising agencies, market segment managers and in this way the marketing department grew in size.

Note that the marketing department is normally separate from the sales department. Its mission is to help the sales force sell better as a result of better marketing research and promotional support. Eventually the marketing department overtook the responsibility of developing a marketing plan that made decisions on the 4Ps – product, price, place, and promotion. The marketing plan had to set the 4Ps in a way that would deliver the expected sales, cost, and profit.

At times conflict would arise between the small marketing department and the large sales department. The marketing plan would set the product features and prices and lead to sales quotas for the sales people. Sales people would often complain that marketing set too high a price or that their sales quota was unrealistically high. Sales people would further complain that the ads were weak, the brochures were dull, and the marketing research was insipid. This lack of alignment between sales and marketing needed to be addressed. The first requirement was that the head of marketing and the head of sales needed to work more closely together. The second requirement was that sales participate more actively in developing the marketing plan so that the goals and tasks would be more acceptable to sales.

Although marketing first took root in large consumer packaged goods companies, it soon spread to business-to-business firms (industrial equipment and commodities), then to service businesses (airlines and hotels), and finally to not-for-profit organizations such as museums, performing arts groups, and social service organizations. Each of these organization types shaped their marketing departments to meet their varying needs.

The whole marketing process can be described as:

R -> STP -> 4Ps -> I -> C

Marketing starts with R or research into the market. The research leads to STP. *Segmentation* calls for distinguishing different groups of customers in the marketing. *Targeting* calls for deciding which group or groups the marketing organization should pursue and serve. And *Positioning* calls for giving a chosen target market a clear message of the distinct benefits that it is offering to that target market. Then the company develops a separate 4P plan for each of its chosen market segments. Then the company implements (I) the plan. Finally, the company collects feedback (C for control) to improve its 4Ps for the next round of serving that target market.

11. THE BROADENING OF MARKETING

One of the charms of my profession is the opportunity to meet outstanding excellent scholars in different fields. Sidney J. Levy is one of those persons and I mentioned him earlier. Sidney received his Ph.D. at the University of Chicago in 1956, and after working for a social research company, he started teaching at Northwestern University's Kellogg School of Management. It took little time before he and I became fast friends. Sidney observed human behavior very expertly, and we began to discuss the possibility of applying marketing outside of the business world. It was in the 1960s, when most marketing scholars gained expertise in specific markets, such as automobiles, home appliances, toys, housing and apparel.

We maintained that the concept of marketing could be applied to places (cities, regions, countries), people (producing celebrities), ideas (gender equality) and beliefs (eating nutritious food, exercising). We published our views in a 1969 article entitled "Broadening the Concept of Marketing." However, some influential marketing scholars said that they did not like the broadening idea, contending that expanding the marketing realm would cause confusion and hurt the definition of marketing.

Because Sidney and I were convinced that expanding the realm of marketing would breathe new life into the discipline, we decided to put the question to a vote by marketing professors. A vote was taken and, thankfully, the large majority supported our view. Sidney and I celebrated the occasion.

Marketing Forges Ahead

- **Commercial marketing**
- **Place marketing**
- **Person marketing**
- **Social marketing**
- **Political marketing**
- **Fundraising**

It remained a question of whether the broadening of marketing would bring fresh insights and whether the 4P framework would be effective in the other fields as well. We also hoped that it would lead to new concepts and theories that could be imported back into commercial marketing. I was hopeful that various marketing problems would be clarified.

Above all, I hoped that people from different fields of study who had not thought about marketing seriously would then have a desire to learn more about marketing. For example, if administrators of art museums, who had thought that their job was mainly to sell admission tickets and collect donations, broadened their view and realized that the essence of their work was marketing a good "product," strengthening their brand, and creating high visitor satisfaction, I would be pleased.

I decided to devote several years to studying new areas for marketing.

I collaborated with Irving Rein and Don Haider and wrote *Marketing Places: Attracting Investment, Industry and Tourism to Cities, States and Nations* (1993). I worked with my former student, Joanne Bernstein to write *Standing Room Only: Strategies for Marketing the Performing Arts* (1997). I worked with my brother Neil Kotler to write *Museum Strategy and Marketing* (1998) that became a museum classic. These two last books constituted what I called Cultural Marketing. Earlier I collaborated with Irving Rein to research and write *High Visibility* (1987) about the celebrity-making business. I was sure that all of these sectors would benefit from applying marketing thinking.

As regards religion, I was aware that introducing marketing could invite criticism. My former student Bruce Wrenn and I and two others wrote *Marketing for Congregations: Choosing to Serve People More Effectively* (1992). We renamed the book *Building Strong Congregations* (2009). We showed that religious organizations could attract, keep and grow church members by understanding their needs and meeting them through faith and religious activities. We applied the marketing concept of STP - S(segmenting), T(targeting) and P (positioning) - to precede the work of setting the 4Ps. This was highly effective.

Expanding marketing to new fields was challenging and full of adventure. And my next interest was directed to applying marketing to social problems.

12. THE FIELD OF SOCIAL MARKETING EMERGES

Can marketing play a role in improving the lives of people beyond simply providing them with a growing variety of goods and services? So many problems plague mankind – poverty, hunger, disease, pollution and environmental degradation – can marketing tools and principles make a dent in these problem areas?

Professor Gerald Zaltman and I considered this question as young professors at the Kellogg School of Management at Northwestern University in 1971. G. D. Wiebe had raised an interesting question many years earlier: "Why can't you sell Brotherhood like you sell soap?" (G. D. Wiebe, "Merchandising Commodities and Citizenship on Television," *Public Opinion Quarterly*, (Winter, 1951-52), pp. 679-691, at p. 679.) Can marketing be used to sell ideas such as brotherhood, peace, exercise regularly, eat more nutritious food, say no to drugs. The more we thought about this, the more excited we became about the possibilities of developing a field that we could call "social marketing."

Marketing is generally thought to be a commercial subject. In my earlier writing, I had alluded to "societal marketing" by which I meant that marketers should consider the impact of their activities on society's well-being. How did the push for more spending by consumers affect our available resources and the quality of our air and water? Were there any limits that should be placed on "economic growth"?

Zaltman and I were looking at a broader question, whether marketing could be used to persuade people to adopt behaviors that would be better for them, their families and friends, and the society in general. We decided to call such marketing actions "social marketing" as a short term for "social cause marketing." Little did we know that social marketing would later be confused with "social media marketing" where some practitioners of social media marketing today shorten their phrase to social marketing.

We published our ideas in the article "Social Marketing: An Approach to Planned Social Change," *Journal of Marketing*, July 1971, Vol. 35, Issue 3, pp. 3-12. The article created a lot of attention and won the Alpha Kappa Psi Foundation Award for the best article published in 1971 in the *Journal of Marketing*.

I felt that there was so much more to say about social marketing that I invited my bright Ph.D. student, Ned Roberto, who came from the Philippines, to join me to co-author the first book on social marketing, *Social Marketing: Improving the Quality of Life* (2002). Social marketing thinking was first visibly applied to the problem of overpopulation and the challenge of getting families to plan more carefully how many children to have. "Birth control" was renamed "family planning."

We witnessed India's efforts to persuade rural families to have fewer than six children which was the norm given that three children might die and one of the surviving children had to be a male. India tried many tactics including showing movies in villages at night to keep parents from copulating when they had nothing else to do, to passing out condoms, to urging men to sterilize themselves so they wouldn't need condoms.

Other countries tried other solutions.

Ned Roberto

Dr. Mechai Viravaidy in Thailand promoted the use of condoms by having them blown into balloons, passing them out in restaurants, and dramatizing publicly the whole issue of safe sex and avoiding HIV/AIDS. He was known as the "Condom King" and persuaded McDonald's to distribute condoms and he helped make them available in toll booths, banks, and hotels. He even had Thai monks bless condoms so that Thai people would know there would be no ill effects from using them. Thailand's fertility rate fell substantially over the next several years.

The second big issue to tackle by social marketing was cigarette smoking. The evidence was clear that cigarette smoking shortened lives by leading to lung cancer and heart attacks. The Surgeon General of the U.S. mounted a public campaign against smoking and he was joined by many health organizations. Different campaigns were designed and targeted to different smoking groups by age, gender, and social class to help them avoid smoking or quit smoking. We believe that social marketing contributed greatly to a substantial decrease in tobacco use.

The next big application addressed the spreading epidemic of HIV/AIDS. Here the challenge was to warn gay men to test themselves and avoid promiscuous sex with partners they don't know. In 1986, the U.S. Surgeon General C. Everett Koop mailed information to every American household explaining AIDS and its dangers. This and other publicity convinced more young people to be tested and to be careful in their sexual choices.

I had the good fortune some years later to meet Nancy R. Lee. Nancy is based in Seattle and she is a professional social marketer who consults clients on campaigns to better the lives of people. I invited Nancy to join Ned and me to prepare a second edition of *Social Marketing* and with her deft mind and wide experience, social marketing took on a new life. *Social Marketing* is now in its fifth edition (2016) and is the most widely adopted book on that subject.

We began to realize that other persons had been working on social marketing. Bill Novelli was a partner in the advertising agency Porter and Novelli that specialized in helping social causes and Bill went on later to become the executive director of AARP. Bill Smith and Craig Lefebvre were also running social marketing campaigns.

Our books helped attract more people to enter and specialize in the field of social marketing. Professor Alan Andreasen of Georgetown University and others arranged social marketing meetings with the Center for Disease Control, the World Bank, the United Nations. The term "social marketing" began to catch on. Andreasen established an Internet application to enable social marketers to raise specific questions and share their experiences with others. He also wrote *Marketing Social Change* where he added the idea that social marketers should not only work with "downstream" social marketing situations but also work on "midstream" social marketing (with peers and family) and "upstream" social marketing situations to influence agencies and organizations that have a high impact on social behavior. For example, to fight the growing problem of obesity, social marketers not only have to persuade us to eat more healthy foods but also persuade food companies, restaurants, and other groups to reduce fat, sugar and salt in their food and drink offerings, as well as school systems to provide better menus.

Other social marketers include Professor Gerald Hastings of Stirling University in the UK who carried out serious research especially on anti-smoking, and who runs one of the best social marketing training programs. Professor Jeff French of the Brighton Business School in the UK has worked with the British public health system to train public health workers in social marketing. Professor Carol Bryant of the University of South Florida in Tampa runs an annual conference in Social Marketing in Clearwater, Florida. At one of the last meetings, Carol asked if she could establish the annual Philip Kotler Prize in Social Marketing. I agreed. The first three annual prizes awarded to Bill Smith, Carol Bryant, and Nancy Lee.

The first World Social Marketing Conference was held in Brighton, England in 2009 and drew over 700 social marketers. Since then, there have been other international meetings and a society was formed called the International Social Marketing Association. Social marketing has become a profession with recognized publications and groups around the world practicing social marketing. My guess is that there are over 100,000 professional social marketers carrying on the work.

Philip Kotler and Nancy Lee

Nancy Lee and I continued to co-author books concerned with improving social welfare through marketing. They are:

- Philip Kotler and Nancy R. Lee, *Corporate Social Responsibility: Doing the Most Good for Your Company and Your Cause*, Wiley, 2005.
- Philip Kotler and Nancy R. Lee, *Marketing in the Public Sector: A Roadmap for Improved Performance*, Wharton School Publishing, 2006.
- Philip Kotler and Nancy Lee, *Social Marketing: Influencing Behaviors for Good*, Sage, 2008).
- Philip Kotler and Nancy R. Lee, *Up and Out of Poverty: The Social Marketing Solution* (Philadelphia: Wharton School Publishing, Spring 2009). (A winner in the 800-CEO-Read

Business Book Awards for 2009)

- Hong Cheng, Philip Kotler and Nancy R. Lee, *Social Marketing for Public Health: Global Trends and Success Stories*, Sudbury, Ma., Jones and Bartlett, 2011.
- Doug McKenzie-Mohr, Nancy R. Lee, P. Wesley Schultz, and Philip Kotler, *Social Marketing to Protect the Environment: What Works*. Sage 2012.
- Philip Kotler, David Hessekiel, and Nancy R. Lee, *Good Works! Marketing and Corporate Initiatives that Build a Better World...and the Bottom Line*, Wiley, 2013. (Voted 4th best marketing book of the year by Expert Marketing Magazine EMM)

I am very proud of where social marketing has come since the first article and I hope that the social marketing movement continues to grow and improve the theory and practice of ameliorating social problems.

When I spoke in Jeddah recently, I was invited to the home of a prominent Saudi Arabian family. During the dinner conversation, one of the brothers said that he hoped I would apply social marketing to one of the world's most pressing problems that clearly, I had not studied. "What is that," I asked him. "Professor Kotler," he said, "can you find a way to market Peace?"

Recently, I co-authored an article with Christian Sarkar in called "Brand Activism, Finally!" We are at last seeing more business firms reaching out to promote better social conditions.

13. CRITICISMS AND CONTRIBUTIONS OF MARKETING

Marketing is a pervasive human activity. Practiced by every business and by countless individuals, it nevertheless manages to draw endless criticism. Woody Allen once remarked: "There are worse things in life than death. Have you ever spent an evening with an insurance salesman?" Why does marketing seem to irritate many people?

Criticisms

First, there is the intrusiveness of millions of brands that want to wrest money from our bank accounts, brands in which we normally have little interest nor that would significantly increase our well-being. It is estimated that we are exposed to 5,000 commercials a day without noticing most of them. These brands are collecting information about us as we use Facebook, Twitter, Instagram, You Tube, or Google and they reach a point of knowing so much about us that they hope to send the right message at the right time and place to incentivize us to make a purchase. We resent our loss of privacy and sometimes wish that we could live in a society free of advertising.

Second, there is frequent exaggeration or deceitfulness of the messages. Charles Revson of cosmetics brand Revlon said it well: "In the factory, we make the product; in the store, we sell hope." Others will hint: "Buy this convertible, and women will swarm all over you." Each medicine will cure the described illness, and each pair of shoes will let you glide through life. Vance Packard, one of marketing's most dedicated critics, wrote the *Hidden Persuaders* and *The Status Seekers* replete with stories of marketing practices to get people to buy things they didn't need or want. Ralph Nader, a major founder of the consumer movement, wrote *Unsafe at Any Speed*, to expose the auto industry's lack of safety in the design of many of its automobiles.

Third, marketing seems to neglect the hidden costs and damage to the environment that our high consumption creates. Businesses in the past were not charged for the air and water pollution that their activities produced. Rachel Carson alerted us in her book *Silent Spring* on the ravages to our rivers and streams by the relentless use and disposal of our natural resources and the weak regulations covering production activity. Add to this that companies gain by continually upgrading their products (called by its critics "planned obsolescence"), turning older versions of products into throwaways that pile up in waste dumps. As the level of world consumption increases, its damaging effects on the environment could make the planet uninhabitable.

Fourth, marketers pay little attention to the five billion desperately poor people in the world (of the 7 billion on the planet) who need much lower cost products. The poor do not have the means to buy even the cheapest bottle of shampoo. This was the case until Unilever started to package shampoo in a very small bag, or sachet. Even here, the price per ounce of shampoo is higher than in a regular bottle. The main point is that marketers go to where the money is which is mainly in the hands of the working class, the middle class, and the rich, all of whom add up to two billion out of the seven billion people on the planet.

Fifth, marketing's job is to increase consumption and it does this by increasing covetousness. Marketers operate on the assumption that there are no limits to human wants and everything could be made and sold as an object of desire. The result is that many people spend more than they can afford, facilitated greatly through the omnipresence of credit cards. The average American household has a credit card debt of $16,000 and what is worse, their interest rate may average 15 percent annually. The U.S. has failed as a society to produce an ethic of sane consumption in its consumers. Many other societies, especially European and Asian societies, have a much higher rate of saving vs. spending. In earlier America, getting into deep debt was regarded as a black mark and even a sin. Today, the motto is "Buy now. Pay later."

Sixth, marketers work hard to differentiate their offerings through the heavy use of advertising and branding, whose job is to hide the commodity nature of most offerings. There isn't much difference between most brands of coffee or aspirin. Advertising and branding increase the cost of most products, sometimes by as much as 10-20%. They don't grow the product category so much as shift brand shares. Naomi Klein is the strongest critic of branding and she provides much evidence of its cost and its false differentiation in her book *No Logo*.

Seventh, marketers are ready to sell anything that consumers want, without regard to its fitness for consumption. For years, marketers sold cigarettes and dismissed or denied evidence of the damaging effects of smoking. Had laws not prevented selling cigarettes to minors, marketers would want to get minors early into the smoking addiction and have them buy cigarettes for the next 70 years. Marketers don't raise questions about marketing alcohol to drunkards, or guns to mentally disturbed people. Marketers are ready to use any appeals that work, such as glamorizing smoking, showing good times with beer drinking, and using fear and security to sell more guns.

I will stop listing further criticisms of marketing. I want to emphasize that not all marketers are the manipulative Mad Men dramatized in the popular American television show. Most major companies and marketers exhibit a high level of integrity and transparency in marketing their products and services. They know that deceitfulness and manipulation can backfire on their reputations and lose customers and damage their reputation.

Contributions

We now will state the other side of marketing, namely its contributions. I would like to point out the major contributions of marketing to society.

First, marketing has raised our standard of living and built the middle class. Marketers, through intensely competing with each other, have developed products with new features, better quality and design, and superior service. Marketing has created the largest array of products, brands, and services that the world has even seen. Consumers today can live a life of affluence, health and entertainment that was not available to even the richest persons in the past.

Second, marketing is a major force in job creation and economic growth. Marketers are relentless in bringing new products and life styles to people's attention and enticing them to try new products, services and experiences. If their marketing succeeds, people spend more money and this creates more jobs. The result is a higher Gross Domestic Product.

Third, marketing improves the ease with which people can obtain the products, services and experiences that they desire. Every town will have a supply of Wrigley chewing gum, McDonald's hamburgers, and Bayer aspirin. Marketers not only ensure mass availability of their offerings but also mass information about their offerings and where they can be found.

Fourth, marketing offers a broad range of prices available for common products. Some businesses supply products priced at the low end, others at the middle, and still others at the high or highest end. Car buyers can choose a cheap second hand car, a medium priced new car, or buy a Ferrari or Rolls Royce for several hundred thousand dollars. A Swedish carmaker, Koenigsegg, prices his car at $3 million and it won't be ready for four years.

14. HOW TO MARKET PLACES

As a marketer, I receive many invitations to consult not only companies but also cities that want to achieve certain marketing objectives. A city might want to attract more tourists, conferences, residents, talented individuals or high net worth individuals. Or it might want to attract factories or company headquarters and branches. It might want a new and fresh branding campaign to help the place become better known in other parts of the world.

Some cities are so unique in their character that most of the world's population wants to visit these cities without needing any nudging or extra inducement. Cities like Rome, Paris, Venice, London and some others are blessed with a powerful history and sights.

But what can be done for an average city that is without an interesting history or character? How can such a city compete for attention and resources?

Consider Bilbao, Spain. I was invited to speak in Bilbao about their challenge of attracting more visitors. Bilbao had been a thriving city in the 1920s; you could tell from the quality of its buildings. But Bilbao could not compete with Madrid, Barcelona, Toledo, Granada or Seville, the Spanish cities that most tourists want to visit. Bilbao thought that the answer would lie in developing an expensive advertising campaign. Many people think that advertising and branding can turn a city from a non-entity into a star. I took a different approach. I told my audience of 600 Bilbao managers and citizens that advertising and branding would cost a fortune and not make much of a difference in Bilbao's attractiveness. What Bilbao needs is an "Eiffel tower," something that everyone in the world would want to see. "You have a nice city but no Eiffel Tower," I said. Bilbao needed a great attraction such as a great museum or theatre or sports arena. Luckily, they turned their thoughts to building a great museum but the problem was that Bilbao did not have a great art collection like that found in Madrid's great Prado museum. I said that the key was not to have great art but to have a great looking art museum. The committee decided to hire the prize-winning architect, Frank Gehrey. And Gehrey built a spectacular museum in Bilbao that itself became the work of art that everyone had to see. People flew in from all over the world on chartered flights to see the inside and outside of this great looking art museum.

Bilbao Guggenheim Museum

The challenge of making a city more attractive led to a research project that I started with two colleagues, Professors Irving Rein and Donald Haider. In 1993, we published *Marketing Places: Attracting Investment, Industry, and Tourism to Cities, States, and Nations*. We subsequently published three different versions of our book for the cities in Europe, Asia, and Latin America. We urged cities to undertake a strategic analysis of their city's strengths and weaknesses, and their opportunities and threats and then imagine some big and small ways to improve the city. Once done, they would be ready to build a strong marketing campaign to draw the attention of those groups that the city wanted to attract.

Phil and Irving Rein

Any city improvement plan should involve not only the city's power brokers but also its citizens. I remember Mendes France, the French Prime Minister in 1954 urging his French citizens to "smile more" so that foreigners would feel more welcome. I remember Singapore coaching its citizens on how to smile. And then there is Thailand where the people smile out of their very nature. "Smile" marketing can go a long way in ingratiating visitors and getting them to want to return again. I would add that cities should also use marketing to encourage their citizens to better attitudes toward Cleanness, Politeness, and Safety.

15. POLITICAL MARKETING AND ITS EVOLUTION

I am often asked what I think about political marketing. Political marketing is nothing new but it is growing more sophisticated and growing excessively expensive.

Let's look at what political marketing was before it became so sophisticated and expensive. We can start with ancient Athens where political oratory to sway audiences became a fine art with Athenians such as Demosthenes and Pericles. Orators either were running for election in ancient Athens or praising some politician or urging some collective action such as going to war against Sparta. The great Aristotle systemized the principles of rhetoric that were used by the great orators to argue for a cause.

For years, political candidates used homespun methods of ingratiating themselves with voters including kissing babies and attending countless teas and coffees, not to mention later using megaphones and sound trucks to call attention to themselves and their cause.

My first hint of looming political sophistication occurred when I studied at M.I.T. and heard about Professor Ithiel de Sola Pool who taught political science. He had developed a huge and representative database of voters and could provide John Kennedy, the democratic candidate for President at the time, with an estimate of how many votes Kennedy would win or lose with each stand that Kennedy might take on a public issue. Every politician in principle wants to maximize the number of votes in his favor. In Kennedy's case, he would sometimes take a stand that lost more votes than he would gain but he would project a more consistent picture of his character.

On this basis, we can distinguish between a political leader and a political hack. The hack is willing to take any position that will deliver more votes. The other characteristic of a political hack is that he or she will adopt the positions that raise the most campaign money. The hack is more interested in representing the interests of those who can donate the most than thinking seriously about representing the public interest.

My wife and I first met Barack Obama at the author Scott Turow's home a few blocks from our home. Scott knew Obama. Both of them were lawyers working to improve the criminal justice system. Scott wanted to help Barack raise money to enter the race to become a Senator. Twenty-five of us had gathered and we were overwhelmed with the brilliance and the human touch of Obama. I remember this as the first-time Nancy and I gave money so enthusiastically to a political candidate. We walked home saying "America needs more leaders like Obama."

Obama won the Senate seat and later the Presidency and both terms. His team made greater use of the newly developing social media that are revolutionizing political marketing. Using Facebook, Twitter, LinkedIn and You Tube helped Obama and the Democratic Party to establish a more intimate and frequent presence to their target voters. The Democrats brilliantly managed to raise small donations from the mass market to be seen as the more representative party for the public interest.

One can easily get cynical about the electioneering process. Independent candidates do not have a chance of winning an election without a party to back them. Each political party needs to spin a story about how it differs from the other party or parties and will deliver superior benefits to the mass of voters. Each political candidate must adhere to the party's principles or lose the party's backing at the next election cycle. So, the candidates are essentially voting for what is in their party's interest, not necessarily for what is in the public's interest.

Funding the campaign is central to the candidate's success. Each election cycle shows more and more money being spent by each party. Are there any solutions to curtail all of this political spending?

One solution is to fund all the candidates with government money and discourage or limit any private donations, but this raises freedom of speech issues. Another solution is to limit public electioneering and spending to only three months before the actual election date, something that the U.K. put into practice. Today we see winning candidates starting to raise money right after their successful election. Electioneering is becoming a continuous process. A third solution is to let the candidates run for longer terms, say four years instead of two years so they would have some time to pay attention to legislative issues rather than fundraising issues.

Two other areas of reform are also needed. A political candidate must first win the primary sponsored by his or her political party. Usually the primary vote is only participated in by party loyalists and ideologues. An extreme unrepresentative candidate can often win the primary. And in many states, the candidates who lose in the primary cannot run in the general election.

The other area is "gerrymandering," whereby a winning candidate may have his district redesigned in a way that leaves him either with more voters who think his way or with fewer who think his way, in which case he won't be reelected. One Democratic winning candidate found his district redesigned with many more Republican voters and he lost the next election.

All these issues led me to research, write and publish *Democracy in Decline* (2016). Now with a new President Donald Trump, who is the most unconventional of all our Presidents, I may have to write a new edition and find a new title.

16. THE FASCINATING WORLD OF MUSEUMS

One can find a museum in almost every city of reasonable size. It may be a museum showing the history of the city or in larger cities, it may be an art museum, a science museum, or a natural history museum. It may be a major museum with thousands of visitors or a lonely museum with many objects but few visitors.

I grew up in the city of Chicago that is rich in museums. We have some of the world's greatest museums - the Art Institute of Chicago, the Field Museum of Natural History, the Adler Planetarium, the Shedd Aquarium, and the Museum of Science and Industry. Even within the category of art museums, Chicago has the National Museum of Mexican Art, the Museum of Contemporary Art, the Polish Museum of America, and the Balzekas Museum of Lithuanian Culture.

These museums are significant contributors to our culture in Chicago and to our understanding of ourselves and our place in the world. They, along with our schools, libraries, and local newspapers, play a major role in shaping our knowledge and our worldview.

The original idea of a museum was to collect, protect and exhibit objects of historical or artistic interest. These objects would be exhibited on platforms and in cases in a well-protected public building for viewers to see, admire, and contemplate. The former director of the Metropolitan Museum of Art in New York City, Philippe de Montebello, held the view that museums are about objects and the reason to come to a museum is to enjoy seeing the objects. All other reasons to come to a museum are secondary.

Many of today's museum directors have a much broader view of what should go on in their museum. Many museums have added music and entertainment programs and have formed different collectors' groups. They feature single nights and senior nights. Museums have added an upper level restaurant in addition to their cafeteria. They have devoted space for children to play and do art under supervision. They want their museum to be filled with visitors who come to enjoy various experiences aside from viewing objects.

Over the years, a number of museum directors have contacted me about how to attract more visitors, how much should they charge for admission, how to attract more donors and larger donor gifts, how to prove that a museum makes a contribution to the economic development of a city, and other questions. I realized that a museum director must have several marketing skills: attracting visitors, donors, talented museum staffers, and support from the city. For a few years, I taught in the Getty Museum program that selected talented curators who wanted to acquire business skills that might lead to becoming the head of a museum.

As a result of my involvement in museums, I published with Neil Kotler, my brother, *Museum Strategy and Marketing: Designing Missions, Building Audiences, Generating Revenue and Resources* (1998). The book was successful and on visits to museums, I would often see a copy on the director's or a curator's desk. When the new digital media came along, we updated the book (2008) and published our second edition with the co-authorship of Wendy Kotler, Neil's wife.

Neil Kotler

I never thought that I would get involved in building a museum but this was the next step in my museum journey. My good friend and from Indonesia, Hermawan Kartajaya, runs the largest marketing research, training and consulting firm in Indonesia called MarkPlus. He and I met three Bali princes on a trip to Ubud. The princes had built two art museums on their land holdings and became very interested in our work in marketing. We proposed to them that Bali could be the first place in the world to have a Museum of Marketing. There is a Museum of Brands, Packaging, and Advertising in Notting Hill, London but our concept was much broader. The Princes were very happy to support the idea and we hired an architectural firm and within a few years a beautiful two-story museum opened up on their land in Ubud, Bali.

Phil and Hermawan Kartajaya

In walking into the museum, you first pass a section celebrating leading business marketers –Steve Jobs, Richard Branson, Anita Roddick, Herb Kelleher, and others -- and you read about their stories. Then you move to viewing some of the world's most customer-oriented companies and institutions such as Grameen Bank, Samsung, and the Mayo Clinic. Finally, you enter an auditorium where you view some of the world's greatest commercials – "I'd Like to Teach the World to Sing" by Coca Cola, "1984" by Apple, and the "RED" campaign by Bono. The Museum also contains a seating section for conversation, a reference library, and a knowledgeable staff.

Museums are like living organisms. They must grow and evolve to meet the ever-changing needs and interests of their audiences, and become relevant to the communities of which they are a part. We hope that many citizens of Bali and visitors to our Museum of Marketing 3.0 gain a new appreciation of the power of marketing to stretch our imagination and serve new needs and wants. I was honored by Indonesia in being featured on the new postage stamp shown below.

In 2007, I was appointed a Special Ambassador at large for Indonesian Tourism. In May 2011, the city of Denpasar in Bali bestowed on me the title of honorary resident of Denpasar.

17. ALL THE WORLD IS A STAGE: MARKETING THE PERFORMING ARTS

I always wondered what a large city or country would be like if there were no orchestra, opera, ballet, theatre, and live performances. It would mean the loss of a huge and precious cultural and entertainment industry.

Of course, people could still see and hear performances. They could view movies and play DVD discs. These performances could be available at any time or place. One would not face the problem of getting into a car, driving and finding a parking space, lining up to enter the theatre, moving to a seat, hoping that a tall person would not be sitting directly in front obstructing your view, waiting for intermission to get to the restroom's line, watching the second half, applauding and then going through a line to get your car, driving home and preparing for bed to end the four hours of intermittent pleasure and discomfort.

Millions of people still choose to attend live performances. Although they could just stay home, turn on a Shakespeare DVD and watch John Gielgud playing Hamlet, and two hours later rise and make a cup of tea, millions still consider this as not the same experience as going to see a live production of Hamlet. They want to experience the real thing, not a copy of the real thing.

Will the copy eventually replace the real? Modern technology and the Internet can deliver a copy of anything you want to see or hear with no exertion. Can the virtual experience suffice and satisfy? If more people become satisfied with the virtual experience, it will ultimately undo the live performing arts.

Technology is not the only noose around the neck of the live performing arts. The other is economics. The live performing arts are very expensive to produce and expensive to attend. Performing halls must be owned or rented. Auditions must be held to find the right persons to perform the roles. The performers – musicians, dancers, actors - must spend countless hours practicing their roles. The marketers must prepare and distribute news items about the events to attract a sufficient number of audience members to come and fill the seats at somewhat high prices.

The rising ticket cost of the performing arts cannot be solved by productivity increases. Playing Beethoven's Fifth faster or shortening it won't help. Reducing the orchestra's size may change the impact of the experience. Reducing the pay of the orchestra members would be wrong because their pay is not high to begin with. In general, it is harder to achieve productivity increases in service industries than in physical goods industries.

Another factor is that sales are limited to the size of the performance halls. A successful program may have to turn people away or invite them to sit in a separate room where they can see or hear a transmitted version. But this is the same as turning the performance into a copy instead of the real thing.

All the production cost cannot be covered by ticket sales except at prices that no one would pay. If the only source of revenue were ticket sales, an opera ticket would cost $500, more than anyone would want to pay. In the U.S., the reason that the ticket is only $150 is that the difference is paid by generous donors. In many other countries, the performing arts get huge support from their governments.

Will there be enough people in the future who will pay for the real experience rather than the copy? This is the existential question that may face the live performing arts. We know that different performing arts have their own popularity cycles. Live theatre may be moving up in attendance while live orchestra may be moving down. The story can be different in different countries. There are 7 full-sized orchestras in Tokyo, all of which attract good sized audiences. The fine arts are more a part of people's lives in Europe and Russia, for example, than in the U.S. In some American cities, ballet is popular and in other cities, poorly supported or non-existent. Ballet and opera typically need sizable cities to support them in the U.S.

We know that most performing arts are patronized by the over-50 crowd, not by the young or by families with children. Will the next generation of the over-fifties show the same support of the live performing arts as today's generation? Do today's marketers have the skills to build larger audiences? Do today's artists have the skills to create more exciting experiences for their patrons? Do they think in terms of creating experiences that are relevant for their target audiences?

I have been fascinated with these questions. My former student, Joanne Scheff Bernstein and I researched the performing arts and published our findings in our Harvard Business School Press book, *Standing Room Only: Strategies for Marketing the Performing Arts* (1997). We looked at the questions of ticket prices, subscription programs, fundraising from donors, building the performing arts company's brand, publicizing performances, focusing on old vs. new music and plays, attracting younger people to attend the performing arts, and dozens of other issues.

Joanne Scheff Bernstein

Our main conclusion is that those managing performing arts programs need the full range of management and marketing skills to put on excellent programs, fill the seats, attract donors, and cultivate public sector support. If they fail, we will all suffer.

18. THE COMPLEX WORLD OF RELIGION

As the field of marketing broadened its applications to nonprofit organizations – hospitals, social service firms, museums, performing arts organizations - I started to receive inquiries from various religious leaders as to whether marketing thinking could help them grow their congregation or at least prevent the congregation's decline. I have always been interested in religion as a force that brings people together to think about the good life and the guidelines for ethical and spiritual behavior. So, I decided to work with my former student, Bruce Wrenn, to research how marketing can help congregations and houses of worship "keep and grow" their "customers."

Even this phrasing of the problem turns off a number of religious leaders. The more conservative and traditional they are, the more they resent talk about applying marketing or business thinking to their religion. Yet we persisted. We remembered that one church - the Western Presbyterian church in Washington, D.C. - was losing members and it turned to the Alban Institute, a church consulting firm, that armed the church leaders with demographic reports and advice to focus on families with young children and adjust the sermons, all of this resulting in a doubling of attendance.

We pursued our fieldwork and finally we reported our findings in a new book *Marketing for Congregations: Choosing to Serve People More Effectively* (1992) along with two other authors (Norman Shawchuck and Gustave Rath). Later three of us published a revised edition and called the book *Building Strong Congregations: Attracting, Servicing, and Developing Your Membership* (2009).

Bruce Wrenn

We recognized that religious organizations are facing a growing number of challenges:

- Secularization had created new questions about the meaning and value of religion in terms of relevance and benefits.
- Marketization had created new ideas about the role of media, goods and services and what they should or could deliver.
- Radio, television and the Internet was competing with local churches and even offering virtual church services.
- Growing social issues of divorce, intermarriage, childless couples, gay marriages, multi-language and multi-cultural congregations, population shifts, and increasingly scarce financial resources all had to be dealt with by religious leaders.
- New immigrant groups were entering the U.S. with widely different cultures such as Buddhists, Muslims, Coptic Christians, and others.
- Independent, unaffiliated "mega-churches" were gaining in popularity as being different from institutionalized bureaucratic denominations.

With all of these developments, we are seeing new adaptations in church life. In San Francisco, the largest mosque took the controversial step of removing the eight-foot wall that separated male and female worshippers. Some males and female members left the mosque and joined a different mosque that retained the partition. In the New York area, a Jewish congregation offers Sabbath programs around tai chi, nature walks, yoga classes and stand-up comedy as a means of Sabbath observance.

In working with congregations' leaders, our approach is to show that there are many different motives that influence the decision to join or stay in a congregation. A church cannot meet the needs of all kinds of seekers. A church needs to define its target market carefully and learn their needs and expectations that would come from worship and social connections and service to the community. We use our marketing vocabulary and ask the congregation leaders: What is your offering (Product)? What are its benefits and costs (Price)? Where and when will it be delivered (Place)? And how would you promote it (Promotion)? We call these the 4Ps and they apply to every organization that wants to attract, keep and grow customers.

We emphasize the importance of first impressions on new visitors to a church. Are they greeted individually? Is there a follow up to find how they felt about the service and what are their good and bad impressions? A little preparation and a little research can go a long way in improving the church's offering. Our objective is to share the exciting ideas coming out of research in the growing field of service marketing.

We stay away from applying marketing to another and more sensitive question, "How to market your religion against another religion." There is a long history of religious clashes between Catholics and Protestants, between Christians and Muslims, between Shia and Sunni Muslims, between Orthodox and Reform Jews. Some religions are active in proselytizing and sending missionaries to other countries.

The Mormon Church has an active program for bringing in new converts to Mormonism. In a deep sense, most religions that grow meet a deep need in people and offer a set of beliefs that meet this need in exchange for their affiliation. One author made the claim that "the Bible is one of the world's great marketing texts." Preachers applied "marketing" practices as far back as Colonial times.

My interest is in learning how the different religions can live in peace with each other. There is no way to prove one religion's superiority to another. Each religion must be humble enough to acknowledge the earnestness of the members of other religions.

19. SEEKING TRANSFORMATION

Most people remain who they are through their whole life. If they are happy, they rarely seek to change. If they are unhappy, they might spend time with psychiatrists, drugs, and support groups. They may try to lose weight or go on a vegan diet or have plastic surgery. They may resort to travel, change occupations or spouses or take other steps to achieve more satisfaction in life.

I have had an interest in people who try to become a very different person. They are trying to trade in their current persona for another and hopefully better one. They are seeking not only some new experiences but also to be "transformed."

That this is possible, consider the life of Count Leo Tolstoy who went from being an army officer to a famous writer to an anarchistic moral thinker and social reformer. Tolstoy observed: "Everyone thinks of changing the world, but no one thinks of changing himself."

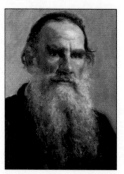

Count Leo Tolstoy

I remember joining a humanistic movement called EST (Erhard Seminars Training). Werner Erhard was a handsome and charismatic humanistic leader who would run a program over two weekends that would attract about 300 people, most of whom were seeking some level of transformation, not just an interesting experience.

They would go through a series of exercises in self-exploration as well as interpersonal interaction that might open their mind to new possibilities and ideas. They would raise their hands to be recognized to share a personal and often very disturbing experience after which others would comment on having similar experiences, showing that these experiences are not that unusual. The first weekend aimed to break down each person's current persona and the second weekend aimed to rebuild the person with new ideas and aspirations. Over 90 percent of the audience would report the weekend as being a major transforming experience in their lives. Some number of them would change their life after that weekend, change their job or relationships or other things that were bothering them.

Werner Erhard

Another transforming experience happens when one joins an ashram. I remember a professor acquaintance living in San Francisco who went through a difficult divorce.

One day he stumbled into a storefront ashram, heard the "guru," and started to attend regularly. He felt a new purpose in life and he decided to take a one year leave of absence from his university and move to India where the main ashram was located. He lived a new rich existence and planned to give up returning to his university.

But toward the end of the year, his guru said to him "It is time to return to your university." My friend objected and said that he would want to stay on at the ashram for the rest of his life. But his guru said "You have much more to offer to the world as a university professor than you could offer by staying here." He finally returned to his university and although conflicted, he has been one of the most popular lecturers at the university, undoubtedly enriched by his Indian experience. Whether he is really transformed, or partially or fully transformed, is not clear.

A more thorough transformation experience occurs when one decides to enter a religious order and become a priest or nun that is more extreme than becoming a minister or rabbi. The priest or nun has to abandon the idea of marriage, itself a transforming experience, and take vows that lead to a very different life. Some of them find that this is the wrong transformation and they return to their former lives.

Probably the most extreme transformation occurs when someone decides to become a monk and abandon earthly values. One acquaintance is a 40-year old Chinese son of a very wealthy family living in Asia whose life was going well but who felt something was missing. He started to study Buddhism in a serious way and then joined a monastery for a month. When I saw him, he told me that many things had changed in his life. He was seriously considering joining the monastery and giving up his present life.

Few of us are driven to seek a brand-new life but I keep thinking about those I know who have undertaken to erase the person they were and create a person that they now want to be.

20. MEETING PETER DRUCKER, THE FATHER OF MODERN MANAGEMENT

From the other end of the phone, I heard a person speaking in English with a German accent. As I listened carefully, he said, "This is Peter Drucker." I was astonished and tried to keep calm. This was because I had closely read his books that are rich in insight and I had great respect for him although I never met him. A call from Peter Drucker meant more to me than if our U.S. President called. He asked "Would you come to Claremont (in California) and talk with me about various things?" I hopped aboard the first airplane the following morning. It was in the second half of the 1980s.

Peter Drucker

Peter is not only the father of modern management. He also is a major pioneer in the discipline of modern marketing. For more than 40 years, Peter had been explaining to managers that the center of the company was its customers. Everything in the company should revolve around meeting and satisfying the needs of their customers. Creating customer value is the purpose of marketing.

I was influenced by four questions that Peter posed to companies:

- What is the primary business of your company?
- Who is your customer?
- What does your customer find value in?
- What should you make your primary business?

Each time Peter came face to face with one of the CEOs of a company such as P&G or Intel, he asked these questions. And CEOs testified that they achieved many insights in trying to answer his questions. I myself put similar questions to many companies I consult.

Peter's books and remarks are full of appropriate sayings about marketing and customers. I would like to mention some of them along with what they imply.

For example, he said: "the purpose of a business is to create a customer." This statement was in direct opposition to the view of most managers in those days that the purpose of a business is to create profit. For Peter, this view of managers is an empty theory that lacks the important idea of how to create profit. The secret is to create customers. To create customers, a company has to provide higher value (benefits minus costs) than its competitors. The only source of profit is customers.

Peter also said: "Business has only two basic functions – innovation and marketing; all the rest are costs." While being fully aware that all business functions are necessary and make a contribution, Peter singled out these two functions. Innovation means that companies cannot stand still when technologies and consumers' tastes are changing. And marketing needs to be strong if customers are to learn about the product and to know its features and price and locations and respect the company's offering. A company cannot be successful if it is strong only in innovation or in marketing but not in both. He also clarified the difference between marketing and sales. He stunned managers by saying that "the purpose of marketing is to make selling unnecessary". He thought that it was important to understand customers' needs deeply and create products that customers line up to buy without any sales prompting.

Peter criticized companies that first designed a product such as a car and only afterwards tried to decide who the car is for and what to say about the car. It makes more sense for the company to start with a full concept of the customer target and the product's purpose and then design the car to meet and satisfy that customer target group.

Back to Peter's phone call and my flight to meet him in Claremont, California. Peter picked me up at the airport, and we went straight to Claremont Graduate University, where he taught. He was a professor of art as well as of management. The university gave Peter a private gallery where he stored his collection of Japanese folding screens and hanging scrolls.

Peter opened and unfolded one hanging scroll after another. We talked about each work of art. The hours passed quickly. We discussed the fact that Japanese people have a different way to interpret and evaluate art. They like "sabi" a quiet quality that a work of art might have. They like "wabi" a feeling that the work of art had "lived" and earned a history. Japan's sense of beauty is quite different from the Western standards. Peter and I finally left the gallery and we lunched at a nearby restaurant.

Peter then invited me to his home. I met Peter's wife Doris, who is trained as a physicist and who was a wonderful tennis player. She greeted me with a wide smile. I was surprised by the modesty of their home. I was even more surprised to think that Peter had entertained top executives coming from many world-famous companies in their not-so-large living room. There was probably no need for Peter and Doris to show off.

On the evening of that day, Peter took me to a recording studio near his home. Peter was doing research on NPOs (nonprofit organizations) as I was. In the quiet recording studio, he asked me to speak about,

"How marketing can help leaders of nonprofit organizations improve their performance."

Peter's questions ranged over various topics and were stimulating. His questions about museums and orchestras provoked me to undertake more research into these cultural institutions. Peter summarized our Claremont discussion about nonprofit organizations in his book *Managing the Nonprofit Organization* published in 1990.

When the Peter F. Drucker Foundation for Nonprofit Management was established in 1990, I was invited to become a member of its advisory board. The foundation was set up to help NPOs learn from other NPOs and from managers and scholars to improve their NPO. I attended several annual meetings of the board and made presentations on how nonprofit organizations can develop exciting, creative marketing solutions to social problems.

Peter and I exchanged letters from time to time. What impressed me is that Peter always wrote letters by hand. He used neither a typewriter nor a personal computer to do so. Of course, he may have used these appliances on other occasions, but he never used them for his private letters to me.

The Drucker Foundation is currently operating under the name of the Leader to Leader Institute. Peter was at first unwilling to set up a foundation with his name and finally agreed on the condition that his name be removed some years later. His modest character showed itself in such gestures.

Each time I met with Peter, I was stimulated by his overwhelming knowledge of history and his prescient insights into the future. I cannot imagine how he acquired his vast knowledge in such a wide variety of fields.

I think of Peter as a rare Renaissance man who is one of the most remarkable persons that I have had the pleasure to know.

21. MY CONSULTING AND BOARD MEETINGS

Most professors of marketing, especially if they have written books on marketing, are likely to be contacted by companies needing consulting. The consulting is likely to enrich the professor's teaching and finances. In my case, I consulted with banks (Bank of America), auto companies (Ford, Hyundai, Kia), pharmaceutical firms (Merck, Johnson & Johnson, Eli Lilly), packaged goods companies (S.C. Johnson, Unilever, Apple), B2B companies (IBM, GE, Honeywell), and many other types of companies.

I have been invited to serve as an expert marketing witness by many law firms who believe that my books on marketing make me an ideal witness. But I decided a long time ago not to accept "marketing expert" invitations. They tend to interrupt one's schedule as legal cases are delayed, moved to other dates. And a witness knows that the opposing attorneys will stoop to anything to disestablish the witness's credentials and testimony.

I have been invited to serve on some company boards. I generally found that board meetings took a lot of time on matters of less interest to me and also exposed me to liability claims if my fellow board members did not exercise enough inspection on the doings of the management.

Boards range all the way from "rubber stamp" boards whose members are picked because they are congenial to management and likely to raise few questions and enjoy the pay and perquisites to other boards consisting of highly independent members who take their responsibilities seriously and raise lots of good questions and offer interesting ideas and proposals.

Most boards have a mix of rubber stampers and independent thinkers. One of the best examples of what can go wrong on a board is the General Motors board in the days when GM was riding high. The GM board generally didn't challenge management's strategy. But one of its new members, Ross Perot, whose company Electronic Data Systems

(EDS) was acquired by GM in 1984, was added to the board. He asked tough questions and expressed openly at the board meetings that GM was not producing great cars. He complained about GM executives lacking initiative, being top heavy in bureaucracy, and being out of touch with customers, dealers and workers. He saw his role as trying to teach "an elephant to dance. "

Ross Perot in 1986

The other board members didn't say much or join with him to criticize GMs policies and strategy. Top management found Ross to be too outspoken and asked him to resign and not say anything publicly about his criticisms or else he would forfeit a large sum of money for his silence. Ross was not one to be intimidated and he quit the GM board and promptly gave an interview to *Fortune* writer Thomas Moore in 1988 on how he would run GM and eliminate most of the senior management.

The best board meeting that I experienced was at a Fortune 500 company. I was consulting the CEO on how to bring more customer-centered thinking into the company. The CEO invited me to sit in and observe the two-day board meeting. The meeting consisted of three fascinating parts.

The first part consisted of hearing from three major customer companies about what they thought of the company's service and equipment. I remember hearing a senior manager from DuPont complain how difficult he found it to reach the right people at this company. The CEO made sincere apologies on hearing this and stressed the importance of his company striving to provide perfect service to its major customers. "That's the reason you are here," he said to the DuPont customer, "to help us improve our service to you."

The second part consisted of listening to three branch managers expressing how they felt about headquarters' branch policies. The well-regarded manager of the company's Chicago branch complained that he needed more leeway in hiring the people he needed to optimize his branch's profits. Headquarters allowed him to hire two new accountants but he wanted instead to hire two marketers. He told the Board: "Let me manage my branch by hiring the people that I need, not the ones that you think I need. I have promised the company a certain performance and budget and I should be free to hire who I want because I am on the line for results." Here the CEO agreed that branch managers should have a larger say in what they need in the way of branch hires.

The third part was fascinating. The CEO had invited a "competitor" to tell the board about the strategy the competitor planned to use to grab market share from the company. The "competitor" eyed the Board members and opened with the statement "Our aim at Sun is to bury your company!" He said that the company focused on improving equipment whereas the future lay in building networks.

This Board meeting example illustrates the need for company boards to hear at least three presentations:

1) Some major customers should be invited to tell the company how it is performing.
2) The company's own branch managers should describe how they feel about headquarter directives.
3) An important stand-in "competitor" should describe how that competitor is planning to attack your company.

22. SAVING BUSINESSES IN THE MIDST OF THE GREAT RECESSION

In 2008, the American economy was thrown into a very deep recession that lasted until 2011. Called the Great Recession, millions of people in the world lost their homes, income or wealth. There were earlier signs in 2007 that much recent economic growth had been built on speculation and over-generous financing. Americans had witnessed a steady rise in home prices and many felt that this would continue for a long time and they borrowed money to buy better homes and cars. They took out large mortgages and leased or bought their cars with small down payments. Mortgages no longer stayed in the issuing bank but instead were sliced and diced and bundled with other mortgages into what seemed like fairly diversified securities. Each mortgage contained a mix of highly secured homes and dubious homes. These mortgages were sold to banks and other institutions around the world.

In March 2008, the investment firm of Bear Stearns went bankrupt but the policy makers at the Federal Reserve chose to lend it money based on the collateral value of Bear Stearns.   Then in September 2008, the large investment firm of Lehman Brothers was facing failure. The government tried to get other investment firms to buy Lehman Brothers and save it. But when Barclays, the last potential buyer, said no, the government let Lehman declare bankruptcy on September 15, 2008. Two days later, the large insurance company A.I.G. was about to fail but the government intervened to save it. Now things got even worse and a clear recession was rolling in. Companies stopped hiring and started cutting their work force. Consumers would have less money to pay their mortgage installments and car loans, and many would find the value of their homes "under water." Economic conditions moved from bad to worse and unemployment rose from 5 to 15 percent.

I held discussions with my friend John Caslione who had authored a number of books on global business and had traveled to many countries. We saw companies desperately cutting their prices and reducing their marketing and sales forces, all of which seemed to us to be counterproductive. Companies were hurting their brand and their future and they failed to think deeply about alternative business strategies.

John and I decided to write a book on what companies can sensibly do in the midst of a growing recession. Because we saw chaos everywhere, we began to think that chaos was the "new normal". In May 2009, we published our new book, *Chaotics: The Business of Managing and Marketing in the Age of Turbulence*. The book drew excellent reviews and we received many invitations to speak on our ideas in the U.S. and abroad.

John Caslione

A few years later, John invited Nancy and me to attend his marriage in Italy to Donatella. Regrettably we couldn't go and we missed one of the great romantic marriages and settings. Later John and Donatella invited me to accompany them to enjoy four days in Florence and Rome where we saw two operas and consumed many great meals.

I was sad to learn several years later that this handsome couple divorced. Donatella wanted to remain in Vienna where she enjoyed a highly rewarding position as a financial advisor to a wealthy family. John wanted to return to the U.S. and make it his headquarters for international consulting. John is now remarried and he lives and teaches in Tampa, Florida.

23. GROWING A BUSINESS IN AN AGE OF SLOW GROWTH

The financial crisis starting in 2007 ushered in a period of low or no growth that spread throughout the world. It left the U.S. with a very low growth rate and it put several European countries – Greece, Portugal, Spain, Italy - into a negative growth rate. At the same time, several Asian countries – China, Indonesia, India, Malaysia - continued their 5-8 percent growth rate.

We know that every low growth public company is under pressure to achieve higher growth and profit. We also know that a company's current strategy, the one that delivered profits in the past, is no longer promising. It's time for the company to design a new strategy.

We do not think that a company in a low growth economy needs to accept low growth as its fate. We believe that a search will reveal many pockets of opportunity waiting to be exploited by those with insight and vision.

The pressure to achieve higher profit growth led my brother Milton and me to identify eight strategic pathways for higher growth. We described them in our book *Market Your Way to Growth: Eight Ways to Win* (2013).

Milton Kotler

Milton and Philip

Top management, in its eagerness to please its shareholders, usually sets an aggressive growth objective for the next year. If the company faces a large "growth gap," the gap must be filled by undertaking new initiatives. Each initiative will come with a certain level of promise and risk.

Here are eight major strategic pathways for growth:

1. Building Your Market Share
2. Developing Committed Customers and Stakeholders
3. Building a Powerful Brand
4. Innovating New Products, Services and Experiences
5. Expanding internationally
6. Considering Acquisitions, Mergers, and Alliances
7. Building an Outstanding Reputation for Social Responsibility
8. Partnering with Government and NGOs

Suppose your company has achieved growth in the past by the first strategic pathway, i.e., winning market share. It added new features to its products and charged a higher price. But in the new low growth environment, customers have more interest in a lower price than getting additional benefits. Your company has to consider one or more of the other seven strategic pathways to growth.

What are the key points involved in each of the eight strategic pathways and what are the pitfalls? Acquiring another firm might close the growth gap but many mergers and acquisitions fail. Entering another country such as China might close the growth gap but international expansion can involve many surprises and difficulties. The aim of the book is to put together in one book the major considerations that arise with each strategic pathway in trying to fill the company's "growth gap." Although execution is important, it adds little value if the company chooses the wrong strategic pathway.

24. MANAGING NONPROFIT ORGANIZATIONS

My mother, Betty Kotler, was in her fifties when she decided to become a volunteer at her local hospital. The manager assigned her to work in the hospital's gift shop. She worked there for the next 30 years, meeting patients, visitors, doctors and nurses coming in to buy flowers, candy, newspapers and sundry items.

Betty Kotler

I noticed how much satisfaction she got from volunteering her time to a good cause while receiving no pay. This hospital was a non-profit hospital. It opened my eyes to volunteering behavior and also to the huge number of organizations in the nonprofit sector: schools, colleges, museums, theatres, churches, charitable and social welfare organizations such as Boy and Girl Scouts, YMCA, health and community organizations such as the American Cancer Society or American Heart Association, and so on. These organizations fill an important and separate sector between the millions of for-profit private firms and the huge government sector.

I used to think that government was supposed to do everything needed in a society that private enterprise would not do. This is more the case in Western Europe than in the United States. Government taxes in Europe are very high to cover the cost of free health, education and other needs that nonprofit organizations (NPOs) (also called the non-government sector – NGOs) often have to cover in the U.S.

In the 1970s, I began to consult many nonprofit organizations on their problems of setting prices, designing services and raising money from the government, business firms, and individual donors. As a marketer, I advised them to adopt a business view of their operations. *Then I realized the problem!* The people running these organizations would say that they were not running a business. "Business" was like a dirty word in their mind. Several said that they chose to work in a NPO to do good and to avoid a business career! The idea of dealing with functions such as marketing, procurement, finance and others turned them off.

In spite of this, my aim became to make business thinking more understandable and acceptable to NPOs. These NPOs needed a plan and many business tools to get good results. In 1975, I wrote one of the first textbooks on NPOs, *Marketing for Nonprofit Organizations*. The term "non-profit organizations" wasn't used very much. Each type of organization – hospital, school, church—thought of itself as operating in a separate world. My book caught on and went through a second edition in 1982. Later I invited Professor Alan Andreasen of Georgetown University to join me as co-author of the third and subsequent editions. The book is now in its 7th edition.

2nd ed., 1982 (1st ed., 1975)

I remember discussing the nonprofit sector with Peter Drucker when he was writing his book *Managing Nonprofit Organizations* (1990). Peter was a major fan of this sector and he wrote about hospitals, churches, orchestras and other types of NPOs. He used the orchestra as a wonderful metaphor of how every organization should work. There is the conductor who rehearses and leads the orchestra. Each performer knows his musical instrument well and knows how to perform his or her work and knows how to work with others so that the whole outcome is beautiful music.

Around 1982, I had a realization. My nonprofit book worked well to introduce management students to the use of marketing in the nonprofit sector. But the book didn't go deeply into specific types of nonprofit organizations. Each type of nonprofit organization has a distinct mission and characteristics. These different types cannot be described richly enough within one book. I decided to carry out research into each major type of nonprofit organization and publish a separate book on each. Starting in 1985, I published books in the following six sectors of the nonprofit world:

Schools and Universities:

Philip Kotler and Karen Fox, *Strategic Marketing for Educational Institutions*, Prentice-Hall 1985, 1995.

Healthcare:

Philip Kotler and Roberta N. Clarke, *Marketing for Health Care Organizations*, Prentice-Hall, 1987;
Philip Kotler, Joel Shalowitz, and Robert Stevens, Strategic *Marketing for Health Care Organizations: Building a Customer Driven Health Care System*, Jossey-Bass, 2008;
Hong Cheng, Philip Kotler and Nancy R. Lee, *Social Marketing for Public Health: Global Trends and Success Stories*, Sudbury, Ma., Jones and Bartlett, 2011.

Social and Charitable Organizations:

Philip Kotler and Eduardo Roberto, *Social Marketing: Strategies for Changing Public Behavior*, The Free Press, 1989;
Philip Kotler, Nancy Lee and Eduardo Roberto, *Social Marketing: Improving the Quality of Life*, The Free Press, 2002. (Latest title is Philip Kotler and Nancy Lee, *Social Marketing: Influencing Behaviors for Good*, Sage, 2008);
Philip Kotler and Nancy R. Lee, *Up and Out of Poverty: The Social Marketing Solution* (Philadelphia: Wharton School Publishing, Spring 2009);
Doug McKenzie-Mohr, Nancy R. Lee, P. Wesley Schultz, and Philip Kotler, *Social Marketing to Protect the Environment: What Works*, Sage 2012, and Philip Kotler, David Hessekiel, and Nancy R. Lee, *Good Works! Marketing and Corporate Initiatives that Build a Better World...and the Bottom Line*, Wiley, 2013. (Voted 4th best marketing book of the year *by Expert Marketing Magazine* EMM)

Religious Organizations:

Philip Kotler, Norman Shawchuck, Bruce Wrenn, and Gustave Rath, *Marketing for Congregations: Choosing to Serve People More Effectively*, Abingdon Press, 1992. (Revised in 2009 as Philip Kotler, Bruce Wrenn and Norman Shawchuck, Building Strong Congregations).

Performing Arts Organizations:

Philip Kotler and Joanne Scheff Bernstein, *Standing Room Only: Strategies for Marketing the Performing Arts*, Harvard Business School Press, 1997.

Museums:

Neil Kotler and Philip Kotler, *Museum Strategy and Marketing: Designing Missions, Building Audiences, Generating Revenue and Resources*, Jossey Bass, 1998, 2008

I realized after this long and gratifying period of research that I neglected a huge sector, the third sector, namely the government. Government agencies need to train their people as "public servants" whose job is to create "satisfied citizens." Many national, regional, state and city governments lack this philosophy of making it easy and convenient to use government services. Thus, government marketing became my next focused research interest.

25. IMPROVING GOVERNMENT PERFORMANCE

I became interested in studying how marketing could improve the delivery of good service by government organizations at the city, state and nation level.

I remember walking into the City of Chicago's Vehicle Bureau to renew my driver license. Renewal involved taking a driving test with a staff person who would verify that I could drive safely. I found myself in a line of over 200 people and realized that I would be spending my whole day waiting for someone to test my driving ability. Waiting time would also be necessary with other government tasks, such as getting a new passport or getting an appointment to speak to an Internal Revenue Service agent.

My thought was that a poor level of service wouldn't happen if I was dealing with for-profit organizations that were competing for my business. Government is a problem in that each agency is a monopoly and you need its service. Government employees are sometimes poorly trained and the agencies lack enough money to hire an adequate size staff.

I thought that if we could give government workers better training and adequate resources, we would get better service. This is not necessarily so. We have to give them a "consumer orientation" and a "business training" so that they set high service standards and collect information about the level of consumer satisfaction with their service.

In some ways, I shouldn't complain because government service is worse in many other countries. The worst cases are in countries where government employees won't do much to speed up unless they receive a "bribe." Citizens, besides having to pay taxes, have to pay extra money to get the services that they were supposed to get from their government.

Most government agencies don't have the incentive or the ability to think innovatively. There are many practices and procedures that can be improved in this new Age of Information. I witnessed this in the case of driver license plates. In the past, the Vehicle Bureau would send a form each year to fill in and to send it back with a check to get the next year's metal license plates. The license plates would arrive by mail in a few weeks, and I would take the plates and a screw driver to my car and unscrew the old plates, throw them away and screw on the new plates to the back and front of my car.

Some bright person suggested that the license plates did not need to be replaced each year. People could keep their old license plates and pay each year a fee to receive a new vehicle sticker to paste in the right upper corner of their old plates. The government would save the annual expense of making new metal plates and the citizens would not have to unscrew old plates and replace them with new plates. Another innovation was the recognition that only one plate in the rear of the car, not two, would be sufficient.

There are many government services that can be improved through innovative ideas and better management. I invited Nancy Lee to co-research this subject with me. In 2006, we published *Marketing in the Public Sector: A Roadmap for Improved Performance.* We describe many procedures and stories about improving public sector performance.

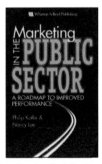

Marketing in the Public Sector:
A Roadmap for Improved Performance

Governments face another challenge beyond delivering better service. That challenge is to become more effective in attracting tourists, visitors, factories, headquarters, and human talent to their city or country. Government agencies need to acquire the skills of "place marketing." In the case of cities, cities need to prepare separate marketing plans to attract different groups.

Along with professors Irving Rein and Don Haider, we researched how cities carry on these city improvement activities. We published our findings in 1993 in Philip Kotler, Irving Rein, and Donald Haider, *Marketing Places: Attracting Investment, Industry, and Tourism to Cities, States, and Nations*. This book was well-received. Afterwards, we invited foreign colleagues to adapt the book to cities in other continents and we published separate editions for Europe, Asia and South America.

Marketing Places:
Attracting Investment, Industry, and Tourism to Cities, States, and Nations

I then recognized that the challenge of marketing a nation differs considerably from marketing a city. Nations carry a brand image from their history, culture, and philosophies. A nation has to examine its image and see how it helps or hurts the nation in accomplishing its objectives. A research field called "country of origin" describes how a nation's image affects its ability to compete in different markets. We would think that a new car made in Germany would be perceived as excellent but if we heard that a new car was made by a Yemen company in Yemen, we would perceive it to be fair or poor. A nation must understand how its current image helps or hurts a product's acceptability.

Many countries need to rebrand their national image. The rebranding cannot be done by words and pictures alone or a huge advertising budget. The rebranding might require a whole new set of behaviors and investments to make the new image believable and effective. Working with two of my students on this challenge, we published in 1997 Philip Kotler, Somkid Jatusripitak, and Suvit Maesincee, *The Marketing of Nations: A Strategic Approach to Building National Wealth.*

Somkid Jatusriptak, Philip and Suvit Maesincee

There is a fascinating change occurring today in the relationship between a nation and its major cities. Historically the nation sets the strategic direction and the cities follow. In the U.S., the hierarchy runs from the federal government down to the 50 states and then down to the cities. The federal government collects taxes and allocates funds to the states that in turn allocates funds to the cities on a need, bidding or political basis. In these circumstances, a city's development is highly dependent on the largess it receives from the federal and state governments.

Today the relation between the federal and state governments and the cities is inverting. The federal government and the states are terribly short of money as a result of the financial collapse of 2008. The political gridlock between Republicans and Democrats has prevented Washington from solving the nation's problems. Many American cities are now taking the initiative to create their own future and set their own goals and objectives. Major cities are going abroad to attract factories, businesses and foreign direct investment from China and elsewhere. Cities are improving the city's quality of life to be more attractive to businesses and skilled workers. We will see major cities become like the old city-states and carry the nation forward rather than the nation carrying the cities forward. This became the theme of my book co-authored with my brother, Milton Kotler, *Winning Global Markets: How Businesses Invest and Prosper in the World's High Growth Cities* (2015).

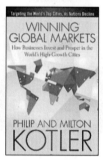

Winning Global Markets:
How Businesses Invest and Prosper in the World's High Growth Cities

26. THE SCOURGE OF CORRUPTION

Most fields have a dark side that its practitioners hardly mention or deliberately bury. Most political science textbooks do not mention the special interest groups and lobbyists and the influence peddling that goes on. History textbooks hide certain facts that would otherwise tarnish the popular view of an event or person. U.S. history books did not mention Thomas Jefferson's failings as a person owning slaves and having children with his personal slave. Science textbooks fail to mention cases of flimsy or fabricated research and widespread plagiarizing of the other's work.

Marketing too has its dark side. We like to think that Lockheed Aircraft won a Japanese bid for its aircraft because it offered the better value proposition. But we learned subsequently that Lockheed gave major bribes to the buyer committees that were choosing the aircraft.

Bribery is a widespread practice but I have never mentioned it in any detail in my textbooks. Why? I certainly do not advocate bribing the customer. Nor do I want to advise a company on how big a bribe they need to offer to win a contract. At best, I would want my students to know that one or more of their competitors may be doing this and they should report it to the authorities or desist from bidding.

I remember a professor friend at the London Business School who decided that the extensiveness of bribery practice needed to be exposed. He decided to collect data from his executive training classes. He would ask the executives in his evening class to raise their hands if their company used bribery to win contracts. No hands were raised. Then he switched the question: "Raise your hands if you know that one or more of your competitors has given bribes." Almost all hands went up. The funny thing is that the same class contained managers from the same companies that didn't raise their hands when the first question was asked.

The professor went further and asked members of his class to send in anonymous descriptions of how specific bribery episodes were performed. He didn't want any company to be named nor even the name of the student, only how the bribe was delivered in a specific situation. He received hundreds of cases over the years. He decided that he would codify the types of bribing arrangements and even figure out the optimal ways to bribe and optimal amounts to offer as a theoretical exercise. He planned to publish a book on his findings and told his wife. At that point, she panicked and warned him not to do this. He would get a reputation that would draw many unsavory characters to seek his advice on how to optimize on bribery. He decided not to write a book or article and all of his research was locked away or destroyed.

The terrible truth is that bribery is very extensive. A business that is planning to enter another country should consult Transparency International to see how the country ranks in bribery and corruption. The most corruption is found in Africa, Asia and South America. But even a relatively clean country such as Germany in the past allowed its business people to write off any bribe they gave as an expense of doing business.

The fact is that most companies do not want to get into the bribery business to win contracts or facilitate performance. The problem is that when a company knows that its competitor is doing this, does the company also have to offer a bribe, or should the company report this, or desist from even bidding.

We know that bribery imposes a great cost to society. It results in a misallocation of resources in that the most valuable and efficient offers do not win. The bribe imposes a tax on profits and does not add any value to the society.

An Indian friend told me a story. He decided to go to the titles office in India to put his property in the name of his son. This should normally take 10 minutes and 100 rupees to execute the application. But the bureaucrat wanted a payment of 5000 rupees to carry out this transaction. My friend asked the bureaucrat why do you do this. The bureaucrat answered that he is poorly paid. My friend decided not to pay this (because no value was created) and asked a high-level friend of his in the bureaucracy to get this transaction done at the regular cost. He told me the story of one of India's ministers who was caught with hundreds of thousands of rupees in his drawer, much more than he could have earned with his salary. The minister was angry, "Why are they picking on me," he shouted. "They are all doing it."

Nations have been largely ineffective in reducing corruption. The U.S. used the most direct approach by passing the Foreign Corrupt Practices Act in 1977 where any evidence of a corrupt act would lead to fines or jailing the perpetrators. On the whole, U.S. companies have behaved ethically under this law. A few managed to distance themselves as far away from the site and agent carrying out a bribe. Police and legislative effort is now moving to reach into the money hiding centers of Switzerland and the Caribbean banks that manage black money. The best piece of news is that many Swiss banks have agreed to pay taxes on the amount of money held in secret accounts. And recently India decided to stop producing notes of 500 rupees because they clearly were used to facilitate black market transactions.

27. THE INEVITABLE RISE OF CORPORATE SOCIAL RESPONSIBILITY

As a marketer, my job is to help companies produce good products and services and be effective in selling them. I always had some concerns about the impact of all this production and distribution on the state of our environment. I was haunted by William Wordsworth verse "Getting and spending, we lay waste our powers: Little we see in Nature that is ours..."

In 1972, the Meadows published a book called *The Limits to Growth* based on a computer model showing that unchecked economic and population growth may cause us to eventually run out of key resources as well as hurt the environment. This would manifest itself by a rise in the price of many key commodities. My friend Julian Simon thought this was nonsense and challenged the Meadows with a bet that commodity prices wouldn't rise. Commodity prices didn't rise and he won the bet.

Nevertheless, I began to think that marketers needed to show more responsibility for their impact on global resources and the environment. I thought that companies needed to give something back to society in return for what they get from society. I became interested in the question of corporate social responsibility (CSR).

Should a public company feel obligated to make charitable contributions? The owner of a private company might want to support some charities and make gifts through the business. That is his or her right. But the management of a public company would be taking the money that belongs to stockholders and deciding on which charities to support. The employees may resent this because they didn't participate in the charity choices and maybe would have preferred that the money go into paying higher wages.

My professor, Nobel economist Milton Friedman of the University of Chicago, was the strongest voice objecting to charity-giving by businesses. "There is one and only one social responsibility of business— to use its resources and engage in activities designed to increase its profits so long as it stays within the rules of the game." He felt that the company's profits belong to the shareholders who put their capital at risk. The shareowners should personally decide whether to give any charity from their income and if so how much and to which charities should the money go. Friedman also felt that companies that spent money on social responsibility will be more vulnerable to competitors who don't do this or who put their money into R&D or other competitive-building investments.

This position was very popular among traditional companies but now is losing followers. Today, most companies are engaged in giving money to good causes. What is the rationale?

There are three rationales.

First, companies have received a lot of benefits from society such as the roads and bridges and ports and other infrastructure that help them be profitable. Therefore, they should return something to society.

Second, CSR will help improve the company's reputation as a good citizen and this will win over more customers and help their employees feel better about their company.

Third, giving charity offsets the wide impression that companies care only about profits and about accumulating wealth.

There is a larger rationale called moral obligation.

R. Edward Freeman made this point: "How are we going to make this company an instrument of service to society even as we fulfill our obligation to build shareholder wealth? ...This country has been too steeped in materialism and self-centeredness...Companies need a soul."

When a company decides to be generous, it must still decide who should get the donations. One possibility is to respond to the many good cause solicitations that come from the community and other stakeholders such as suppliers, dealers, and so on. The other possibility is for the company to choose an important cause and direct most of its donations to that cause. For example, Avon chose to support research and treatment of breast cancer, an extremely important issue to women. In this way, Avon's reputation strengthens for its supporting a cause that most of its customers care about.

I am inclined to favor this focused approach to donation-giving. Nancy Lee and I studied this question by interviewing 25 well-known companies – among them IBM, Johnson & Johnson, Microsoft, American Express, Starbucks, Ben & Jerry's, Timberland, McDonald's, Motorola, Hewlett-Packard – and asking them several questions, including: How did you decide on your cause? How do you measure the impact of your gift to know how much good it is doing for the receiving group? How do you measure how much your giving is doing for your reputation and in attracting new customers and keeping present customers? We published our results in our book *Corporate Social Responsibility: Doing the Most Good for Your Company and Your Cause* (2005).

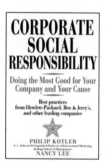

Corporate Social Responsibility:
Doing the Most Good for Your Company and Your Cause

Here is a sample of companies and their causes: Kraft (reducing obesity), General Motors (improving traffic safety), Levi Strauss (preventing AIDS), Motorola (reducing solid waste), Shell (cleaning up coasts), and Starbucks (protecting tropical rainforests).

Most of the companies made an effort to measure how the donations helped the recipients. The task of measuring the return to the company

– in terms of stronger customer and employee results - remains more difficult to measure, because so many other variables also affect the company's reputation. In the end, one might say that helping others is a good enough reason and does not always have to be measured in dollar terms. My co-authors and I reported our latest research on corporate social responsibility in *Good Works* (2012).

Good Works

We distinguished between six ways in which a company can manifest its corporate social responsibility (CSR):

1) Cause Promotion,
2) Cause-Related Marketing,
3) Corporate Social Marketing,
4) Corporate Philanthropy,
5) Community Volunteering, and
6) Socially Responsible Business Practices.

I also devoted Chapter 7 in my recent *Market your Way to Growth* (2013) to describe how companies can use CSR as one of eight winning strategies.

28. THE CONSCIOUS CAPITALISM MOVEMENT

Winston Churchill made the following observation about democracy: "It has been said that democracy is the worst form of government except or all those other forms that have been tried from time to time."

I am sure that the same defense can be said about capitalism. Capitalism has its faults but all the other systems are worse. Yet capitalism sure has a litany of faults. Legions of critics complain that capitalism is based on materialism, greed, and financial self-interest, three forces most likely to injure "community." Here are the Big Nine shortcomings of U.S. capitalism:

1. Proposes only a weak solution to poverty.
2. Fails to charge businesses with the social costs of their activities.
3. Capable of exploiting workers in the absence of collective bargaining.
4. Capable of exploiting natural resources in the absence of regulation.
5. Sees citizens as mainly consumers who should be persuaded to buy more and more goods and services even beyond their means.
6. Exhibits a very high level of income and wealth inequality.
7. Emphasizes individualism over community.
8. Encourages greed + financial creativity + materialism.
9. Produces periodic business cycles and economic instability.

Yet when Communism came along as an alternative system promising to build community and equality, it created some of the unhappiest citizens in the world. Its sway during the period 1920s-1980s cost millions of lives and set back dozens of national economies.

Capitalism emerged from the end of the Cold War to become, ironically, the operating principle of the Russian and Chinese economies, as well as the economic system of most of the world's other nations.

Today there is broad consensus that when capitalism works well, it leads to higher productivity and standards of living.

Yet the urge to find something better than capitalism persists. The proposed "middle way" would be something like "socialism" or "social democracy" where private property exists and businesses can pursue profits under the discipline of various regulations and social norms. The government would operate some industries in the public interest – defense, electricity, public infrastructure, waste management, public health – and would tax private incomes substantially enough to fund virtually "free" education and health, the two biggest concerns of most citizens.

Scandinavian countries illustrate that it is possible to reconcile socialism and democracy. These countries have avoided slipping into authoritarianism or tyranny, the so-called "slippery slope" of socialism feared by its critics.

A less drastic improvement of capitalism has been proposed by a handful of academic and business personalities that they call "Conscious Capitalism." When I first heard this term, I wondered if it implied that normal capitalism is "unconscious" and what does that mean. Why didn't they call the new movement "Responsible Capitalism" or "Reform Capitalism"?

Who launched this movement and what are its principles? The principal academic co-founder is Raj Sisodia, a professor of marketing at Babson College and the principal business co-founder is John Mackey, who created the Whole Foods Market chain of food supermarkets. Other businesses that have supported the movement are Southwest Airlines, Costco, Google, Patagonia, The Container Store, UPS, Joie de Vivre hotels and dozens of others.

All of these businesses are successful and practice an enlightened form of capitalism. They are not pretending to be "social businesses" which just aim for a little profit. Instead these companies pursue normal profits in socially responsible ways. Much of their thinking is described in the new book, *Conscious Capitalism: Liberating the Heroic Spirit of Business* (2013) by John Mackey and Raj Sisodia.

According to MacKay and Sisodia, Conscious Capitalism is based on four principles:

Higher purpose. Companies will be more successful if they exist for a higher purpose beyond profit-making, a purpose that inspires its owners, employees, middlemen, and customers. Management's task is to propose an inspiring higher purpose meaning for the company. This would happen when an agricultural company says that its purpose is to help end hunger in the world, or a food producer says that its purpose is to improve the nutritional quality of food.

Stakeholder integration. Companies will be more successful when they build a team feeling among the various stakeholders who contribute to its success. The stakeholders – customers, employees, distributors, suppliers, community, and environment – all commit to the higher purpose and are rewarded fairly for their individual contributions to the success of the company. They work together to find ideas for improving the performance of all the stakeholders. No longer do the investors treat the other participants in their ecosystem as "resources" to be exploited for the well-being of investors. Stakeholder integration should lead to higher satisfaction of customers, employees, distributors, suppliers and other stakeholders. Conscious Capitalism challenges the old dogma that profits are optimized by companies focusing exclusively on the bottom line.

Conscious leadership. Business leaders must be motivated primarily by service and creating value for all stakeholders. The leaders need to be sensitive to conflicts and trade-offs but try to reach higher consensus solutions that ultimately benefit all the stakeholders

Conscious culture and management. The company is built on a set of values that encourage innovation, collaboration, and empowerment of the participants. The values include trust, accountability, transparency, integrity, egalitarianism, love and caring.

It is too early to tell whether the Conscious Capitalism movement and its principles will endure and re-pattern the thinking of an increasing number of business leaders. But if those companies that now practice Conscious Capitalism continue to outperform their competitors in their profitability and level of stakeholder loyalty, other companies will be persuaded to start turning their practices toward a higher company purpose. I have had the pleasure of speaking at ones of their large annual conferences on how Marketing 3.0 fits in with Conscious Capitalism. I left with a positive feeling that Conscious Capitalism will contribute to improving the performance of capitalism.

29. THE CURSE OF POVERTY

For all of marketing's sincere emphasis on serving customers, it has all but ignored five billion of the seven billion "customers" in the world. Marketing has catered brilliantly to the working class, the middle class, the affluent and the superrich. But those groups only add up to two billion people. Of the seven billion people in the world, marketing has paid continuous attention to only two billion.

Dorothea Lange's iconic 1936 photograph, Migrant Mother

The U.S. Census Bureau reported in 2012 that 15 percent of Americans live below the poverty level. That means 46.5 million Americans are poor. One in four American children are poor.

How can marketing ignore the poor? A superficial defense of marketing is to point out that "the poor do not have money." Or "There is no profit in selling to the poor."

This was our mindset until the great and late C.K. Prahalad and Stuart L. Hart wrote their ground-breaking article *The Fortune at the Bottom of the Pyramid* (2006). Professor Prahalad said that there are billions of dollars actually in the hands of the "poor" that can be activated.

Prahalad pleaded with companies to build less expensive products and services that the poor could afford. Even if poor consumers cannot afford Coca Cola or a McDonald's hamburger, why can't creative entrepreneurs bring out drinks or fast food items that the poor can afford? Isn't it the modern company's high spending for "branding" and advertising and packaging that is increasing the cost of ordinary products?

A few large companies are now beginning to pay attention to the poor. Hindustan Unilever in India introduced sachet ("small bag") size shampoo so that a poor woman can buy a little amount of shampoo who otherwise could not afford a bottle-size shampoo. Unilever also makes smaller size soaps with the purpose of affordability in mind. (Ironically, the smaller sizes are priced higher per pound but we should be thankful). Coca-Cola has worked hard to bring water purification systems into rural area so that safe drinking water would be available and affordable. These and other companies also contribute by building more efficient supply chains to deliver their goods to remote rural areas, managing thereby to bring down the cost of these products. For example, Coca-Cola delivery trucks can rent space on their trucks to suppliers of other goods that need to reach remote areas.

There are other companies that are managing to lower costs and prices to the poor. A poor Indian who needs cataract eye surgery can go to the Aravind Eye Care System. Aravind is a network of hospitals, clinics, community outreach efforts, factories, and research and training institutes that has treated more than 32 million patients and has performed 4 million eye surgeries. Aravind patients pay only what they want to pay. Even though the majority of patients pay very little or nothing, Aravind is financially successful without relying on government aid or donations.

A poor Indian who has lost a foot or leg in an injury or amputation need not lose the capacity to walk. An Indian entrepreneur solved this problem with the "Jaipur foot" which costs about 1/100 of the prices charged in the West. If the Indian government can't subsidize this cost, hopefully the poor person's neighbors will collect enough money to help pay for the Jaipur foot.

In 2009, Nancy Lee and I published the book *Up and Out of Poverty: The Social Marketing Solution*. The book describes many ways to help the poor escape from poverty. It is important for nonprofit organizations, entrepreneurs, companies, and governments to work together to reduce poverty.

Fortunately, this book was chosen as a winner in the 800-CEO-Read Business Book Awards for 2009.

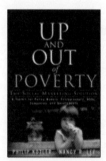

Up and Out of Poverty:
The Social Marketing Solution

30. THE CURSE OF CONCENTRATED WEALTH AND GROWING INEQUALITY

The curse of poverty cannot be analyzed without examining the high and growing concentration of income and wealth. Income inequality is measured by the "Gini coefficient" which ranges from zero percent in which case everyone earns exactly the same income to one hundred percent in which case all the income goes to only one person. The Gini coefficient stood at 38 in the U.S. in 1968 and now stands at 45. The Gini coefficient is even higher in Brazil (57) and South Africa (63). But it is much lower in Sweden, Norway, Finland and Denmark at around 25.

The fact is that wealth begets wealth. Wealthy family members get a better education, enjoy more access to health, get higher paying jobs, have funds to invest in property and financial instruments, and have more influence on public policy. A nation's income and wealth concentration is likely to increase in the absence of any government interventions. Every time I hear news about the high compensation paid to chief executive officers of big American companies, I feel that they are taking advantage of their shareholders and their workers and the American consumers.

One striking fact is that CEO pay used to average about 40 times that of the average worker. Today's U.S. CEOs are compensated at around 350 or 400 times the rate earned by average workers. Some managers draw lavish pay: David Tepper of Appaloosa made $2.2 billion in 1212; and Lawrence J. Ellison of Oracle drew $96.2 million. And if the CEOs draw high pay, surely the other chief officers under them have to receive hefty pay. This means that the senior management cost structure in U.S. companies puts the company at a cost disadvantage in competing against the Chinese, Japanese and the South Koreans. This is aside from the question of whether anyone is worth that much yearly pay or whether this is a scam on the public shareholders.

Yet conservatives argue against higher tax rates for the wealthy by saying that wealth creates jobs and needs a sufficiently high expected return to cover the investment risk. They further argue that "all boats will rise with higher income." But the recent experience in the U.S. is that workers' real incomes have not increased since the 1980s while the rich have enjoyed a substantial increase in income even during the financial collapse.

I would assert that the wealthy are hurting themselves by accumulating too high a proportion of the world's income and wealth. This leaves less purchasing power in the hands of the middle class and very little purchasing power in the hands of the poor. Therefore, consumer demand remains flat or down. The less the spending, the fewer the number of jobs that can be supported. So, I would counsel that the superrich should be in favor of some redistribution to keep the workers buying at their stores and keeping their factories busy.

The stagnant GDP fires up potential anger in the population. It led to "Occupy Wall Street," a protest movement that took place in New York City's Wall Street financial district in September 2011. It was a symbol of the American public's discontent and frustrations. While watching mass demonstrations on TV, I thought that the protests might develop into a more radical mass movement aimed at social transformation. Right now, there is a growing demand for a higher level of minimum wages from the woefully inadequate $7.25 an hour to something like $10 pushed by McDonald's workers or $15 pushed by airline cabin crew members.

The super-wealthy are short-sighted and cannot see beyond their mansions and swimming pools. We can hope that more members of the superrich such as Bill Gates, Warren Buffet, Ted Turner and others see the big picture and support a tax system with a higher tax rate for the rich and no loopholes that embarrass Warren Buffett about the fact that his secretary pays a much higher tax rate on her income than he does.

Bill Gates and Warren Buffet organized The Giving Pledge and 132 billionaires have signed up and pledged to give a substantial amount of their wealth in the next ten years to improving conditions in the country.

31. HANDLING NATIONAL DISILLUSIONMENT

Every nation does what it can to make its people feel special. The French felt exceptional in launching the French Revolution for liberty, equality, and fraternity. Britain at the height of the British Empire felt exceptional. And so did Russia at the height of its Communist state.

In the U.S., we call this "exceptionalism" and claim that we are a people gifted with talents and a democracy found nowhere else. Political scientist Seymour Martin Lipset saw America as developing a uniquely American ideology, based on liberty, egalitarianism, individualism, populism and laissez-faire. We prided ourselves in lacking social class barriers and as having more upward mobility. Some Americans see America as "God's country" and setting a fine example of science, technology, democracy and human rights

Yes, Americans can be proud of several contributions that they have delivered to the greater world. First, there is the establishment of one of the most successful democracies and constitutions in human history. Second, the U.S. became the most powerful nation in the 20th century in military power, trade power, and GDP size. American companies and brands are known throughout the world. Third, the U.S. has been a major contributor of new science and art to the rest of the world. Its companies such as Facebook, Google, YouTube, Twitter, Amazon and others are known and used around the world. In these and many other ways, the U.S. has made a distinct number of contributions to the rest of the world.

When I traveled to Europe and Asia in the past, I felt that the citizens in the other countries had a widespread respect for citizens from the U.S. At the other extreme were individuals and groups who preferred to attack us for our policies and our materialistic bent and acquisitiveness.

On a recent trip in Asia, I noticed a different attitude toward the U.S. Instead of a concern with the U.S. and its impact on their lives, there was an absence of thinking very much about the U.S. Asia was focused more on its own successes, particularly the fact that their economies were growing over 6 percent annually while the U.S. barely grew by 2 percent annually. Asia didn't think about the U.S. very much because it was focused on its own "exceptionalism."

Back in the U.S., I realized that U.S. citizens had suffered a number of shocks that shook their self-image.

The Soviet Union launched Sputnik 1 into an elliptical low Earth orbit on 4 October 4, 1957. Americans were stunned and immediately increased the funding of our space program to regain leadership in space. We managed to recover space leadership by putting the first man on the moon, Neil Armstrong, on July 21, 1969 who spoke the famous words "That's one small step for man, one giant leap for mankind."

Japan's fantastic growth in the 1970s-1980s in industries such as automobiles, motorcycles, watches, cameras, optical instruments, steel, shipbuilding, pianos, zippers, radios, television sets, video recorders, and hand calculators taught us that we were losing leadership in certain industries and that Japan was outperforming us in management and marketing. The blow to our ego came on October 31, 1989 when the Rockefeller Center, Radio City Music Hall and other mid-Manhattan office buildings had sold control to the Mitsubishi Estate Company of Tokyo, one of the world's biggest real estate developers.

The September 11, 2001 Al Qaeda air bombing of our Twin Towers in NYC created a deep wound in our national soul. We lost 3,000 persons and this was the first time an enemy brought destruction to our own shores.

We began to hear that our students were lagging behind students in other nations. The Program for International Student Assessment in 2009 ranked American 15-year-olds at 14th in reading, 17th in science and 25th in math in relation to students in Belgium, Estonia and Poland. In the STEM areas – science, technology, engineering, and mathematics

- our upper middle class students were significantly outperformed by students in 24 countries in math and by 15 counties in science. Countries in Asia and Northern Europe trained many more engineers than we were training. Chinese students were spending 12-hour days at school while one-third of U.S. college-bound students needed remedial education.

We had prided ourselves on thinking that our health system was the best in the world but studies showed that we were spending almost 20 percent of our gross domestic product on health care, twice as much as most other developed countries that were getting the same or better health outcomes.

We fought several wars at great costs and failed to achieve our objectives. We lost the war in Viet Nam and had poor results in Iraq and Afghanistan. Consider what this money would have accomplished if it had been spent on improving U.S. infrastructure, health and education.

Americans always prided themselves on having high mobility for escaping out of poverty. Yet most Western European and English-speaking nations now have higher rates of mobility than does the United States. Our mobility is less than in Canada, Australia, and the Nordic countries, and probably less than Italy, France, Germany, and the United Kingdom.

Then came the financial collapse in 2008 resulting from bad banking practices and over liberal mortgages causing not only the largest financial loss to the U.S. but serious damage to the worldwide economy. The result was widespread massive unemployment and bankruptcies and nations such as Portugal, Italy, Greece, and Spain in danger of not being able to pay their bills. Increased questions arose about the ability of the capitalist system to provide rising growth and jobs for all. In the U.S., evidence indicated that while the rich kept improving their income and wealth, U.S. workers were no better off in 2013 than they were in the 1970s.

All of these events have led more Americans to question their "exceptionalism." The future of the U.S. will be determined largely by the younger generation's attitudes toward work and opportunity. Many of our young people are cynical about foreign involvements leading to successful results. They are cynical about whether their education will get them a job. They are cynical about whether their job will pay enough to achieve a middle-class standard of living. They are cynical about whether they can pay off the huge debt they incurred by going to college.

When a nation loses its major definition of self, it is time to develop a new or stronger identity. What can America stand for in this rapidly changing world? For a long time, Americans stood for "freedom," "democracy," and "capitalism." It will continue to stand for these appealing ideas. America has also stood for the American Dream, visualized as "a happily married family living in a suburban home with the latest appliances and acquiring a new automobile every few years." This American Dream is losing out in the face of lower incomes, more joblessness, growing foreign competition, and environmental restraints.

The new needed identity hopefully will be a force that brings about a better world, not just a better American life. We believe that we helped make the world safer through our military operations. But now let's become the architect of creating a more peaceful and prosperous world.

We may think that we have been doing this through our generous aid packages to emerging countries such as Egypt, Jordan, Lebanon and others. But these are grants with no long-lasting value.

Let's go back to the vision that created the Peace Corps under John Kennedy.

Let's go back to mounting a serious United Nations effort to end world poverty and hunger.

Let's go back to the vision of helping countries protect the natural environment from erosion and air and water pollution.

Let's think more basically about what constitutes a good life in a world that is increasingly income and resource-constrained. Thomas Jefferson saw America as a model for helping other nations secure ends based on the natural and universal rights of man through moral force rather than military force.

Yet America is entering a new stage by electing Donald Trump as President. He doesn't think this way. He wants America to withdraw and reexamine our foreign relations and commitments. He has disparaged NATO and the European Union. He wants to round up the eleven million illegal-aliens and send them all back to Mexico and other countries and build a wall separating the U.S. and Mexico and get Mexico to pay for it. He asserts that our media is dishonest, our justices are not trustworthy, our intelligence system is biased. He is very sloppy on facts and relies more on opinion and hearsay. He thinks that Hillary Clinton's greater popular vote by 3 million was the result of illegal voting.

I have been busy writing articles warning that President Trump has the makings of an authoritarian or dictator just judging by his attacks on our valued institutions. See my article "The 'Terrorist' in the White House" published in the *Huffington Post* on Monday, February 20, 2017. Ironically, this was President's Day in the U.S.

32. WELCOME TO THE AGE OF DEMARKETING

Most of the commercial world spends its time trying to increase the demand for products and services. But we also need a science of "Demarketing" to help reduce the demand for certain products and services. It would be applied to reduce the demand for "vice" products such as hard drugs, cigarettes, and fatty foods. It would also be used to reduce the use of scarce resources, such as water, clean air, certain fish, and certain minerals. California doesn't have enough water and in Beijing, 9,000 citizens are in hospitals with respiratory sickness because of the lack of clean air. For some things, the task is not marketing but demarketing.

In 1971, Sidney Levy and I published an article in the *Harvard Business Review* entitled "Demarketing, Yes, Demarketing." We argued that shortages can be as much of a problem as surpluses. We defined demarketing as ". . . that aspect of marketing that deals with discouraging customers in general or a certain class of customers in particular on a temporary or permanent basis."

Today many people are concerned about the planet's "carrying capacity" to provide the resources on the scale needed to support the world's growing population and the needs of this and future generations. The "ecological footprint" concept says that we would need the equivalent of six to eight more earths of resources if all people in the world want to achieve the US living standard at the current rate of resource consumption. One generation can exploit the existing resources – oil, water, air, timber, fish - so intensely that the next generation is doomed to accept a lower standard of living. As the earth's resources diminish, we may have to move from the Age of Marketing to the Age of Demarketing.

How does this bear on business decision making? Companies that embrace sustainability need to make some basic changes in their production and marketing strategies and practices. Paul Polman, CEO of

Unilever said: "Our ambitions are to double our business, but to do that while reducing our environmental impact and footprint… It has to be done via more responsible consumption…"

If every company sets the goal of doubling its business and if all succeed, sustainability would be impossible to achieve. If the less developed countries achieve middle-class living standards, the pollution, road and air traffic, and energy power outages would smother their quality of life. Something between a zero-growth goal and a modest growth goal would make more sense.

Sustainability-driven companies need to introduce clear criteria to direct their new product development programs, invest more in reuse and recycling, and convince their stakeholders - employees, channels, suppliers, and investors – to fight waste and accept some limits to growth. Companies will have to change their compensation package to set a better balance between the goals of growth vs. sustainability. The CEO needs to earn a pay-out based on achieving the planned growth rate while reducing environmental costs by a planned percent.

Enter Demarketing

Companies need to build demarketing thinking into their demand management strategy. Demarketing is another name for demand reduction. Four situations call for demand reduction.

- *Managing an existing shortage.* The Middle East is short of water and must ration it to competing users. Frequent energy blackouts in various countries require campaigns to discourage unnecessary or wasteful energy consumption.
- *Avoiding potential shortages.* Overfishing must be curtailed in order to maintain the fish supply. Timber cutting must be followed by active replanting.
- *Minimizing harm to individuals.* Efforts are needed to reduce cigarette smoking and hard drug use and eating foods too high in sugar, salt, and fat.

- *Minimizing harm to nature or unique resources*. Discouraging overcrowding at Yellowstone National Park or other over-attended tourist areas.

What are the tools of demarketing? Let's examine Russia's effort to discourage its citizens from overdrinking vodka and other alcoholic beverages. Vodka dependency results in fights, marriage breakups, injuries and deaths. The 4Ps serve as an initial marketing framework to be used by the Russian government and NGOs to reduce vodka consumption:

Product. The government would order lower production of vodka. It might also limit consumers from buying more than one quart a week.
Price. The government would substantially increase the price of vodka.
Place. The government would limit the number of distribution outlets that sell vodka and make these outlets more difficult or inconvenient to visit.
Promotion. The government would run advertising and news campaigns on the harm done to individuals and families by excessive vodka consumption.

Demarketing efforts have been applied in a wide range of situations: to persuade legislators to limit the number of licenses for hunting and fishing, to discourage the number of visitors to overcrowded national parks, to persuade hotel guests to request fewer towels, to persuade homeowners to use less air conditioning and electricity, to persuade car buyers to purchase more fuel-efficient cars.

There are cautions, however, when trying to reduce demand for a desired object. First, the demarketing campaign might make the product or service more desirable: banning a book or movie often has this effect. Second, it can create a criminal class that will prosper during the induced scarcity, as happened in the "prohibition era" in the U.S. when liquor was banned. Third, human rights advocates will complain about the government's interference with what they consider citizens' rights.

Demarketing poses difficult choices between individual freedom and the public good. Without demarketing, we experience the Tragedy of the Commons where everyone uses too much of a public good. With demarketing, we experience a limit on our individual freedom. Demarketing works best when there is high citizen consensus that the consumption of some good or service should be reduced.

33. LAUNCHING AND MANAGING THE WORLD MARKETING SUMMIT (WMS)

In 2010, after publishing my co-authored book with Nancy Lee entitled *Up and Out of Poverty: The Social Marketing Solution*, I realized that a marketing forum was needed that would bring experts together who wanted to create a better world with fewer social problems. Of course, the World Bank, the International Monetary Fund and the United Nations work toward creating a better world. But I had something else in mind that was inspired by the World Economic Forum (WEF) that is held annually in Davos, Switzerland that attracts major government officials, CEOs, and leading academics to discuss the economic problems of the world. I had been an invited speaker some years ago. I remember landing in Geneva, greeted by the WEF staff and escorted to a limo in which sat another Davos invitee, the Finance Minister of Brazil. We chatted while the limo drove for over an hour on snow covered and treacherous roads to get us to Davos.

The WEF gave me the idea to launch a smaller but similar non-profit annual event that would focus more on strategy, management and marketing issues. The event would feature how management and marketing sciences and arts can make the world a better place. We would call its purpose "to make the world a better place through marketing." We would focus on the eight United Nations Millennium Development Goals (MDGs) agreed to by the majority of nations in 2000. These included reducing poverty and hunger, improving education and health and the environment.

We held the first session of the World Marketing Summit in Dhaka, Bangladesh on March 1-3, 2012. Bangladesh, a poor country of 150 million people, had to address all the problems mentioned in the MDGs. Bangladesh's Prime Minister Sheikh Hasina was eager to support our meeting and she asked the other major Ministers of energy, education and finance to prepare talks as well. We invited over 60 experts on social problems who addressed our audience of 4,000 over a three-day period.

The speakers included were:

- Professor Donald Schultz from the U.S. who formulated the field of Integrated Marketing Communications (IMC)
- Hermann Simon of Germany who is an expert on "hidden champion" niche companies
- Evert Gummesson of Sweden who is a leader in services marketing
- Walter Vieira of India who shared observations about programs in India dealing with poverty and hunger
- Hermawan Kartajaya who proposed programs for improving conditions in Asia
- Nancy Lee who shared powerful stories of successes in social marketing

We also invited executives from Unilever and other companies to tell us what they were doing to create a better world through marketing.

Walter Vieira and Philip

Facts about World Marketing Summit

- This is the world's first World Marketing Summit.
- Eminent speakers (economists, marketers, psychologists) coming from many countries.
- Over 3,000 delegates expected to attend the talks and coming from several countries.
- Theme is "Creating a Better World Through Marketing."
- WMS will focus on how marketing can improve lives in four areas: Health, Education, Environment, and Food
- WMS is unique in establishing eight continuing incubators around these themes to advance human knowledge and well-being.

The three days were a beehive of activity. Experts met other experts for the first time. We not only heard excellent talks but we also invited academics to initiate incubators, each incubator dealing with a different problem and we invited cross-country researchers to participate in incubators. Four incubators were signed up with the aim to present their findings at a subsequent annual meeting of the WMS.

One of the highlights of the trip for the speakers was to visit the famous Bangladesh Parliament building designed by the famous architect Louis Kahn. It has the appearance of a fortress that will be here for the next 1,000 years. The parliament was not in session that day and we roamed the huge chamber imagining the politics and wrangling that must take place during a daily session.

Our success with the first year in Bangladesh was followed with a successful WSF 2013 conference in Kuala Lumpur. We began to think about whether we want annual WMSs to be in a different location each year or follow the model of Davos and give it a permanent home. We decided to choose a permanent home somewhere in Asia. When we met with the Prime Minister of Thailand, Yingluck Shinawatra in Bangkok on March 7, 2013, she said that she would like WMS to be in Bangkok in 2014 and after that event we would discuss Bangkok as a possible permanent location. Several Thai companies were ready to provide support for the conference.

Meeting with the Prime Minister of Thailand, Yingluck Shinawatra

Unfortunately, a strong protest movement started in Thailand against a proposed piece of legislation that would allow the former Prime Minister Thaksin to return to his country. Because of the deep political disturbances, we decided to move WMS 2014 to Tokyo instead.

The Japanese were very welcoming and gave us major support. WMS2014 took place on September 24-25, 2014. Tokyo is surely one of the most interesting cities on the planet. We invited a new set of 20 presenters to the Tokyo meeting. So successful was WMS2014, that we were invited to present WMS2015 and subsequently WMS2016 in Tokyo. It began to look like Tokyo might be the future home of our annual World Marketing Summits.

34. JAPAN'S PROWESS SHAKES THE WORLD IN THE 1980S

In early 1980, I taught a CEO executive class at Kellogg's School of Management. I was surprised when one CEO leveled the charge that I had contributed to America's deep economic losses to the Japanese. I asked him to defend his statement. He said that the Japanese had read my *Marketing Management* and took it to be their "marketing bible" and rigorously applied the marketing principles to defeat the U.S. in industry after industry. I immediately countered: "But every business person reads *Marketing Management* and can apply the same principles and strategies. Maybe the difference is that the Japanese believe what I say about marketing principles and many Americans don't. Maybe the Japanese believe that "better products" are the essence of marketing while Americans believe that "better advertising" is the essence of marketing."

This episode raised an interesting question. How did the Japanese manage to miraculously recover from the devastation following the Second World War to become a major industrial leader in: autos, motorcycles, watches, cameras, optical instruments, steel, shipbuilding, pianos, zippers, radios, television sets, video recorders, hand calculators? Japanese companies were rapidly moving to the number two position in computers and construction equipment and making strong inroads into the chemical, pharmaceutical, and machine tool industries.

In the summer of 1982, I published my view of the answer in "The World's Champion Marketers: The Japanese" (Journal of Business Strategy, Vol.3, Issue 1, pp. 3-13). It took a little courage for me to use this title because Americans thought that they invented and remained the leaders in marketing. I said that many factors helped Japan win leadership in several key markets including their superior understanding of marketing. Among the factors:

- Japan used a consensus system of decision making. They used bottom-up communication with multiple participants to take a deep look at decision alternatives. Although this was a slow process, once the decision was made, the company was fast in implementing the decision.

- Japanese personnel practices such as lifetime employment, worker suggestion systems, excellent training and rotation systems and quality circles all contributed to high company loyalty. Japan also ran a very tight system of cost containment, production efficiency, and product design and quality.

- Japan's close working relations between government, business, and labor played an important role. The integrated trading companies, government support and subsidies and easy access to Japanese banks contributed to company success.

- Japan benefitted from the close ties between manufacturers and their suppliers and distributors and the high work ethic of their employees. Japan's low wages also gave Japan a competitive advantage, as well as its willingness to accept a lower profit level in reaching for a higher market share.

- Japan's own industries benefitted from a great amount of internal competition. Japan's auto industry included nine auto companies, not the three in the U.S.; four motorcycle companies vs. one, Harley Davidson in the U.S.; a dozen camera manufacturers, and several manufacturers of hand calculators and appliances. Clearly Japanese companies were highly skilled in competing with each other.

Although all these advantages worked, Japan had learned one more critical lesson, namely that "customer value wins." You can always beat your competitors by "offering a better product at a lower price." We know that offering a lower price is often enough to take sales away but it won't bring the customers back if the product is average or disappointing. Japanese companies made sure that their products had higher quality, better design and some innovative features to ensure that the customers would come back even if the price had to be increased.

Japan's practice of marketing included carefully determining what industries to enter, which market segments to serve, and the appropriate strategies to penetrate each market segment. I was so impressed with Japan's superior understanding of customer-driven marketing that in 1985 I published *The New Competition* (Philip Kotler, Liam Fahey, and Somkid Jatusripitak) to explain Japan and the new competition.

A few years later, Japan began to lose some of its upward surge. A lawyer friend asked me, "Why is Japan's economy slowing down." I said "It is only temporary. The Five Tigers are coming on strong and China is emerging. But Japan will keep its leadership and even win more industries."

Another five years passed and Japan's stagnation continued and my lawyer friend asked "Why is the Japanese economy stagnating?"

Why did the Japanese economy stagnate for 20 years? I think that I know some of the answers:

- Japanese success led to some degree of arrogance or complacency that its success would continue indefinitely.
- The great early leaders and entrepreneurs who founded their companies were not followed by CEO successors with the same level of creativity.
- Japan's domestic economy was growing and provided enough domestic opportunity without going abroad.
- Japanese companies understood manufacturing but did not continue to understand marketing. They saw marketing as a one P subject – promotion. They didn't appoint Chief Marketing Officers who could participate in planning the company's future.
- Japanese companies were slower in making decisions compared to their competitors, especially in comparison to their South Korea and Taiwan competitors.
- Lifetime employment and seniority rather than merit were limiting Japan's resilience.
- Japanese companies were coming under the influence of Wall Street capitalism by focusing on short term results rather than planning for long term results.

What does Japan have to do to reignite its economy? I would recommend the following recipe of initiatives:

- Japanese companies must become more innovative in developing new products, new business models, distribution systems, and pricing. They need to make more use of co-creation and crowdsourcing.
- Japanese companies need to shift some money from 30-second commercials to social media campaigns and listening posts.
- Japanese companies need to appoint Chief Marketing Officers that participate in strategy setting for the company's future.
- Japanese companies need to build their brands and take higher purpose stands on what they are contributing to making the world better.

I visited and spoke in Japan in June 2013 to 1,000 managers from various industries. I spoke about my new book, *Market Your Way to Growth: 8 Ways to Win*. There was much enthusiasm. I profoundly hope that Japan will enter a new cycle of growth.

Kotler articles on the Japanese economy:

1. Somkid Jatusripitak, Liam Fahey, and Philip Kotler, "Strategic Global Marketing: Lessons from the Japanese," *Columbia Journal of World Business*, Spring 1985, Vol. 20, Issue 1, pp. 47-53.
2. Philip Kotler and Liam Fahey, "Japanese Strategic Marketing: An Overview," in *Strategic Marketing and Management*, ed. Howard Thomas and David Gardner (NY: John Wiley & Sons, Inc., 1985), pp. 441-451.
3. Philip Kotler, "Meeting the New Competition from Japan and the Far East," *Journal of Global Marketing 4*.

35. WONDERFUL EXPERIENCES IN JAPAN

Over the years, I have made several trips to Japan. Every trip has been interesting and intriguing.

My introduction to Japan first came through my friendship with Professor Ferdinand Mauser, who taught marketing at Wayne State University, but subsequently moved to Japan and taught at Keio University. Ferdinand was dedicated to thinking about larger values and virtues, such as supporting sustainability and telling his students to respect nature, an attitude he picked up from living in Japan. He influenced many Japanese students. I knew him because he had selected his finest students from Wayne University and convinced them to come to the Kellogg School of Management for their Ph.D. in marketing. As a result, Kellogg trained Richard Bagozzi, Gary Armstrong, and Randall Schultz…all of whom became distinguished marketing scholars.

Professor Ferdinand Mauser

After teaching 20 years at Keio University, Ferdinand did a surprise career turn when a Japanese talent agent recognized that Ferdinand would be an ideal model for a Westerner in Japanese ads. Suddenly Ferdinand appeared in ads for blue jeans, famous brands of Italian shoes, and Western suits and even appeared in a few Japanese videos. We corresponded many times about world affairs and I learned a great deal from Ferdinand's Japanese outlook. Sadly, he had a stroke some years after retirement and I lost a dear friend.

Ferdinand had befriended Mr. Masatoshi Ito, founder and chairman of Ito Yokado that runs the famous 7-11 chain of convenience stores, Denny's restaurants and several other retail businesses. Ferdinand introduced me to Mr. Ito who received me very graciously. Mr. Ito is a lifetime learner. We had many conversations about retailing and economics and he always took notes, as I did while talking with him. Not much later he wrote that he wanted his son Yasuhisa to study with me at Kellogg and I was happy to receive Yasuhisa. Yasuhisa was an excellent student and I recently met him again in Tokyo.

Philip and Ito Masatoshi

I taught many excellent Japanese students at Kellogg who later managed large companies:

- Haruo Naito, CEO of Esai
- Tadahiro Yoshida, Chairman of YKK
- Yoshimi Inaba, President of Toyota USA
- Mitsuhiro Shibata, who went on to work for Ito Yokado, then Disney, then Loro Piana, and finally became an active member of the Club of Budapest working for the cause of peace.

Philip and Mitsu Shibata

Ferdinand introduced me to Professor Shoji Murata. His students greatly admired Shoji and once every year on a special day his former students returned to greet him and bring him up to date about their activities. The event took place in a swimming pool with Shoji in the water at one end and with each student swimming to him in turn to greet him. To me, this was high drama. It was also high drama when my wife and I were invited to Shoji's home for dinner and we entered to find Shoji not in his everyday Western clothes but in an elegant traditional Japanese gown looking like a Samurai warrior. He welcomed us with his deep voice. We enjoyed a fine evening with him and his wife. Shoji also introduced me to Mitsuaki Shimaguchi, an exceptional scholar on distribution at Keio University.

My wife and I enjoyed Japanese culture, including the tea ceremony, flower arranging, bonsai art, Japanese gardens, and Japanese food. We visited and enjoyed the beautiful Japanese gardens in Kyoto.

One of my special friends at Northwestern University and in Japan, Hiroko Osaka, who helped me during my visits to Japan, invited me to attend her brother's wedding in Tokyo in February 1995. I was so pleased to be able to attend a Japanese wedding because I had never seen one. I was looking forward to see what kind of Shinto ceremony takes place at a Japanese wedding. I had completely jumped to conclusions. It turned out that the young Japanese bride and bridegroom wanted a

Western-style wedding. It was a fashion trend at the time and they became short-term Christians only during the wedding process. I never ended up seeing a traditional Japanese wedding!

Hiroko Osaka and Phil, Feb. 1995

I remember an unusual experience that I had in another Japanese city where I spoke. My host arranged a dinner with two special guests who I remember vividly. One is Japan's "national treasure" person in the art of swordmaking. He knew that I collected Japanese swordguards (called tsubas). He brought along a beautiful sword that he recently made that I admired greatly. A sword of his would sell for $1 million to collectors. I said that I regretted not collecting swords because my wife refused having swords in our home where our children were growing up.

The other person at the dinner was a beautiful Japanese woman. She sat next to me at the dinner and we chatted. I noticed that some guests were tittering as they observed our conversation. Then my host said that this female guest can give a great massage. Would I be interested? I said yes. I retired at 10pm and there was a knock on my door. Instead of the beautiful guest appearing, a large older woman appeared saying she came to give a massage. So, a joke had been played on me by my host. But the joke was deeper than that. The beautiful slim woman with whom I had chatted was not a woman! If I had watched Japanese TV, I would know that "she" was a famous man who passed himself off as a woman! It could have been Akehiro Miwa or Karsele Maki. I never forgot this sense of humor that my host had orchestrated for that evening.

36. COLLECTING JAPANESE NETSUKES AND TSUBAS

One day many years ago, my 11-year old daughter Amy and I wandered into an antique store in Harvard Square in Cambridge. Amy spotted a "cute" little ivory figure of a monkey for sale. The dealer wanted $100 and I bought it for Amy. Little did I know that I would subsequently become a major collector of Japanese netsukes.

Netsuke of a mother and child monkeys playing

Those "cute" little ivories helped build my love and understanding of Japanese culture. I am surprised that many Japanese, mostly younger Japanese, know little about netsukes. In meeting younger Japanese, I proceed to tell the following.

Before the 1870s, Japanese men and women wore kimonos and a belt called an obi. Kimonos didn't have pockets. How were Japanese citizens to carry their coins, tobacco and medicines? The answer was to attach a chord to their purse or medicine case (inro) and pass the chord around the obi with the end of the chord tied to a weighted object with a hole (himotoshi) in it. The weighted object was usually made of ivory (or wood, whalebone or other materials) and carved into a familiar Japanese theme, such as an animal, vegetable. person, or imaginary character

Often a wealthy Japanese landowner would commission an expert netsuke carver to make a netsuke of personal interest to the landlord. The landowner was happy when his companions would notice this fine netsuke at tea gatherings and public meetings. The netsukes were always visible.

I began collecting netsukes by visiting Japanese art and antique galleries in New York, San Francisco, London, Hawaii, Tokyo and Kyoto. I met many interesting and knowledgeable dealers who guided my wife and me in the fine points of netsuke connoisseurship. I joined the Netsuke Society and I received their monthly well-illustrated magazine. I looked forward to receiving each issue with its beautiful photos and articles on netsukes.

I remember attending the World Netsuke Society's week-long meeting in Hawaii where three hundred collectors from all over the world gathered including notables such as Hans Conried (former Hollywood movie star) and Arthur Murray (founder of the famous dance studio). We swapped stories and bought and sold netsukes. I fell quickly under the sway of Raymond Bushell, an American lawyer married to a Japanese woman who became a famous collector and authority on Japanese netsuke. His books on netsukes are classics and his famous collection is now on display in San Francisco in the famous DeYoung Museum. Another great collection of netsuke was donated by Virginia Atchley and can be found in the Victoria and Albert Museum in London.

One of the finest collections of netsukes is the collection by Prince and Princess Takamado. I had the pleasure of meeting Princess Takamado in 2014 and exchanging stories about netsukes. She has published a few books on their netsuke collection.

Princess Takamado

A wonderful book - *The Hare with the Amber Eyes: a Hidden Inheritance* - was published recently that revived world-wide interest in netsukes. The author, Edmund de Waal, is a descendant of a famous European Jewish family that owned a brilliant netsuke collection that was passed on from generation to generation but which had to be hidden and managed to be saved from the Nazis.

My love of netsukes culminated in my publishing "Judging Quality in Netsuke" in the March-April 1976 issue of *Arts of Asia*. My article describes the ten characteristics of a netsuke that turn it into a masterpiece: originality, aesthetic merit, functional suitability, craftsmanship, life force, tactile appeal, age, condition, popularity of subject, and signature and pedigree.

I hope that more Japanese people return to knowing and appreciating the wonderful and gifted carvings of the netsuke artists. So impressive is their work that to this day, some independent artists living in different parts of the world are still carving netsukes, even though they have lost their function of being a weight to balance a purse or inro on the other end of a chord.

Tsubas (Swordguards)

My other collecting love of Japanese objects are the fine swordguards (called tsubas) from the Japanese swords. Japanese swords were prohibited from being won in public after March 28, 1876 (The Sword Abolishment Edict) as a measure of public safety. Yet people continued to collect these beautiful swords and their several components such as tsubas, menuki, fuchis, and kashiras.

My wife sensibly doesn't want swords in our home and so we are satisfied collecting the beautiful sword guards.

They are made of iron or finer metals and often carry silver or gold in their pictorial scenes. My sadness is that every Japanese tsuba was once a part of a full sword, but time and circumstance has led to sales of these separate components of a complex Japanese sword.

The Japanese sword is another fine example of the superior aesthetic and technical skills of the Japanese craftspeople. The following picture shows a Samurai warrior with two swords and the swordguards are clearly visible.

Japanese samurai warrior

Two Swordguards (tsubas)

37. COLLECTING CONTEMPORARY STUDIO ART GLASS

There are two classes of people in the world: those who collect something and those who don't. The first group is very diverse in that they collect so many things: art, coins, stamps, buttons, baseball cards, autographs, and even Japanese netsukes and tsubas as in my case. My wife and I also collect one other thing that goes under the name contemporary studio art glass.

Everyone knows about glass in its practical form of windows, test tubes, bowls, plates, and glass tiles. The public knows less about glass as an artistic medium. Even in ancient Rome, some glassmakers created beautiful glass vessels. In the 1840s in France, glass artists created beautiful paperweights featuring flowers, fruit and other pictorial elements. French, German, Italian and Czech glass artists also began to make beautiful paperweights. Paperweight were so named because they could be put on a pile of paper to prevent the paper from being blown away by a wind.

Paul Standard paperweight

It wasn't until 1962 that Harvey Littleton doing work first at the University of Wisconsin and then at the Toledo Museum of Art started the Studio Glass movement. He and Dominick Labino figured out how to craft larger glass objects in a small kiln without needing the resources of a large glass factory. This marked the beginning of the studio art glass movement that today numbers thousands of artists and collectors worldwide.

Harvey Littleton and one of his contemporary glass pieces

Nancy and I saw our first examples of contemporary glass art in the home of friends who had an early collection. We were fascinated with the beauty and intricacy of these glass art works and shortly grew into enthusiastic collectors.

The most celebrated glass artist is Dale Chihuly whose studio is known as the Boat House in Seattle. Dale had lost the sight in one eye in an auto accident and had to give up glass making but he sketched pieces to guide other glass artists working for him. He created many series:

- Seaform Series, transparent sculptures of thin glass, strengthened by ribbed strands of color
- Macchia Series, featuring every color available in the studio
- Persian Series, inspired by Middle East glass from the 12th- to 14th-century, featuring more restrained color and room-sized installations
- Venetian Series, improvisations based on Italian Art Deco
- Ikebana Series, glass flower arrangements inspired by Ikebana
- Niijima Floats, six-foot spheres of intricate color inspired by Japanese glass fishing floats from the island of Niijima

- Wall Hangings, Chandeliers and Glass Trees and Botanicals

It is said that Dale Chihuly's art glass is found in more museums around the world today than the works of any other living artist.

Dale Chihuly and his Ikebana glass creation

Whereas Dale's pieces are primarily known for their beauty, we were attracted more to pieces that carried a narrative quality or meaning.

One of our pieces shows a woman and man seated on comfortable chairs facing each other. The woman is leaning forward talking and the man is leaning back listening. Who are they? Is this a female patient and her male psychiatrist? Or is it a wife sharing her news with her tired husband? The piece elicits different interpretations from different viewers.

Another piece in our collection shows four persons, three of whom look like they are shouting while a fourth person is looking down and reading a book. Are they at a football game where three are highly involved in the spectacle and the other is less interested? Or are all four holocaust prisoners facing their grim fate in different ways?

We also collect more abstract works but usually ones that suggest meanings beyond the piece. One work of ours shows two circular rolling objects – one larger than the other - resting on an inclined and titled platform which itself is resting on a strong rock. My interpretation –

Nancy is running after one of our children while I (the rock) support the platform and family although even I am not on firm ground.

We realized that collecting art is about collecting collectors and dealers as well. We were invited to join the Board of Directors of the Art Alliance for Contemporary Glass (AACG) and instantly met 60 other enthusiastic glass art collectors. We visit dealers in Chicago, New York City, Detroit, Denver, Venice, and Prague and know them well. We attend the Glass Weekend in Wheaton, New Jersey every two years to meet dealers and collectors and hear lectures by studio art glass artists and critics.

The bottom line is that we have thoroughly enjoyed collecting 150 works of contemporary glass art. We open up our home to visitors and collectors. We have fond memories of so many interesting experiences in our adventure in the glass world.

We arrived at a point in collecting glass art for twenty-five years when we started to think about where our collection should go. Our three daughters favored a few pieces but their homes could not accommodate such a large collection. We faced the alternative of selling our pieces through one of the large art houses such as Sotheby's or Christies. Or we could gift our glass collection to a major museum.

We chose the latter. Living in Sarasota, Florida, we contacted the Ringling Museum of Art, the 16th largest art museum in the United States. Ringling has a magnificent collection of Baroque art and recently added a contemporary art wing and an Asian Museum. Ringling recently acquired a major collection of photographs and expressed a strong interest in acquiring our glass collection. We were happy to gift them 30 pieces for an opening show in November 2013 and with more to be gifted in the future. The show continued through June 2014 and drew huge attendance and wonderful comments.

Ringling Museum of Art, Sarasota, Florida

In the meantime, we enjoy having much of our art glass in our Sarasota home. We will also be able to visit and see the pieces that we gifted to the Ringling that is only 10 miles away from our Sarasota home. The pieces will be displayed in a new wing of the Ringling Museum of Art called the Kotler-Coville Glass Pavilion. This way we share our glass collection with a much larger world audience.

38. MY LOVE AFFAIR WITH SWEDEN

Many years ago, I read a book by Marquis Childs called Sweden: *The Middle Way* (published 1936). Childs was showing how Sweden was shaping a society that stood between the extremes of capitalism and communism. It might be called "liberal socialism." The book describes the cooperative movement in Sweden, state-sponsored worker housing, the welfare movement, free college education and other developments.

Sweden has long been committed to build a better and healthier society. For example, Sweden rationed alcohol and citizens over 21 had to register their purchases. How much you could buy was restricted. The state monopolized the distribution of alcohol with the stores run by a state monopoly. From the beginning of their schooling, children would learn the dangers of cigarette smoking, overdrinking of alcohol, and hard drugs. This picture of Sweden delighted me in the sense that the Swedish society was trying to raise its people to be responsible citizens who would enjoy being healthy and productive.

I was impressed with Sweden's brilliant management when they changed their road rules from driving on the left to driving on the right. At the time, Sweden was the only country in continental Europe to drive on the left side of the road. The government set a specific day and time when all Swedish cars must switch from one side of the road to the other. Four years went into informing all Swedish drivers to switch at exactly 5am (time of the lowest traffic intensity) on September 3, 1967. The big cost was to change bus and streetcar traffic with the vehicles, platforms, etc. and to change road exits and entries and not least road signs. Stockholm started a big program for reconstructing streets and roads. The switch took place everywhere in Sweden on September 3, 1967 with loudspeakers blaring "Now it is time to change over." Although this caused tremendous traffic tie-ups, no one was hurt. *This was one of the biggest and most successful social marketing campaigns in the world to change behavior.*

In 1991, I received a phone call from a Mr. Christer Engleus who ran a speakers' bureau called Informationskollegiet inviting me to come to Stockholm and give a whole day presentation on the important role of marketing in creating economic prosperity. The day would start at 9am and run to 5pm, six hours considering the two coffee breaks and lunch. We agreed on the financial terms and thus began a relationship and friendship that continues to this day. Christer is one of those rare marketing entrepreneurs who could run any business successfully.

He subsequently invited me to come each September to Stockholm for a "Kotler Day." My annual seminar attracted between 800 and 1200 managers and CEOs. I remember the last session in 2005 when Christer put signs all over Stockholm that "Kotler is coming." And when each seminar took place, Christer introduced the program without me being visible and he would turn on the theme song from the British film Chariots of Fire… and I would walk from behind the curtain to the podium with applause and begin my talk.

Christer Engleus

The last annual Kotler Day in Stockholm took place in 2005, after a run of 14 years. Christer Engleus told me that he was changing his career from running a leading speakers' bureau in Scandinavia to launching a new online dating service in Scandinavia. He joked that this would be a good way to meet new women now that he had ended his marriage. He launched First Date in Sweden (firstdate.com) and it is now one of the most successful dating services. In a letter to me he said "we are about to leave the runner up position and become #1 in less than 24 months." His ambition is to expand the site to Europe and become Europe's leading dating service. He also offers a Date Guarantee to his Gold Club Members that if they have not met anyone in six months that they like, he will refund a 100% of their money. There is nothing more effective than a person who combines "marketing + innovation" to guarantee success.

In 2016, Christer sold his dating service and he returned to sponsoring management seminars. He invited me to debate with Koenigsegg, Sweden's inventor of the world's fastest car (270 miles an hour). Koenigsegg was determined to build this car and did little market research about whether there would be enough buyers. I argued that he put his idea at great risk by not doing market research. But Koenigsegg's instincts must have been right because he is now selling his $3 million-dollar car and he is backordered by 4 years.

Earlier in 1998, I had received a phone call from the University of Stockholm that they wanted to award me an honorary degree. Professor

Evert Gummesson of the University of Stockholm had nominated me. I was delighted and I flew to Stockholm where I joined several other distinguished recipients who were also receiving honorary degrees in areas of their expertise. Each of us received instructions on how to greet the King of Sweden Carl XVI Gustaf and his lovely wife Queen Silvia. This was my first meeting with royalty and I paid careful attention on how to move my hand to receive the honorary degree and use my other hand to shake the King's hand. These sorts of things are more important than we give them credit for.

Professor Evert Gummesson

Professor Evert Gummesson has had a great influence on my thinking. While most U.S. marketing academics were theorizing about the marketing of products, Evert pioneered thinking about the marketing of services and he published his book on services marketing in 1977. Later he published another innovative book, *Total Relationship Marketing*, covering 30 relationships that marketers might conceivably have to manage. It was cited as the Best Marketing Book of the Year by the Swedish Marketing Federation and in 1999 it won the Chris Ottander Prize and it is now in ten languages and will be published in the 4th edition. Evert and I have been the closest of friends for over 20 years and I greatly respect his ideas.

Sweden remains a country that has a special place in my heart.

39. BEAUTIFUL INDONESIA AND THE MUSEUM OF MARKETING 3.0

My first occasion to visit Indonesia came in the form of an invitation from a Mr. Hans Mandalas. Hans ran a speaker's bureau and at one time had brought Peter Drucker to speak in Indonesia. He wrote and invited me to give a one-day seminar in Jakarta. Although travel from Chicago to Jakarta involves at least a 17-hour flight, I wanted to see this country of 242 million people and experience its history and treasures.

In 1981, I spoke to 700 Indonesian managers and Hans invited me to return another time and speak in Bali. My wife and I stayed at a famous eco-luxury resort where we reveled in the beauty of Bali and the wondrous paintings and sculptures of its artists. I knew that we would return to Bali on future trips.

My next return to Indonesia resulted from a fortuitous meeting in Moscow. I was invited to speak in Moscow on *What is Marketing and How to Use It*. My book *Marketing Management* was the first translated marketing book in Russia.

The word "marketing" didn't exist in Russia and the publisher had to use that word because there wasn't an equivalent word. The odd thing is that the Russian edition arrived and it only contained 222 of the 600 pages of my U.S. edition, leading me to think that they left out all references to capitalism and serving consumers well. The translator told me that every translation had to be approved by censors and obviously, the censors were busy reviewing my book.

The first Russian edition of Marketing Management

One of the other speakers in the Moscow program was Hermawan Kartajaya. I didn't know Hermawan and he approached me saying that he learned his marketing from my books. Hermawan had founded a company in Jakarta called Mark Plus that provided marketing consulting, marketing training and marketing research to Indonesian clients. We had a great deal to talk about and it was one of those moments that I realized that Hermawan would become a close friend, although one living 8000 miles away.

It wasn't long afterwards that Hermawan invited me to speak in Jakarta. He also took me to visit his five-story building and he introduced me to a very talented staff of marketing people. Later he introduced me to his son Michael and his daughter Stephanie. Michael came later to Kellogg to study for his MBA and he was a fine student. Stephanie studied marketing in Kellogg's campus in Singapore.

What impressed me about Hermawan was his enthusiasm and his original mind in marketing. He built theories of marketing processes and life cycles. He showed me his article "The Eighteen Guiding Principles of the Marketing Concept" in Warren Keegan's *Global Marketing Management* textbook. Hermawan's article was an insightful summary of the main ideas in the marketing discipline.

Hermawan Kartajaya with a 3.0 gesture

I was also impressed with Hermawan's extensive contacts with high level persons in Indonesia. He knew the Prime Minister, several other ministers, and many social and political figures in Indonesia. I remember Hermawan taking me to meet the President of Indonesia, Susilo Bamban Yudhoyono. The President's first words after greeting me was that he has read my book *Marketing of Nations* (1997) twice, once when he was a minister and later when he became President of Indonesia, and that he applied many of my ideas on how to accelerate economic growth.

Susilo Bamban Yudhoyono, President of Indonesia

My relation with Hermawan has been one of deep friendship and continual intellectual stimulation. We have co-authored the following seven books:

- Philip Kotler and Hermawan Kartajaya, *Repositioning Asia: From Bubble to Sustainable Economy*, Wiley, 2000.
- Philip Kotler, Hermawan Kartajaya, Hooi Den Hua, and Sandra Liu, *Rethinking Marketing: Sustainable Marketing Enterprise in Asia*, Prentice-Hall, 2003.
- Philip Kotler, Hermawan Kartajaya, and David Young, Attracting Investors: *A Marketing Approach to Finding Funds for Your Business*, Wiley, 2004.
- Philip Kotler, Hermawan Kartajaya, and Hooi Den Hua, Think ASEAN: *Rethinking Marketing Toward ASEAN Community 2015*, McGraw-Hill, 2007.
- Philip Kotler, Hermawan Kartajaya, and Iwan Setiawan, *Marketing 3.0: From Products to Customers to the Human Spirit* (Wiley, 2010).
- Philip Kotler, Hermawan Kartajaya, and Iwan Setiawan, *Marketing 4.0: Moving from Traditional to Digital* (Wiley, 2017).
- Philip Kotler, Hermawan Kartajaya and Den Huan Hooi, *Marketing for Competitiveness: Asia to The World: In the Age of Digital Consumers*, World Scientific Press, 2017.

Our book, *Marketing 3.0*, opened up the idea that marketing practice can pass through three stages, with most firms being in 1.0, followed by many firms in 2.0 and a few in 3.0. Firms in 1.0 are functionally efficient and they win by presenting a better value to customers than their competitors. Marketing 2.0 firms are emotionally effective in winning and bonding with customers through excellent service and empathy. Marketing 3.0 firms go further and express their caring for the world in addition to their caring for their customers. These 3.0 firms show compassion and offer more affordable versions of their products in poor countries and contribute money to important social causes. We expect more companies to practice Marketing 3.0 and then move on to Marketing 4.0 to join the digital revolution.

Marketing 3.0

We opened the new Marketing Museum 3.0 in Ubud (Bali) on May 27, 2011. The museum celebrates the best marketers, products, companies, and advertisements that illustrate a 3.0 marketing consciousness.

Attending the museum opening was a great pleasure for my family and me. Nancy and I invited our oldest daughter Amy and two of our grandchildren, Jordan and Jamie, to fly with us to Bali and join some thousand-people attending the opening. My grandchildren were very moved by the ceremony and by the evening dinner where a few thousand Indonesian guests celebrated my eightieth birthday.

My relationship to Indonesia is continuous. In 2005, the Indonesian government honored me by issuing a postage stamp honoring Hermawan, Hooi Den Huan, and myself. In 2007, I was appointed a Special Ambassador at large for Indonesian Tourism. In May 2011, the city of Denpasar in Bali bestowed the title to me of honorary resident of Denpasar.

40. THAILAND - LAND OF KINGS

My first acquaintance with Thailand came not from a visit but from a movie that left a deep impression on me, namely *The King and I* starring Yul Brynner and Deborah Kerr. It was the lovely story of Siam's King who invited an English woman schoolmaster to come to Thailand to teach the King's children and share news about the rest of the world.

Yul Brynner

Thailand's population today is 65 million. The large majority of Thais are Buddhists and they are very friendly to visitors. Their people smile most of the time. Many visitors come to see the beautiful temples and sights in Bangkok as well as to visit the city of Chiang Mai and the island of Phuket.

The first person I remember meeting from Thailand was my Ph.D. student, Somkid Jatusripitak. Both Nancy and I became very fond of Somkid. Only later did I learn that Somkid came from a very influential Thai family and that his brother was a major figure in Thai's banking world. Somkid wrote an excellent dissertation on International Trade, graduated and returned home to Bangkok with his new Northwestern Ph.D. degree.

Some years later, Somkid phoned me from Thailand and asked my advice on whether to stay in academia or go into politics. I thought about the tradeoff between him contributing new knowledge in the field of marketing or entering politics and contributing to his country. I advised him to enter politics. He would be able to make a great contribution to Thailand, given his fine character and knowledge. He entered politics.

A few years later I received a phone call from a Thai newspaper reporter asking me what I thought about my student Somkid becoming the new Minister of Finance in Thailand, especially given that his training was in marketing, not finance. My answer: "Most Ministers of Finance fail. It's good that Thailand is the first country to appoint a marketing Ph.D. to be the Minister of Finance." I followed his career and heard that Somkid was one of the best Ministers of Finance in Thailand's history. I remember that he implemented a program "one village-one product" so that each Thai village made something that it could export to other parts of Thailand or abroad. Soon after Somkid became the Vice-Prime Minister, second in command.

A later political conflict in Thailand led to another political party taking over. Somkid was relieved and under Thai law could not enter politics again for five years. Somkid spent his time running a leading think tank in Bangkok devoted to solving Thailand's economic and social problems. When Thailand's political turmoil settled, Somkid went back into politics. Today he is the Deputy Prime Minister of Thailand.

Some years earlier, Somkid sent another talented Thai student – Suvit Maesincee - to get a Ph.D. degree at Kellogg. I was delighted with Suvit who turned out to be an original thinker in marketing with new ways to systematize and broaden our understanding of marketing phenomena. He joined Somkid and me as a third author in writing our book, *The Marketing of Nations* (1997).

The Marketing of Nations

My relation with Suvit was far from over after he returned to Bangkok to teach at Sasin Graduate Institute of Business Administration at Chulalongkorn University. We had talked many times about writing a book with a new view of marketing and capitalism. Then something happened that led me back to Thailand and working with Suvit.

A new neighbor had joined our home owner's association in Glencoe, Illinois. He was Mr. Yothin from Bangkok. He told me that he had learned his marketing from *Marketing Management* and wanted to meet me. Not long after, he invited Nancy and me to join him on his yacht and enjoy a week sailing along the coast of Montenegro and Croatia. We spent a wonderful week with his wife Ladawan and three other couples traveling the Croatian coast.

Ladawan, Yothin, Philip, and Dr. Fahim Kibria

Yothin's yacht

Yothin runs a major Thai paper company called Double A and has been a wonderful host to me when I spoke in Bangkok. He showed me his impressive factory in the North of Thailand. He introduced me to Thailand's Prime Minister Yingluck Shinawatra. We told her that we would like to base a future meeting of the World Marketing Summit in Bangkok. We would bring many prominent marketing and business speakers to Thailand and consider ways WMS can contribute to Thailand's further economic growth. The Prime Minister thought the project idea was excellent and gave us her blessing.

This is where Suvit comes back into the picture. Suvit also knows the Prime Minister, having worked earlier as a high official in the government. He accepted the challenge of working with us to run the 2014 World Marketing Summit in Bangkok. We could think of no better person than my former student to become engaged in planning the 2014 WMS in Bangkok.

Unfortunately, Thailand became embroiled in political protests in February 2014. It looked like the protests would continue for some months. We decided not to do WMS2014 in Bangkok and we moved it to Tokyo, as I mentioned earlier.

41. BRAZIL RISING AND THEN FALLING

My first visit to Brazil came about in an unusual way. I received a phone call from my friend, Harvard Professor Steven Greyser, that he and his Harvard colleague, Robert Buzzell had been invited to Rio de Janeiro to speak about marketing on condition that they would invite me as well. Steven said that all three of us would bring our wives and enjoy a great holiday on the beach of Copacabana. Nancy thought that this was a good idea and the three couples boarded the plane in Boston to fly to Brazil.

Bob Buzzell, Philip, and Steve Greyser in Rio

I knew enough about Brazil not to make the famous mistake that an exporter made in sending his merchandise to Brazil with all the instructions in Spanish. I knew that Brazilians speak Portuguese, not Spanish!

After arriving in Rio, I remember that the six of us were hosted by a Harvard trained Brazilian billionaire in his fabulous home who introduced us to a large gathering of his friends. Besides a wonderful Brazilian dinner, he had invited a full orchestra to play dance music and we had a great evening.

We also spent time sunning on the beach in Rio de Janeiro. We even invented a summary that we called the five S's that made Brazil famous. They were: Sun, Samba, Sex, Soccer, and Stones (famous gemstones marketed by H. Stern), and Socks (that we suspected men work in their bathing trunks).

After returning to Chicago, I did not expect to return to Brazil. But a few months later, I received a phone call from a person called Jose Salibi who invited me to present a one-day seminar on marketing in Sao Paulo. I politely told him that the flight from Chicago to Sao Paulo was long and I was not in the mood to travel so far. I had been spending my speaking engagement time in London, Frankfurt, Vienna, and Stockholm and these trips were much shorter. Jose mentioned what he could pay well and it still didn't cover in my mind the three or four days of flying back and forth and speaking in Sao Paulo.

Then he popped an interesting question. "Do you play tennis?" I said yes. Jose said that he was number 19 in the tennis world and I didn't quite know if he meant the whole world or the Brazilian world. He said that he would throw in an extra week of lessons if I would come to Brazil. That persuaded me and I was off to my second visit to Brazil, with at least another 12 trips to follow.

Jose Salibi is an extraordinary entrepreneur. He had phoned his invitation from a telephone booth in New York City with barely enough money to finish the call. Subsequently he co-founded a company called HSM (he is the S) that revolutionized the speaker world.

Philip and Jose Salibi

He paid exceptional attention to the happiness of his guest speakers, his audiences, and his sponsors, making sure that he created and delivered value to all of them. He supplied the conference attendees with free international phone calls and even arranged with Amil, a Brazilian health insurer to supply an ambulance and physician in case any guest got ill during the seminar.

Jose began to invite speakers such as Jack Welch (CEO of GE), Louis Gerstner (CEO of IBM), John Chambers (CEO of Cisco), Tom Peters, Alvin Toffler, Jim Collins, and others. HSM ran an annual EXPO event drawing 5,000 business attendees, including the CEOs of many Brazilian companies. I was a featured speaker every few years in Brazil and I loved seeing how Brazil was moving from a developing economy to a more developed economy. Jose invited me to speak in other Brazilian cities such as Porto Alegra and Fortaleza, as well as to speak in Argentina (Buenos Aires) and Uruguay (Montevideo).

My message was that Brazilian companies needed to adopt marketing thinking as distinct from sales thinking and to apply it not only to selling more of its current products but also to imagine future business and market opportunities. We started to list Brazil as one of the major BRIC countries (Brazil, Russia, Indian, China) experiencing high economic growth. I believe that Jose and his HSM team contributed greatly to Brazil's development. Jose is now busy creating an innovative business school in Sao Paulo with branches in other Brazilian cities, in this way also contributing to Brazil's future.

One of the byproducts of my relation with Jose is that he urged me to write a book on sports marketing, based on his and Brazil's love of sports. I undertook to co-author this book with my colleague Professor Irv Rein and his research assistant Ben Shields. We named the book *The Elusive Fans*. We argued that sports teams do a poor job of thinking about their fans and customers. Most sports teams lose in every season and it is important for them to keep their fans interested in their activities throughout the year.

The Elusive Fan

The Chicago Cubs baseball team hadn't won a pennant since 1908 but the Cubs retained some of the greatest fans found in baseball. The managers and team players spend time with the fans and invite their ideas and the fans themselves are organized. Finally, in 2017 the Cubs won their pennant in an amazing game.

Ben Shields, Irv Rein and Philip

As you can tell, I admire this exceptional person, Jose Salibi, for his personal encouragement and his long-lasting contributions to Brazil.

42. MEXICO AND KIDZANIA FOR KIDS

I usually speak each year in Mexico. Mexico is a country with 117 million people (we are not counting the 32 million Mexican Americans who do not live in Mexico). Mexico City's metro area contains 23 million people. That led me to propose to a Mexican audience that public talk needs to go beyond focusing on the BRIC countries – Brazil, Russia, India, China. We must add the MIST countries – Mexico, Indonesia, South Korea, Turkey – because they are large countries and they are growing their GDP at the same or even a faster rate than some of the BRIC countries. Let's call this whole set of important countries the BRICMIST countries.

Mexico has a lot of positive factors in its future. It has a young population. It trains a large number of engineers. Many of its people are entrepreneurs. The U.S. invests lots of money in Mexico. Manufacturing is picking up. Some Mexican companies - Grupo Bimbo, Grupo Modelo, and Televisa - have moved successfully into the U.S. and will spread into other countries.

Mexico is our neighbor to the South. I have spoken many times in Mexico City and Monterrey. I have enjoyed visiting their museums showing the great sculptural artifacts of many ancient cultures of Mexico. I am partial to their tasty cuisine found in the best Mexican restaurants.

Many Mexican students have come to Kellogg to study for their MBA degree. I meet our active Mexican alumni every few years when I lecture in Mexico. Here I want to talk about one of my favorite Mexican students who took seriously my call that businesses should use business and marketing to create a better world.

Xavier Lopez was my student over twenty-five years ago. In the last fifteen years, Xavier created an amazing new theme park called KidZania. KidZania is like Disneyland in creating rides and fun for kids, usually ages 4-14. But it differs by also adding learning to their experience. Most kids between the ages of 4-14 know little or nothing about the world of work. They do not know what their fathers and mothers do when they leave in the morning for work. They do not think about what they might like to do when they grow up and are finished with their schooling. They don't know anything about most of the jobs, careers, and professions in the world that they can learn and be trained for.

Xavier Lopez and Philip

Kids visiting KidZania can work in a bottling plant or different factories making candy, cereal, chocolate, pastry and jelly. They can choose to work in a bank, beauty salon, hospital, hotel, vet clinic, advertising agency, newspaper publisher, radio station, or TV station. There is a police station, fire station, prison, courts and a city hall for children to work in. There is a disco lounge, theatre, culinary school, modeling studio, art school, and a university. KidZania can handle 3,600 visitors a day and it draws 800,000 visitors a year.

I watched a group of children wearing doctors' uniforms operate on a "dummy" patient in the virtual hospital. I watched a trial taking place in a courtroom with an accused person, prosecuting and defending attorneys, a judge, and a jury. I watched the young mayor of a city give a speech to the legislature consisting of other legislators who would vote on a public issue. I watched a building on fire with young firemen spraying the building to put out the fire. I watched children being taught on how to take care of a dog, brush its teeth, and train the dog. I watched a set of young children learning to change a car tire, run a supermarket or run a restaurant.

Kids do not have these experiences in school. At school, they learn to read and write, math, geography, and history, but there is little time to have contact with the world of work, entertainment, civics, and so on. KidZania supplies this missing experience.

Xavier launched the first KidZania City in Sante Fe, Mexico (a suburb of Mexico City) in September 1999. Xavier gathered some investors, raised money, and designed the park and leased space at the leading shopping center in Mexico City, Centro Santa Fe, which has over 300 stores and parking for 5,000 cars. There I watched children choose their occupations. KidZania occupies several acres and features small buildings such as a hospital, hotel, bank, TV station, police station, fire station, law court, cooking school, and model studio.

Xavier told me that KidZania aims to give kids not only wonderful work and play experiences but to raise their consciousness about five important themes that kids need to understand:

- Kids need to learn how to drive carefully and know the basics of fixing a car, motorcycle or bike, all of which they can learn at KidZania.
- Kids need to learn the importance of conserving water and how a city's water treatment system manages to supply clean drinking water.
- Kids need to think of themselves as voting citizens in a democracy that has elections, legislators, and judges.
- Kids need to adopt sustainable behaviors and know how waste collection and recycling and reusing works.
- Kids need to meet and respect diverse people, especially those with handicaps such as blindness, deafness, being crippled, or aged people.

Parents or school teachers bring the kids to KidZania at 9 am in the morning. Upon arriving, the kids get a Kidzania passport, visa, boarding pass and Kidzania money to spend on various items and services. Each child gets a wristband that monitors where he or she is in Kidzania and each event or store he or she enters. It would be easy for a parent or school teacher to know where a particular child is at any time.

Kidzania is now located in over 11 countries with 10 more locations being planned. Today there are 15 KidZania cities – Santa Fe, Mexico; Monterrey, Mexico; Tokyo, Japan; Jakarta, Indonesia; Koshien, Japan; Lisboa, Portugal; Dubai, United Arab Emirates; Seoul, South Korea; Kuala Lumpur, Malaysia; Cuicuilco, Mexico; Santiago, Chile; Bangkok, Thailand; Kuwait City, Kuwait; Cairo, Egypt; and Mumbai, India. Nine other world city locations are now under consideration or development.

I believe that kids who go to KidZania - many go several times because there is so much to do and see – will turn out to be better citizens than those who do not have this experience. It is very important to bring in poor children or children from orphanages to experience KidZania. Hopefully the KidZania experience will lead to a more capable and wiser generation of children and adults.

You can understand how a business school professor like me feels when one of his students creates and becomes the CEO of a major multinational which has happened with Xavier López. I am prouder of what he has done to make the world a better place than if he was the CEO of any other major Mexican company.

43. ITALY'S PAINS, PLEASURES AND POTENTIALS

At one time, I had the thought to visit every country in the world at least once. When I found out that there are 193 countries, I dropped the idea. I realized that it might be more meaningful to me to visit a few countries frequently rather than trying to visit many countries once. Consider Italy, for example. I cannot say that I have seen Italy by seeing only Florence and Venice. There are too many other treasured cities in Italy that would give me great pleasure given my interest in Italian art and culture. Italy has become one of my most frequently visited countries.

Someone once asked me "What country has contributed the most to the intellectual and aesthetic level of the Western world?" I can imagine someone naming ancient Greece whose philosophers raised profound questions about the nature of the true, the good, and the beautiful. Or how about France which set such a high standard for elegance in the 18th century that Russia under Peter the Great panted to imitate France. Surely Germans would say that they contributed the most with their great universities and research breakthroughs and their great composers such as Bach, Beethoven, Brahms and Mozart. Britain would argue that Shakespeare's plays are the greatest literary achievement of all time.

Friends, my vote goes to Italy. The Italians contributed to the flowering of so many areas of human excellence. What would life be like without the sculptures of Michelangelo and Bernini and the paintings of Leonardo da Vinci and Caravaggio? What would our life be like without the operatic music of Puccini and Verdi? What would our intellectual and scientific life be without Galileo, Alessandro Volta, Guglielmo Marconi, and Enrico Fermi? What would our apparel be like without the gifted work of Ferragamo, Gucci, Armani and other Italian couturiers with their textiles for clothing and leather for shoes? What would our life be without the mighty pasta and risotto and pizza? How could we define beauty if we didn't know about Sophia Loren and Gina Lollobrigida?

Sophia Loren

Gina Lollobrigida

Every year for eleven years my friend Pietro Guido invited me to present a full day workshop on marketing to Milan's business community. Pietro had worked for Montedison but he eventually left and entered the management education business. He produced audiences for me that varied from a few hundred-business people to over a thousand. He credited me with having brought a rich understanding of marketing to the Italian business community.

Pietro Guido and Philip

Each time I landed in Milano, Pietro picked me up. My first question was always about the condition of the Italian economy. How troubled is it? We used a 10-point scale. "Pietro, how troubled is the Italian economy this year?" For many years, he would put it between 5-7. But he grew more pessimistic over time and say 8 or 9. "Why don't you move to another country that is not economically troubled?" He said "I love Italy too much for all of its faults."

Having sponsored so many speakers, Pietro himself turned to writing a number of books. He called one *The End of Marketing.* In another book, he argued that Italy is actually three countries and it should be broken up. The North of Italy makes all the money. The South of Italy destroys all the money. And Rome and its government siphons off all of the money.

I remember when Pietro invited me to dinner at his home for the first time. I walked in and I couldn't believe what I saw. Hanging on the wall were outstanding paintings from the Impressionist period. I recognized a Pissarro, a Degas, a Renoir, a Sisley. "Pietro, you need a permanent guard in your home to protect these paintings." "No," he said. "I painted them myself." Little did I know about his talent as a painter to copy beautifully any painting that interested him. He ended up sending a "Pissarro" to me which hangs in my office.

When I say that Italy has contributed so much to Western civilization, I know that I have neglected to comment on Asia's contributions to the world. So much of our lives are more enjoyable because of great ideas coming from China, Japan, India and other great Asian civilizations. The West is increasingly looking to Asia for answers to the question of the good life.

44. THE ECONOMICS AND ART OF NATION BUILDING

Most nations never reach their potential!

This statement applies not only to economically wrecked nations such as Haiti and Yemen, or even struggling nations such as North Korea and Laos. We can make the same statement about most industrial nations, including Italy, Spain, Portugal and Greece. Do you think that the United States has reached its true potential with 15 percent of its people living in poverty and 30 percent of its students who do not go to college after high school?

What do we mean by a nation reaching its true potential? Every nation inherits a set of natural resources and its people have a certain history, culture and aptitudes. Does that nation make good use of its human capital and natural resources? Do its people have aspirations and manage to achieve them? The answer is no in virtually all cases.

Economists have developed a whole field – economic development theory - to help nations do better. Some development economists emphasize the idea of capital formation to increase labor productivity. Some emphasize international trade where the nation strives to export more than it imports. Some see the answer in human capital development where education and training would confer the skills needed for the nation to grow and prosper. Others see the key to lie in entrepreneurs who build new enterprises to provide the needed jobs.

To facilitate world economic growth, two international organizations play that role - the World Bank (WB) and the International Monetary Fund (IMF). Other economic players helping nations succeed are Central Banks such as the Federal Reserve in the U.S., the Deutsche Bank in Germany, or the European Central Bank. Their job is to facilitate and regulate the local, regional and national needs of businesses for borrowing, lending and investing. Good banking facilities and practices are essential to help nations reach their potential. But banking practices sometimes fail to work, as when large banks resist extending needed loans or are overgenerous in extending credit. Central Banks have to steer the economy between these two extremes.

In 2005, I co-authored with Somkid Jatusripitak and Suvit Maesincee *The Marketing of Nations* to explain the economic forces that could be harnessed to improve a nation's economic standing. I realize that the task of a nation reaching its full potential goes far beyond the role of economics. Good economic theory is often twisted and defeated by political factors, geographic factors, and cultural factors. Greed, corruption, cronyism, and cultural clashes play a role in keeping a nation from fulfilling its potential. The "Arab Spring" nations – Libya, Egypt, Tunisia – are saddled with many problems and need to move to a new constitution and the rule of law if they want to make any progress.

What I realize today is how complicated it is to run a nation well. How can the different vested interest groups inside the country find common ground? How can the nation adapt to the rapidly changing world with its technological advances and its globalization push? Consider that a nation's future is determined by its dependency on foreign markets, foreign funds and foreign oil. Does it even make sense to consider a nation to be in control of its destiny? How autonomous is Italy, Spain, Greece, France or any of the Euro zone nations, which are held in check by the European Central Bank? How autonomous are the developing and emerging nations that depend upon foreign and domestic investment for economic growth?

No nation is independent anymore. Today's nations exist and operate in a complex network and web of international coalitions, institutions, and dependencies.

Yet I hope that each nation finally discovers the appropriate pathway to arrive at its own true goals. I am taken by the story of the King of Bhutan who not only told his people that his goal was to increase their happiness but he went on to invent a system for measuring happiness. This way he could see whether GDP and *happiness* would both rise together. The two might not rise together and countries have to decide whether to focus on achieving more production or more happiness.

45. MEGACITIES, THE DRIVING FORCE IN ECONOMIC DEVELOPMENT

In 1973, Richard J. Barnet and Ronald E. Mueller published *Global Reach: The Power of the Multinational Corporations*. The authors criticized the growth and power of Multinational Corporations and their role in America's expansion abroad in empire-building and colonization. They warned that multinational corporations are designed to exploit other nations. They would make advanced nations richer and poorer nations poorer. The authors advocated policies to curb U.S. and other corporations from expanding without limits. Had their proposals gone into effect, the economically disadvantaged nations of the world would have grown poorer, not richer! In fact, less developed nations improve as the result of letting commerce and trade occur between the advanced and developing nations. Developing nations need capital and investment. Discouraging investment from flowing into needy nations is the way to keep them poor.

The real driver of economic growth is not nations as much as their megacities and urban centers. Most global economic activity takes place in the 600 largest urban centers – places like Beijing, Tokyo, London, Sao Paulo, Mexico City, and Jakarta. Ten U.S. cities - NYC, San Francisco, Miami, Boston, Chicago, Dallas, Houston, Atlanta, LA, and Seattle – account for a substantial amount of the U.S. GDP. The top European cities – London, Frankfurt, Berlin, Paris, Geneva, and Milan – account for a good percentage of European GDP. Today 54% of India's GDP is transacted in 10 cities. Three million Chinese are moving to cities every month!

If GDP is getting more and more concentrated in the megacities and their satellites, then marketing has to shift from mass marketing that focuses on national GDP to urban marketing that focuses on the megacity and its middle classes. These megacities and their satellites are globally interlocked in investment, trade and consumption.

Megacities can be viewed as "quasi-nations" or "city states." Consider that in the 11th century, many cities in Europe, including

Venice, Milan, Florence, Genoa, Pisa, Siena, Lucca, and Cremona each became a large trading metropolis and operated with great independence. Megacities have to form positive and mutually satisfying relations with several groups, including the national power, other global centers that act as rivals or allies, international organizations (World Bank, International Monetary Fund), major banks and multinational corporations. Major megacities must learn how to negotiate their various relationships and opportunities. They need to know how to work with entrepreneurs and other companies that can assist or oppose their policies.

What role does a nation play when economic development is largely in the hands of its major urban cities? One can raise a more basic question. Why are nations needed? Can't a group of major cities achieve their goals better without being part of a nation? What is added by forming a nation which has the power to tax and then allocate resources among the communities according to political compromises and power differentials.

The answer is that nations create a set of benefits that otherwise would not be available to the separate megacities. The nation can shift resources from the richer communities to the weaker communities. We call this the redistributive function of national government. The nation also develops a history of exploits and leaders that give its people a sense of pride and purpose. We call this the heroic function of national government. We know how people in some nations call their nation the Fatherland (Germany) or the Motherland (Russia) to give identity and meaning to the lives of these people. And the nation serves another purpose, its defense function, in that individual cities would be subject to attack from rapacious outsiders and need to formally join with other communities into a nation that provides self-defense. Sadly, most of the world's population over historical time has been oppressed by their national governments. Most European nations were run by a monarchy and aristocracy to serve their own interests. Most citizens lived under feudal and subsistence conditions, with little hope of advancing their well-being. The idea that the citizens of a nation should participate in determining its destiny—the idea of democracy—came to life 2000 years after Athenian democracy with the American and French Revolutions.

How do urban centers work out their own destinies? Clearly each urban center rallies its major power groups to work together toward a vision of urban economic growth. Its power groups include its major corporations, banks, hotels, media and community organizations. Each urban center forms relationships with the nation itself, other urban centers within the nation, feeder cities and resource pools in the nation, other nations and particularly other urban centers outside the nation, and international organizations.

What role is played by global corporations in selecting urban cities to work with? Global corporations moving into a new region of the world such as Asia first need to choose a nation and then an urban center within that nation to become its regional headquarters. Often in Asia, Hong Kong or Singapore will be chosen because these cities have excellent transportation, telecommunications, banks, and services and a high degree of political stability. The power of a major urban center to attract interest and resources from relevant major corporations is key to its urban growth, even more so than its work to wrest resources from its own nation. Urban centers compete with each other to attract foreign capital and resources. They compete by offering free land, tax rebates, a high quality of life. Urban centers improve themselves by building adequate infrastructure - airports, highways, telecommunications, and electricity grids.

The bottom line is that major urban centers need the freedom, opportunity and incentives to build their own power and brands and this will all redound to the success of the nation as a whole. Milton Kotler and I analyze this problem of the relationship between major city centers and major multinationals in our latest book, *Winning Global Markets* (2015).

46. CHAUTAUQUA, N.Y. - A CULTURAL AND INTELLECTUAL OASIS

Starting in the middle of June each year, Nancy and I pack our car with clothing and other goods that we need for our annual nine-week sojourn at the Chautauqua Institution in Chautauqua, New York. Other families look forward to spending their summer vacations in Cape Cod, Upper Wisconsin, Michigan or other places that cater to the summer vacation crowd.

Why Chautauqua for our summer retreat? Where is Chautauqua anyways and what is special about it?

Chautauqua is the name of small town that borders Lake Chautauqua in northwestern New York about a 1 ½ hour drive from Buffalo, New York. Chautauqua was settled in 1874 and soon afterwards the city dwellers invited speakers to bring education to the people in this area. There was the Lyceum movement that brought well known speakers and preachers to different cities and towns in the U.S – persons such as Mark Twain, Theodore Roosevelt, and Franklin Delano Roosevelt spoke at the Chautauqua Institution. Almost every evening features some performance: the Chautauqua Symphony Orchestra, or the North Carolina Dance Troup, or some plays, singers or comedians.

For the last fifty years, the Chautauqua Institution has run a nine-week summer program featuring speakers and artistic performances and diverse religious activities. Each week centers on a different theme. Here is a list of the week-long topics that took place during the 2013 summer program:

- Our elegant universe
- The next greatest generation
- America, 1863
- Markets and morals: reimagining the social contract
- The pursuit of happiness
- Crime and punishment

- Diplomacy
- Turkey: model for the Middle East
- Health care: reform and innovation

Here is my experience on a typical day (June 24, 2013)

10:45 am. Nancy and I and 4,000 other visitors to Chautauqua heard a dazzling lecture by Harvard's Brian Greene, author of *The Hidden Reality*, at the Amphitheatre. Brian explained Einstein's search for a unified theory of the universe. He described how other scientists pursued this dream with formulating the "big bang," quantum theory, string theory, dark energy and matter, and other theories of physical phenomena.

2:00 pm. We attended the talk by Mary Evelyn Tucker from Yale University about her film "The Journey of the Universe."

3:30 pm. We heard Dr. Ann Kirschner of Princeton University speak about "Lady at the OK Corral: Lessons from the American Frontier."

5:30 pm. We went to the cinema to see the film "Journey of the Universe" about the universe's evolution and its fragility today in the face of unregulated forces damaging the environment.

8:15 pm. Attended a concert by two performers singing Broadway melodies.

A Lecture in the Amphitheatre at Chautauqua

This can go on day after day for nine weeks. Usually we reach a point of surfeit and take a respite by spending the greater part of a day on our porch looking at the trees or listening to some music.

Or visitors can turn off the heady lectures and turn to sailing, swimming, golf, tennis, or other sports all available at Chautauqua. Chautauqua can be seen as offering lifelong learning in a beautiful setting. We have the feeling of being fully engaged and fully alive.

One of the most wonderful parts of the nine weeks is sharing it with our children and grandchildren: Melissa, our middle daughter, and our grandchildren Olivia) and Sam, and Louie (their Havanese dog) and our son-in-law Steve.

One can argue that at the end of nine weeks, we are a walking encyclopedia of topics and tidbits that we will share with different friends and acquaintances when we return to normal city life.

Olivia and Sam

Olivia today is now 21 and Sam is 17. Olivia is now a talented singer/songwriter with several albums and attending Clark College after spending a year in Nashville making contacts. Sam is in his third year in high school and deeply involved in robots, gene theory, fish and aquariums, and baseball. Kids grow up very fast, as you can tell from these photos.

Olivia and Sam

47. LONGBOAT KEY, FL. - DON'T TELL OTHERS ABOUT THIS PARADISE

Nancy and I decided in the 1980s that we should consider setting up a second living location, one to which we could escape each Winter when the bitter cold hits Chicago. We didn't plan to build a home so much as to rent a place on a short-term basis. Chicagoans often choose Florida's east coast, or Scottsdale or Tempe, Arizona, or some key city in California.

My colleague, Louis Stern, said that Nancy and I don't have to search for a location because he and his wife Rhona are spending time sampling different locations to find the best vacation area. So, we deferred hoping that Louis will discover Shangri-La. I remember the day when he came to my office and said that he and Rhona have found the perfect location. "Where?" I asked. "Oakland, California!" Louis said they found a beautiful home on the top of a mountain where they could view San Francisco's Golden Gate Bridge and the city in its splendor. Besides, he said, he wanted to be in driving distance to professor friends teaching at the University of California in Berkeley, California.

Well, clearly, we had delayed too long. California was out of the question for three reasons: earthquakes, hard drugs, and long flights. We settled into thinking that the answer has to be Florida, a simple two-hour flight from Chicago.

But isn't Florida a state with little culture and many rednecks? Or are there some intellectual oases in the desert called Florida? Three were mentioned by friends: Miami, Naples and Sarasota. We had been to Miami and we concluded that it is an interesting city to visit, but not one to live in. Traffic congestion is terrible and the city is too large and busy. Naples was much smaller and drew a wealthy winter clientele, had excellent restaurants, and required only a two-hour drive across Alligator Alley to reach Miami. Naples had wealth and good golf courses but not much culture. Sarasota, also a small town. but a town with a long history of culture. John Ringling, of circus fame, and his wife Mable, had built a beautiful home on a large property and built the Ringling Museum of Art to exhibit the many baroque works of art that he acquired on his European trips. Sarasota also had a symphony orchestra, an opera company, a ballet company, two playhouses, and plenty of educational programs offering lifelong learning. We quickly decided that Sarasota would be our Winter retreat.

I told Nancy that we would only spend two weeks in the winter in Sarasota. I had courses to teach at Northwestern. All my books were in Chicago and the computer and the Internet was only just coming into our lives. Eventually I managed to do all my teaching in the Fall and Spring Quarters, leaving the Winter Quarter free. We went from spending two weeks in Sarasota, to four weeks, to two months and eventually to six months, running from December to May.

Our first purchased apartment was in condominium located in a section of Sarasota known as Siesta Key. Siesta Key's beach was rated as one of the best sandy beaches in the U.S. The Florida palm trees, sunrises and sunsets were beautiful to view. Our apartment was on the fifth floor of a six-story condominium of about 100 units. We gradually came to appreciate that condominium living beats owning a private home. We didn't have to cut grass, fix the roof, or have any of these problems that go with owning a private home.

After a while, we wanted to find a better condominium. Our agent suggested that we would probably be happier moving to Longboat Key, Florida. Longboat Key is a long key that runs north and south parallel to Sarasota and connected to Sarasota by two bridges. The agent took us to see the Water Club that consisted of two 12-story buildings, a club house, beautiful grounds, concierge service, and handsome apartments. We saw a few available apartments and made a choice. Since then, we have moved three times within the Water Club and now we have the most perfect apartment. The views are spectacular, we are on the ninth floor, and we enter our apartment directly, not through a corridor.

The people living in the Water Club are accomplished and friendly. The social committee sponsors events such as dinners, dances, and performing artists. There is a large ballroom, a book club, an excellent gym, an Olympic size swimming pool, and a sandy beach. We are near to easy shopping at the Publix food store and CVS pharmacy and other small stores. We take delight in a ten-minute drive to St. Armands, a circular shopping area with hundreds of stores and restaurants. It is a destination for many tourists and very lively in the evening.

Longboat Key has an Education Center where I give a two-day course on Capitalism and Democracy each year, and I take other courses with some fine retired scholars. Longboat Key has some excellent restaurants and we go often into Sarasota to see plays and movies. Sarasota now has four theatres instead of two and we subscribe to all four. We are delighted to be close to the Ringling Museum of Art where we can view our glass collection in the new Kotler/Coville Glass Pavilion. We also can view a selection of our netsukes and tsubas in the new Asia Museum wing of the Ringling Museum.

In 2017, Sarasota was voted the number one city in Florida for quality of life. It is fast becoming a "mecca" for art glass lovers with two great collections of contemporary studio art glass. Sarasota is on a building spree of new hotels and condominiums. This is a sign of its growing popularity and that people see it as a paradise. But paradises might ultimately be hurt by more traffic congestion and the "canyon" look of tall buildings. As the city grows, it is apt to lose some of its beauty and convenience. Hopefully, Sarasota will strike a healthy balance between growth and quality of life.

Longboat Key, Florida

48. THE PLEASURES AND PAIN OF FAME

As a marketer, I have been approached by many aspiring performers – singers, musicians, actors and actresses – asking for my help to become better known by more people. They want to become "famous" or "more famous." They want a marketing plan, a brand-building plan.

Why would they want "fame?" A female singer might want to share her beautiful voice with a larger audience, or meet more people, to draw more admiration, or to increase her income. Why not try to be a Barbra Streisand, a Madonna, or a Lady Gaga? What a charmed life these ladies must lead living in beautiful mansions, catered to by servants and many admirers?

Any young singer should be aware that there is a dark side accompanying a life of great fame. Her success goes with the loss of privacy and anonymity. Her face becomes public property. People will spot her and follow her. They will plead for her autograph and for a photo or selfie to be taken with her. The paparazzi will pursue her and photograph her wherever she can be found.

She will need protection against this intrusion. She will need an agent who will fend off the crowds. The agent will know the right hotels and the quiet corners in special restaurants where she could dine without intruders. She will start to wear sunglasses and dress in a way to be less noticed.

There is a deeper psychological challenge that she will face. The mass media will represent her as a certain type of person. She is a brand and the public expects her to live up to her brand. Her public self may not be her real self.

Norman Mailer, the famous novelist, shared that the media chose to represent him as a tough guy. Therefore, he would project this role in public so that the public would continue to see him that way. His real self was quite different and yet he had to act out his public image. Psychologically, his real self may become less real to him.

I remember the life of the Harvard psychologist Dr. Richard Alpert who changed his name to Ram Dass and converted to Hinduism and wore a Hindu robe. He became a legend for his wisdom and his work with all kinds of people including prisoners and sick people. One day, after many years, he decided to shave off his beard and return to wearing Western clothes. Quite suddenly, he lost his following. He no longer was the symbol that his followers had become attached to. He was another Westerner.

Dr. Richard Alpert

In following the lives of famous people, I researched and co-authored with Irv Rein and Marty Stoller the book High Visibility: *The Making and Marketing of Professionals into Celebrities* (1987). We updated the book in 1998 and 2006). Our main purpose was to provide marketing guidelines for persons who wanted to become well-known. We described the "industrialization of celebrity," namely that an industry – agents, personal managers, promoters – existed to help people become well-known. They approached the person as a product to be improved and promoted and sent into the right channels of distribution and priced higher as they rose in prominence.

A young singer might first sign up to appear in an amateur talent contest, hoping to do well and be noticed by an agent. She might get a singing job in a small nightclub. She might get an interview on a minor talk show and eventually be invited to perform on a major talk show watched nightly by millions of people. Barbra Streisand's break came in this way when she was invited to sing on the *Tonight Show* by its popular host Johnny Carson. The audience was overwhelmed by her performance. Barbra went on to live a fairy tale life with concerts, acting and producing roles in movies, and supporting a variety of causes to help others.

2nd edition 2006, 1st ed., 1997

Would Barbra, in looking back, regret this path that she has taken? I doubt it. The pleasures are too many and the pains are worth it. She can relish how many millions of people she has given pleasure to with her treasured voice and performances.

Most people attain their fame in much more limited geographical and professional areas. There will be the well-known personal injury lawyer in Chicago, the best-known plastic surgeon in Los Angeles, even the best regarded carpenter in the small town of Peoria, Illinois. They command respect and are talked about on a local level without drawing crowds of picture takers and autograph seekers. Their faces may not be noticed in a crowd. They can live their lives more peacefully with their family and personal friends. I remember the novelist Graham Green remarking that he was happy that people didn't know his face as they would if he had been a movie star.

I have been asked whether I developed a marketing plan to become a well-known professor of marketing. No, I hadn't. I just enjoyed thinking, researching and writing about marketing and other topics. Much of fame is produced by working hard at what you love and hitting a high level of performance.

49. INNOVATION AND DISRUPTION IN THE NEW INTERNET ECONOMY

I have had a long-term interest in innovation. We have lived through technological, social, economic and political changes that would have been hard to imagine 50 years ago. Our lives have been changed by computers, microwave ovens, birth control pills, smart phones, the Internet, robotics, nanotechnology, new drugs and surgical procedures, all of these recent innovations.

I engaged in my first systematic research into innovation with Fernando Trias de Bes, a gifted professor at ESADE, the Barcelona Business School. We both felt that innovators had to think more laterally rather than vertically to create new ideas. Instead of the Kellogg company thinking only about launching a new box of cereal (vertical thinking), Kellogg management should think of something else to do with cereal (lateral thinking). How about incorporating cereal into a candy bar or health bar? How about adding a small cup on top of a yogurt container that carries loose cereal that could be added to the yogurt?

We were inspired about thinking laterally, or "out of the box," by Edward DeBono and his book, *Lateral Thinking*. We ended up publishing *Lateral Marketing: A New Approach to Finding Product, Market, and Marketing Mix Ideas* (2003). Fernando subsequently was invited by the Nestle company to use our methodology to help Nestle think up new ideas for marketing coffee. The Nestle group generated over 50 ideas, a few of them being very original and appealing.

Fernando and I felt that the next task was to help companies become truly innovative. It is one thing to use different methods of creativity to find a new idea; it is another to build an innovative DNA into a company.

Philip and Fernando Trias de Bes

We recognized that several roles are played in an innovative organization. Someone has to come up with ideas (Activator). Someone has to examine whether the idea is really original and exciting (Browser). Someone has to turn the idea into a testable concept that proves worthy (Creator). Someone has to turn the idea into a physical prototype or a business model (Developer). Someone has to have the skills to launch the new product or business (Executor). And someone has to supply the money for all of these preceding activities (Financer). If you look at the first letters of these six roles, we can call it the ABCDEF model of innovation or the A to F model of innovation.

We needed to list the tools and skills needed by each A to F player and the relationship between each pair players. We spelled this out in our new book, *Winning at Innovation: The A to F Model* (2012).

The interesting thing about innovation is that it is essentially disruptive. The famous economist Joseph Schumpeter said that innovation involves "creative destruction."

Winning at Innovation: The A to F Model

More recently, Clayton Christensen of Harvard has written widely about "disruptive innovation" and has illustrated it with many examples. A new technology might emerge that initially is no threat to an existing business. The new technology might be cheaper but it performs more poorly and is only of interest to a small group of buyers seeking a lower price. If the disrupter gathers enough customers to make a profit, the disrupter will use the profit to improve the technology's performance or lower its costs further. The leading companies will abandon their lower profit businesses and concentrate on higher profit businesses, as the steel industry did when mini steel mills began to invade their lower product profit space. But the process continues where the innovator keeps getting better and invades more of the space of the leading firms. We don't hear much today about Bethlehem Steel or U.S. Steel, former giants of the steel industry.

Industries have experienced slow change through most of their history but today's industries are disrupted more frequently and severely. Is any industry safe from disruption? Will your industry be next? If yes, what can you do about it?

We expected Kodak to last and lead forever in the film business. Film was the only medium at the time for capturing and distributing pictures. Kodak was blind to the new digital media that could also take and carry pictures. Now every picture is captured by a series of zeros and ones on your iPhone and you can print the pictures in your office or home.

We have witnessed the digital revolution hurting the music business (with MP3 and peer exchange), movie attendance (downloading movies and hurting cinemas), bookstores (downloading e-books), and newspapers (much lower readership). We are now witnessing the digital revolution challenging store retailing itself. Consumers need not leave home to get whatever they need or want. They click on their iPhone to reach Amazon and order common products that will be delivered in a day or two.

The latest industry to face an uncertain future are our colleges. The threat is coming from online courses featuring some of the nation's finest professors from Harvard, M.I.T., Stanford and other schools. Will students continue to spend $45,000 a year for a four-year college degree when they can watch lectures and videos at home and get a college online degree? The Internet and Google can provide training in any area that students desire. As more colleges introduce these online resources, they may be able to trim their costs. Colleges that don't invest in these new learning systems may be disrupted. Top colleges will continue to thrive with their lavish campuses but many marginal colleges may have to close down. Some online disrupters are aiming to produce a $10,000 a year MBA.

This is just the beginning of what the Internet will do to established businesses. Consider the rise of *collaborative consumption* where owners of homes, cars and other hard assets are using them in new ways. Many car owners have joined Uber and are able to taxi people around at a lower cost without joining and paying dues to a taxi company. One can click on Airbnb and find a huge list of homeowners offering a bed at night in their home for a price much cheaper than going to a hotel. Or one can go to Relay Rides and rent the use of someone else's private car that would otherwise stay idle. This practice is spreading as consumers rent from others loft storage space, lawnmowers, parking spaces, speedboats, and other items. The movement toward *shared consumption* doesn't bode well for established companies in the taxi, boat, or hotel business. People increasingly want access, not ownership. And it certainly reduces their cost compared to the alternatives.

Another big source of disruption are new business models. Innovation goes far beyond just creating new products. When Fred Smith built FedEx, the U.S. Post Office should have been warned. It was a success because enough people were willing to pay a little more to get their mail delivered by 1030am the next morning. When Ingvar Kamprad launched Ikea, furniture stores should have noticed this newcomer who was offering good quality furniture at a much lower price. When Leonard Riggio launched the large bookstore of Barnes and Noble, small bookstores should have realized that they would lose most of their customers to this giant intruder. When Jeff Bezos created Amazon as a way to sell books online and through downloading, even Leonard Riggio needed to take note of this potential disrupter to his store-based book selling business. Now, of course, Amazon threatens just about all of retail.

Anthony Ulwick has created a process to optimize innovation outcomes. For 25 years, he has worked to guide companies to success. He has done this by introducing us to what is now called Jobs-to-be-Done theory, and converting it to practice using his rigorous innovation process known as Outcome-Driven Innovation.

In his latest book, *Jobs to be Done: Theory to Practice*, we learn that the vast majority of innovation projects fail. With Ulwick's process we finally learn what the best know already - innovation cannot be left to chance. It can and should be managed for successful outcomes. I call him the "Deming of Innovation" because, more than anyone else, Tony has turned innovation into a science.

Here is a list of entrepreneurs who have introduced new business models to replace older models that used to run our normal businesses.

- Anita Roddick — Body Shop
- Fred Smith — Federal Express
- Steve Jobs — iTunes, iPad, iPhone
- Bill Gates — Microsoft
- Michael Dell — Dell Computer
- Ray Kroc — McDonald's
- Walt Disney — Disneyworld
- Sam Walton — Wal-Mart
- Tom Monaghan — Domino's Pizza
- Gilbert Trigano — Club Mediterranee
- Ted Turner — CNN
- Richard Branson — Virgin
- Charles Lazarus — Toys R Us
- Les Wexner — Victoria Secrets
- Ingvard Kampard — IKEA
- Howard Schultz — Starbucks
- Charles Schwab — Charles Schwab
- Mark Zuckerberg — Facebook
- Larry Page, Sergey Brin — Google

Every company must be alert to new threats that might disrupt their existing business. Senior management needs to meet and consider what changes in technology, consumer tastes, and business practices might pull the rug out from under their enterprise.

Once they discover any serious threats, they have two major recourses. One is to sell their business before most of its value vanishes and before their competitors recognize the threat. The other is to move into self-disruption, namely to invest in disrupting their old business model before someone else does.

50. SPECULATING ON THE DIGITAL FUTURE OF MARKETING

Kevin Roberts, CEO of the advertising agency Saatchi and Saatchi, gave a speech in which he spoke about "the end of marketing." He then explained that he meant the "end of the old marketing." For over 100 years, companies had high control of what consumers thought about the company and its products. Each company used the power of mass communications to shape the customer's attitude and knowledge of the company and its offerings.

That old marketing world is slowly dying with the explosion of the digital world. Today's consumers learn about a company and its products by chatting with friends on Facebook and going on the Internet to find abundant information on every aspect of the company. Today's consumers also treat the retailer as running a "showroom" instead of a store and insist that the retailer match the lowest price for the same product that shows up from other stores on the customer's smart phone.

Today's companies have lost control over building their brand. The brand is shaped more and more by customers talking to each other over the Internet. A company still achieves some influence through its 30-second commercials. But I predict that companies five years from now might spend as much as 50 percent of their communication budget on social and digital media. This will happen as young people stop reading newspapers and add TIVO to their TV equipment and bypass watching TV commercials out of impatience.

Marketing, when it works, is much more than communication.

Marketing's primary aim should be to add value to the customer's life.

Marketing must influence all the factors that affect the customer's satisfaction with company offerings.

Marketing must have an influence on the product, its features, its price, its availability and its accompanying services, popularly known as the 4Ps (product, price, place, and promotion).

A company's Chief Marketing Officer (CMO) should be in charge of defining and delivering customer value. The CMO sits with the other chiefs -- finance (CFO), research and development (CDO), operations (COO), information (CIO) -- in developing the company's current plans and future offerings. My observation is that today the CMO's role is still limited. The other chiefs still see marketing as primarily a communication and selling function.

Marketing may be losing some of its traditional functions to other departments in the company:

- New products   >   R&D product development
- Innovation   >   Operations
- Media   >   Management science
- Channels   >   Logistics and supply chain
- Market strategy >   Strategy department
- Service   >   Customer service department
- Data mining   >   IT and computer science

That leaves marketing with managing:
- Communication
- Pricing
- Branding and differentiation
- Consumer behavior

We are even hearing critics ask whether the CMO position is the right position to serve the interests of customers. Dominque Turbin, CEO of the IMD business school in Switzerland, published an article in the Financial Times (November 19, 2012) titled "The CMO is Dead...Welcome to the COO! How to Breathe New Life into Marketing."

He cited four failings of the current CMO position:

1. Most CMOs are not really immersed in marketing activities. They focus on communications and not on products and pricing.
2. CFOs have become more powerful and have taken control of pricing because of the tough times and are more likely to rise to CEO and give less attention to CMOs.
3. Marketing impact is often hard to measure to know what was accomplished with the millions spent and marketing's budget is most likely to be cut in hard times.
4. Nobody has a clear idea of what marketing is, whereas most people understand what production or finance is.

Dominique argues that the power of the CMO is being eroded and that the CMO title should be dropped and replaced by a new title, that of CCO – Chief Customer Officer. The CCO would know the customers, what they want and where they are trending. The CCO will use customer knowledge to influence company discussions of product features and pricing. A few companies have already appointed CCOs.

But I am not convinced that a CCO would be doing anything different than would be done by a good CMO. Someone needs to manage the full range of marketing work and I am satisfied that that person should be the CMO.

51. BRAND ACTIVISM, THE NEXT STAGE OF BRANDING

Christian Sarkar and I recently wrote an article on "brand activism."

Historically, most brands have been promoted on their performance characteristics. "Our toothpaste is better than yours." "Better at 'whitening teeth,' 'preventing cavities,' or 'fresh breath.'" *Positioning* is the name of the game in brand marketing. *But positioning is no longer enough* in our highly competitive markets. Just consider marketing to millennials. Millennials have high expectations for brands. Millennials live in a world filled with constant problems – air pollution, bad drinking water, crimes. Many would like brands to show concern not just for profits but for the communities they serve, and the world we live in. More and more, we see a yearning for jobs that have a higher meaning than profit-making.

The Body Shop was one of the first companies to broadcast its ethical values and beliefs. Its founder and CEO, Anita Roddick, not only wanted to make really fine skincare lotions but also care for "animal rights," "civil rights," "fair trade," and "environmental protection." Many Body Shop clients said they were mainly interested in her products but many more approved of her activism and often gathered to march together for the causes they shared.

So, what is brand activism? Wikipedia tells us:

> "*Activism consists of efforts to promote, impede, or direct social, political, economic, and/or environmental reform or stasis with the desire to make improvements in society. Forms of activism range from writing letters to newspapers or to politicians, political campaigning, economic activism such as boycotts or preferentially patronizing businesses, rallies, street marches, strikes, sit-ins, and hunger strikes.*"

Brand activism can be regressive or progressive. The poster-child for regressive activism is Big Tobacco that for so many years denied the harm their products did to consumers. They promoted the "virtues" of smoking in a way that actually hurt consumers by leading to a higher incidence of heart attacks and cancer.

On the progressive activism side, we see more companies seeking to have an impact on the biggest societal problems. These companies have a larger purpose than simple profit-seeking, and they are increasingly seen as leaders in their fields.

Harvard Business Review's 2015 ranking of the Best- Performing CEOs in the World was surprising to many. The world's top-performing CEO isn't a household name. Lars Rebien Sørensen, the CEO of Novo Nordisk – the Danish pharmaceutical company that was ranked #1 – says: "Corporate social responsibility is nothing but maximizing the value of your company over a long period. In the long term, social and environmental issues become financial issues."

The rankings weigh long-term financial results at 80% and ESG (environmental, social, and governance) performance at 20%. On the basis of purely financial metrics, Amazon's Jeff Bezos leads all other CEOs, but Amazon's *relatively weak ESG score* places him at #87 overall.

When did brand activism become a thing? It's a natural evolution of the Corporate Social Responsibility (CSR) and Environmental, Social and Governance (ESG) programs that are transforming companies across the world. Previous efforts were identified as marketing-driven and corporate driven initiatives.

Brand activism emerges as a values-driven agenda for companies that care about the future of society and the planet's health. The underlying force for *progress* is a sense of justice and fairness for all.

The Domains of Brand Activism

So, what domains come under the umbrella of brand activism? We identify six areas that will be familiar to all:

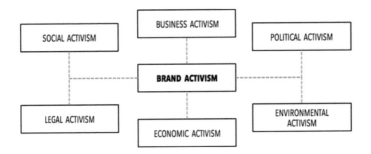

- Social activism includes areas such as equality – gender, LGBT, race, age, etc. It also includes societal and community issues such as education, school funding, etc.
- Legal activism deals with the laws and policies that impact companies, such as tax, workplace, and employment laws.
- Business activism is about governance – corporate organization, CEO pay, worker compensation, labor and union relations, governance, etc.
- Economic activism may include minimum wage and tax policies that impact income inequality and redistribution of wealth.
- Political activism covers lobbying, voting, voting rights, and policy (gerrymandering, campaign finance, etc.).
- Environmental activism deals with conservation, environmental, land-use, air and water pollution laws and policies.

Brand Activism Scorecard

These six domains of brand activism can be combined to create a brand activism scorecard to measure the extent of firm's commitment to the issues.

Different industries have different norms, but even within industries such as oil and gas, for example, there will be leaders and laggards in each domain. It would be an interesting and meaningful exercise to measure and rank all businesses by industry with clear indicators of where they stand. It might be even more interesting to measure their long-term success in the market as well.

Brand Activist Businesses

Let's look at a few examples of companies that are taking brand activism to new heights. These are brand-activist leaders in a field that is growing rapidly.

Patagonia

Patagonia is proud of its conservation ethics. Patagonia wants you to use and reuse your clothing items and eventually give it away to someone else who can use it. But their commitment to social and environmental justice goes a lot further:

- **$10 Million For the Planet** – On Black Friday, Patagonia donated 100% of sales to grassroots organizations working to create positive change for the planet in their own backyards. They state: "In these divisive times, protecting what we all hold in common is more important than ever before."

- **radically///resourceful** – 100% recycled down, polyester and wool. This season Patagonia introduces a new line called re\\\collection—styles made with all sorts of recycled materials, including 100% recycled down, 100% recycled wool and 100% recycled polyester with 85% recycled polyester labels, 80% recycled zippers and 50% recycled buttons.

- **Fair Trade** – Patagonia pays a premium for every Fair Trade Certified item that carries their label. That extra money goes directly to the workers at the factory, and they decide how to spend it. The program also promotes the workers' health, safety, social and environmental compliance, and encourages dialog between workers and management.

- **Regenerative Organic Agriculture** – Patagonia is working to incorporate regenerative organic practices into its supply chain—and work collaboratively with other companies and organizations to further this important work.

Unilever

Here is the powerful values-driven statement by CEO Paul Pohlman of Unilever:

"A year after they were launched it is clear that the UN's Sustainable Development Goals to end extreme poverty, fight inequality and tackle climate change are needed more than ever. That is why we have put them at the heart of Unilever's own model."

Unilever's vision is to grow the business, whilst decoupling their environmental footprint from their growth and increasing their positive social impact. The Unilever Sustainable Living Plan sets stretching targets, including how they source raw materials and how consumers use their brands. Faced with the challenge of climate change and the need for human development, Unilever wants to move towards a world where everyone can live well and within the natural limits of the planet. Their purpose is "to make sustainable living commonplace." The plan covers three key areas:

- Improving Health and Well-being
- Reducing Environmental Impact
- Enhancing Livelihoods

Unilever also co-developed a Circular Business Model, or CBM, that aims to link up all material flows in an infinite process circle in order to use resources most efficiently and ideally don't create any waste. Through this circular approach, the sustainability of a whole business network can be driven. CBMs are useful for translating products and services designed for reuse into attractive value propositions.

Ben and Jerry's

In 1988, Ben & Jerry's was one of the first companies in the world to place a social mission in equal importance to its product and economic missions. Ben & Jerry's operates on a three-part mission that aims to create linked prosperity for everyone that's connected to the business: suppliers, employees, farmers, franchisees, customers, and neighbors alike.

Since being acquired as a separate division of Unilever, Ben & Jerry's has grown and now has a unifying set of principles and criteria on which to evaluate socially responsible businesses, it's called the "B Corp" movement (or Benefit Corporation movement). Certified B Corps satisfy a rigorous set of standards to achieve certification. Ben and Jerry's became the first-ever wholly-owned subsidiary to gain B Corp Certification.

Specific activist issues supported by Ben and Jerry's include: Democracy, Climate Justice, GMO Labeling, LGBT Equality, overturning *Citizen's United*, Fairtrade, opposing rGBH, and Peace Building.

In 2016, Ben and Jerry's publicly announced their support for Black Lives Matter and opposition to systemic racism. In many ways Ben and Jerry's is a justice-brand – taking a stand for social issues most businesses avoid by design.

Seventh Generation

Seventh Generation, another Unilever subsidiary, is also B-Corp-and a mission-driven company. The mission – to inspire a consumer revolution that nurtures the health of the next seven generations – is based on the Great Law of the Iroquois – which holds it appropriate to think seven generations ahead (about 140 years into the future) and decide whether the decisions they make today would benefit their children seven generations into the future.

Seventh Generation is also leading a campaign to reduce the exposure to toxic chemicals that impact human health. Despite the recent passage of the *Frank R. Lautenberg Chemical Safety for the 21st Century Act*, Seventh Generation feels the law does not go far enough:

Many of chemicals in products we use in our homes and around our families are not listed on the label. That's why we've redirected our passion prioritizing your right to know what's in the products you buy. In January, we hosted a rally of mothers, janitorial workers, NGO's and progressive business on the Statehouse steps in California, kicking off our #comeclean campaign calling on legislators to require cleaning products to fully list ingredients they contain on their label and online.

Becoming a Brand Activist

Our economic system of Capitalism is both praiseworthy and blameworthy at the same time. We need to acknowledge that worldwide Capitalism has lifted many out of extreme poverty. But almost half the world — over three billion people — still live on less than $2.50 a day. While we have seen substantial worldwide growth in basic education and literacy and health systems, there is much to be done. Capitalism is also blameworthy. There is no justification for 62 persons in the world owning as much wealth as half of the rest of the world. Our companies have historically practiced "pirate" Capitalism that aims at making the rich richer.

Peter Drucker, in his early writings, saw companies not as our oppressors but more as our possible saviors. He developed the idea of management as a science. Companies would be run by enlightened managers who pursued profitability and sustainability and rewarded all the stakeholders. Drucker saw business management and unions working together as our bulwark against instability – both fascism and communism. He saw companies not as our threat but as our salvation.

This can't happen unless more of our companies go through a transformation. CEOs must become servant-leaders, not emperors. Workers need to be represented on the company's Board of Directors, as in Germany. Companies must formulate a set of principles and values to guide their behavior. Much of the answer now lies in whether more of our companies can adopt a new set of values that go beyond just making profits for their stockholders and managers.

The evolution of brand activism in business is an opportunity for differentiation and purpose-driven engagement. The aim should not only be "profit maximization" that primarily addresses the interests of the investors. The aim should be "stakeholder optimization" where all the parties contributing to the success of the company are well-rewarded.

Will companies embrace brand activism? Elsie Maio, a leading Business Values guru, helps companies undertaking a process of/or spiritual awakening. We see this happening in a handful of companies around the world. A company that wants to be a brand activist must ask:

- What kinds and how many consumers are likely to care about our company's level and type of activism?
- Will consumers believe that our company authentically and passionately believes in the cause(s) we support?
- Will the cost of implementation require us to raise our prices? Will our consumers be willing to pay a little more?
- Does the governance structure and executive leadership

understand how and why brand activism makes a difference?

- How does our activism make us a workplace of meaning to engage and inspire our employees?

Also needed is a way to recognize and award those companies that practice sustainable, stakeholder-oriented business management.

We need to set up a **Brand Activist Award** for Business and each year cite and award certain companies as being leaders in brand activism. Our hope is that more buyers will make their purchases from activist brands, in recognition of their enlightened business practices.

52. HOW I RETURNED TO THE FIELD OF ECONOMICS AND CAPITALISM

When Nikkei invited me to write 30 columns, I couldn't be more delighted. To write 30 columns about my life and ideas in the same series that has featured Peter Drucker, Tony Blair and other notables is an honor. Hopefully the invitation was based on my work of 50 years to restructure the field of marketing into a more scientific and comprehensive discipline about markets, market behavior, and marketing decision making. The fact that most of the world's marketers and managers have been raised on one of my 15 editions of *Marketing Management* or 15 editions of *Principles of Marketing* is gratifying and is at the same time terrifying.

What if my theory and recommendations for the practice of marketing are wrong or underpowered? Although no counter-theory has yet emerged, this doesn't prove that my approach will or should continue to prevail. I have always encouraged counter-theories and debates to take place in marketing because that is how a field advances. If our marketing field suffers, it is from too few debates rather than too many.

Marketing Management, 15th edition

I have said many times that I felt good about my decision to study the discipline of economics as a prelude to my work in marketing. Economics taught me to reason carefully about how different economic variables can be measured and how they interact with each other. I have gained an appreciation of the role of free enterprise in making capitalism dynamic, the role of government policy and regulation in preserving competition and high standards, and the needed role of government in re-stimulating the economy when it has been flattened by a financial disaster or previously bad practices on the part of private enterprise or government.

I finished my new book called *Confronting Capitalism: Real Solutions for a Troubled Economic System* (2015). Capitalism is the major economic system used around the world, even though it takes on many different forms. I examined the fourteen major shortcomings of Capitalism.
Capitalism is falling short because it:

1. Proposes little or no solution to persistent poverty
2. Generates a growing level of income inequality
3. Fails to pay a living wage to billions of workers
4. Not enough human jobs in the face of growing automation
5. Doesn't charge businesses with the full social costs of their activities
6. Exploits the environment and natural resources in the absence of regulation
7. Creates business cycles and economic instability
8. Emphasizes individualism and self-interest at the expense of community and the commons
9. Encourages high consumer debt and leads to a growing financially-driven rather than producer-driven economy
10. Lets politicians and business interests collaborate to subvert the economic interests of the majority of citizens
11. Favors short-run profit planning over long-run investment planning
12. Should have regulations regarding product quality, safety, truth in advertising, and anti-competitive behavior
13. Tends to focus narrowly on GDP growth
14. Needs to bring social values and happiness into the market equation.

For each shortcoming, I describe the major solutions that have been proposed. Some of capitalism's shortcomings include the widening gap between the rich and the poor, the neglect of the protecting the environment, the role of greed, the debt burden, questionable products, the impact of automation on reducing jobs, the over- financialization of economies, the tenuous relation between GDP and human happiness, and other issues. As we move to having over nine million people on the earth in 2050, the challenge will be to provide enough resources and jobs to support the earth's people with a decent standard of living.

Confronting Capitalism

Three concerns stand out. The first is that capitalism, while capable of generating more wealth than other economic system, seems to create great wealth for a few people and a low income for the many. The gulf between the rich and the poor is getting so wide that Capitalism is only serving a small percentage of the population. Prosperity needs to be shared more widely, especially if the majority of consumers are to have enough purchasing power to meet their needs and support further economic growth.

The second concern is that economic theory does not factor in the whole issue of sustainability and preserving clean air and water. Companies proceed to maximize their profit independent of any charges for negative externalities. Companies want to go on forever creating more wants and more goods and services as if this does not risk running out of natural resources or damaging the climate, air and water. We know that it would take several earths to bring everyone in the world up to the American standard of living.

The third concern is that classical economic theory is too abstract to take into account many forces and nuances that affect market behavior and market institutions. Classical economic theory does not pay sufficient attention to the role of many types of marketing channels and forces such as advertising, sales force, and sales promotion in influencing the level of demand and supply. Classical economic theory still assumes rational and maximizing behavior on the part of consumers, middlemen, and producers when this assumption is coming under increasing challenges.

The new economics is now given the name of behavioral economics. The Nobel Prize in Economic Science has recognized Kahneman and Tversky, two psychologists, for their research and findings on economic irrationality.

Behavioral economics is, in truth, another word for Marketing. For over 100 years, marketers have been researching how consumers and other economic players make their decisions. The role of emotion, impulse and other factors have been amply documented. If more economists were to follow the developments in marketing theory, the whole field of economics would be enriched with new theory and findings.

53. DOES CAPITALISM HASTEN THE DECLINE OF DEMOCRACY?

The more I thought about our economic system, the more troubled I became about the state of our political system, Democracy.

How could our Democracy remain unimpaired by an economic system that produces so much one-sided wealth, campaign finance money, and incessant lobbying activity? How could we claim that the citizens of the United States actually run the country? I concluded that the public really do not run our political system. We have moved from being a Democracy to an Oligarchy. An Oligarchy is a government run by a few, not the many. Here is my logic:

1. The public votes for the political candidates that the two political parties have put forth.
2. Each political candidate needs to raise an enormous amount of money to stay in the race and win the race.
3. They raise their money from the major corporations and the wealthy 1 percent donors, obligating themselves to vote favorably toward the interests of these groups if they hope to be reelected again in the future.
4. Therefore, the real policies of the American government are determined not by Congress but by the big corporations and the wealthy 1 percent donors.

Once I grasped this, I initiated a research project to evaluate the state of our Democracy.

Once again, I sought to identify the major shortcomings in our democracy that need correcting. I identified fourteen shortcomings:

1. Low voter literacy, turnout and engagement
2. Shortage of highly qualified and visionary candidates
3. Blind belief in American exceptionalism
4. Growing public antipathy toward government
5. Two-party gridlock preventing needed legislation
6. Growing role of money in politics
7. Gerrymandering empowering incumbents to get re- elected

forever
8. Primaries leading candidates to adopt more extreme positions
9. Continuous conflict between the President and Congress
10. Continuous conflict between the Federal and State Governments
11. The Supreme Court's readiness to revise legislative actions
12. The difficulty of passing new amendments
13. The difficulty of developing a sound foreign policy
14. Making government agencies more accountable

I will briefly comment on some of these issues. Gerrymandering is one of our major problems. The leading political party in a geographical area will modify the shape of the Congressional district to include more of the voters who favor the incumbent candidate. The result is that over 90 percent of incumbents are reelected and they become the most powerful members of Congress who run the key committees determining legislation.

Another major problem is political gridlock. The Republican House leader Mitchell McConnell openly stated that the Republicans want President Obama to fail to accomplish any of his goals. The Republican party used long filibusters and even threats to close down the government to stop voting from taking place on proposed legislation. Even when Obama scored on a new piece of progressive legislation, the Republican Party spends its time to weaken or rescind the new laws. They have tried to destroy the Patient Protection and Affordable Care Act (PPACA) (called Obamacare) and to weaken the *Roe vs. Wade* decision allowing women to choose abortion, and other passed legislation.

Another major problem is that our system of caucuses and primaries is manipulated by more extreme members of both parties leading to more extreme candidates. The electoral college system itself and the use of super delegates by both parties tend to weaken the voice and political preferences of our citizens.

What can be done about the increasing "corruption" of our democracy? The first step is to end the infamous *Citizens United* 5-to-4 decision of the U.S. Supreme Court that made it possible for Big Business and rich donors to spend so much money influencing voters. It is estimated that over $6 billion was spent to influence the outcome of the local, State and Presidential elections in 2016. The second step is to reign in the huge amount of lobbying spending and activity that influence so much of our legislative outcomes. The third is to limit all political advertising to 30 days before the voting as they do in Britain. The fourth is to prevent the efforts to make voter registration and voting hours difficult for a great many citizens. The voting day should be shifted to weekends or to online mailed-in ballots.

In July 2016, I put my research findings together and I published *Democracy in Decline: Rebuilding Our Future* (Sage, 2016). I hope that the readers of *Democracy in Decline* will get a much better understanding of how our major political institutions actually work, including Congress, the Supreme Court, Presidential power and its limitations, States protecting their rights, and how foreign policy is developed. Most people never took a civics course or read a deep treatment of how things actually work in our democracy. I hope that readers will get upset enough with the current weaknesses and abuses that they will talk to others, join discussion groups, and think more deeply about which candidates they believe in and can trust that these candidates really care about making life better for our citizens.

Democracy in Decline: Rebuilding Our Future

I confess that my views about democracy are tilted to the liberal side.

No one can write an unbiased book about democracy. All that one can ask is that the author reveal his biases. My biases are transparent. I have always been a believer in efforts to improve the lives of people and I believe that liberal thinking will do a better job of improving people's lives than conservative or reactionary thinking.

I sincerely want Republicans to read this book. Otherwise my book will only appeal to the converted. For each issue, I try to show the historical sources of the issues, the effects of the issue on the lives of people, and the alternatives that voters might face in voting or acting on the issue. In my last chapter, I discuss sixteen issues presently facing Congress and the American people and I spell out all the possible positions that could be taken on each issue. Any reader who proceeds to choose the alternative on each issue that he or she favors would get a clear idea of where his or her political interests lie and why.

I know that some people will question my writing a book on Democracy given that I am not a trained political scientist. My answer is quite straightforward. There is a disturbing interaction between Capitalism, our economic system, and Democracy, our political system. Features and trends in our Capitalist system are doing great damage to our Democracy.

The major problem in our Capitalist system is the growing level of income inequality. There will always be some income inequality but it has moved to a level that is corrupting both Capitalism itself and our Democracy. Capitalism is doomed to grow at a much slower rate because most of the gains in income are going to the 1%. During the recovery from the 2008 recession, income of the top 1% increased by 31% but just 0.4% for 99% of Americans.

A great number of our workers earn less today in real terms than they earned in the 1970s. Capitalism and capitalists are dooming themselves by not paying higher wages to our workers and opposing raising higher taxes on the rich, many of whom even pay a lower income tax rate than their own office and factory workers.

The growing gap between the rich and the poor is putting major political power in the hands of the 1%. They can convince low income people to vote against their own best interests. They can get voters to vote for an obsessively self-absorbed President named Donald Trump who claims that he can create more jobs and build a wall on our border to keep out illegal Mexicans and to ban Muslims from coming into the U.S. He wants citizens to have guns that can even be carried by students into schools to protect themselves. Trump is a salesman steeped in real estate and the deal making world. He also has the inexcusable habit of calling all of his political opponents insulting names. Now he is attacking the media, the judiciary, and our intelligence service whenever they say anything unflattering or that he disagrees with.

Democracy was in decline long before Donald Trump but he is the most recent contributor to the embarrassingly low level of political discourse in this country. There was a time when most politicians debated issues rather than just engaged in sending insults. Hillary Clinton sticks to issues and so does Bernie Sanders. Two of the Republican aspirants, Jeff Bush and John Kasich, stuck to issues. But the deeper problem is that our democratic government is no longer working to improve the lives of our low income and middle class citizens. Recently John Stewart put it well: "The problem in this country is you have one party in America whose sole purpose is to freeze the government." (May 2016)

Every day brings new issues in front of our voters. To keep my readers informed, Christian Sarkar and I created a website called **www.democracyindecline.com**. This website carries very current and thoughtful new articles on how we can improve our democracy.

We have also created a website for the other half of the problem, namely our Capitalism, called **www.fixcapitalism.com**. These websites and the two books go well together to keep our citizens well informed and actively involved in improving our democracy.

54. CAN AMERICAN DEMOCRACY SURVIVE TRUMP?

I was heavily engaged in writing my book, *Democracy in Decline*, and I finished it just before the 2016 Presidential election. The Republican Party had just announced that 17 Republicans would compete to be their Presidential candidate. Sixteen men and one woman! Such a large number of Presidential "would-be's" had never happened before. And one of them was Donald J. Trump, thought to be one of the weakest and most embarrassing candidates.

The Democratic Party, by comparison, had only one strong candidate, Hillary Clinton. Bernie Sanders had a strong following but Hillary was clearly the consensus candidate. Unfortunately, she had a lot of shortcomings that the Republican candidates incessantly magnified and harped on, so she entered the race as "damaged goods."

This was not a political contest that would be won by the democratic principle of "one citizen, one vote." This contest would be won by "one dollar, one vote." Never before had a Presidential election attracted so many billionaire backers of the Republican candidates. This election contest ran three years since the first candidates announced their candidacy and ended up costing the candidates and the parties the most in American history, $7 billion.

I began to realize that Capitalism and Democracy were not fully-compatible systems. They operated on different principles. Capitalism was more exclusive; Democracy was more inclusive. Without the rule of law and a democratic check-and-balance system, Capitalism could devour Democracy.

The Republican contest among the 17 candidates devolved into a circus with a lot of name-calling. Most of the clowns fell by the wayside. The biggest clown, Donald J. Trump, carried on continual scraps with Senators Ted Cruz and Marco Rubio. In the end, Trump surprised everyone and became the Republican candidate. Hillary became the Democratic candidate.

The two candidates fought each other with live speeches, public television debates, and news conferences. In the end, Hillary won the popular vote by receiving 3 million more votes than Donald. But the Electoral College, which was set up to prevent a fool or incompetent from winning the election, voted Trump in, raising the question again whether the Electoral College system makes any sense to retain.

Donald Trump was inaugurated on January 20, 2017. He claimed that it didn't rain during the inauguration and he claimed a much larger turnout than could be seen by aerial photographs. He claimed that he won the popular vote but for the votes cast by illegals.

The first 100 days of his administration were marked by a fury of Presidential executive orders and high appointments. He had trouble with his immigration executive order and a terrible defeat of the new health bill pushed by Representative Paul Ryan.

I watched with amazement and disbelief what was happening to our democracy with this new leader. I began to think of writing my sequel to *Democracy in Decline* with the new title, *The Death of Democracy*.

What were my concerns about Trump?

- This man illustrated in his campaigning and in his Presidency, that he was full of himself, running on "braggadocio" and "bombast." He is sensitive to any slight and comes back with a nightly tweet or two to destroy any adversary.
- This man is an inveterate liar who may not even know when he is lying. Now the nation has to deal with untruth and alt-facts.
- This man has a limited knowledge outside his field. He doesn't read. He prefers TV and Fox and dismisses the idea of getting daily intelligence reports.
- This man is playing the role of a part time president and weekend golfer. He flies on weekends to Mar-Lago at a $3 million cost to taxpayers and fraternizes with the wealthy members who pay $200,000 in annual membership dues. He would rather play golf or watch a golf match than think deeply about the nation's problems.
- He picks the wrong priorities. His first steps included pushing for

the building of a Mexican Wall that might cost up to $40 billion and requesting a $54 billion increase in the military budget where our military budget is higher than that set by the 7 top military spending nations.

- He alienates our allies by the way he talks about the Japanese, Germans, Mexicans, the European Union, NATO, and other political powers.
- He is prejudiced against Muslims by his immigration policies and he thinks little of Black Americans.
- He attacks our major democratic institutions: the media, the courts and judges, and our FBI and CIA intelligence system.
- He cares little for our culture by wanting deep cuts in our Corporation for Public Broadcasting (CPB), our National Endowment for the Arts (NEA), and our National Endowment for the Humanities (NEH).
- He cares little for our poor and our seniors, focusing mainly on selling fables to the white Christian working class.
- He screwed up the healthcare issue without even understanding its complexity.
- He operates with a badly fractured Republican party and will not be able to deliver on his promises. Our political system fortunately has some checks and balances that stop him in ways he didn't experience as a CEO.
- He is a President with little respect for science. He denies climate change. He is reducing the money that goes to research on healthcare issues and diseases. He is a President who has not declared his income tax and who has not appointed a blind trust to run his businesses but openly gets reports from his children about his property.
- He purchased the Old Post Office Pavilion and spent $200 million to turn it into a luxury Trump International Hotel with 270 rooms and presidential suites with bulletproof windows. Foreigners have oversubscribed to have this chance of getting close to the President who spends some of his lunches at his Washington Hotel.
- He has not severed his business ties. (His sons report to him). His hotel in Washington is replete with foreigners.
- He can cut the Meals on Wheels program to save $3 million but doesn't think twice about flying at a cost of $3 million to his Mar-

a-Lago Club. His wife Melania continues to live in New York and her family is protected at a huge cost to the taxpayers.

It is too early to assess the damage. My profound wish is that he is forced to retire or is impeached. This can happen if he clearly violates the emolument clause by accepting any gifts from foreign sources, or his Republican Party sees him as an embarrassment and prefers to operate with Pence as President, or if he fails to produce jobs but instead produces high inflation and his white, evangelical-Christian audience turns against him.

Pence, for all of his faults, at least would operate with fewer surprises and follow the rule of law with more consistency.

55. SAVING THE U.S. HEALTHCARE SYSTEM: IT'S TIME FOR SINGLE-PAYER

We have had "Obamacare" and now the Republicans have fallen short in replacing it with "Ryancare" (a.k.a. "Trumpcare"). Both plans have their unforgiving and deep critics and enemies.

I think that it is time to adopt the healthcare system that Canada and most other nations have: a single-payer healthcare system.

A single-payer healthcare system will be simpler, more efficient, involve less cost, and satisfy more consumers. The U.S. healthcare system is a compromise between the Democrats wish to expand healthcare coverage to more citizens and the Republicans wish to work with private insurance companies that compete by offering different plans.

Let's first examine the criticisms of Obamacare and then the criticisms of the Republican proposal - "Ryancare" - and finally see what a single-payer healthcare system offers.

What about Obamacare?

"Obamacare" is the political name given by Republicans to the healthcare plan passed by Congress and signed by President Barack Obama in March 23, 2010. The technical name is the Patient Protection and Affordable Care Act but for short, it is called the Affordable Care Act (ACA).

The ACA sought to correct many problems of the previous "free enterprise" health care system. Here are the problems:

1. About 45 million Americans lacked health insurance coverage. Such persons would have pay their own full medical bill out of their income or rely largely on the emergency room services of local hospitals.
2. Health insurance companies did not have to accept

applicants, especially if they had a health problem.

3. Health insurance companies could terminate AIDS patients and many insured persons complained about poor service from the insurance companies.
4. Health care coverage and service varied greatly from area to area. Many rural areas had only one or two health insurance providers.
5. Many patients experienced high and rising costs of health insurance and resented the limits placed on their choice of physicians and procedures.
6. Patients complained about the high prices for medications that were cheaper in many countries.
7. Physicians were unhappy because of falling remuneration, restrictions on their freedom to choose procedures and the high cost of malpractice insurance in an overly litigious society.
8. Employers were unhappy because their medical premiums kept rising.
9. Hospitals faced rising costs of new technology that rapidly needed to be replaced by still newer technology.

Clearly most people and many stakeholders were dissatisfied with the quality, access, and cost of our "free enterprise" healthcare system. Many people argued that health care was a right, not a privilege and that new legislation was needed.

The Obama plan (ACA) set three aims: (1) to increase health insurance quality and affordability, (2) lower the number of uninsured people, and (3) reduce the costs of healthcare. To accomplish this, the ACA set up mandates, subsidies and insurance exchanges. The mandate was the requirement that all persons and families needed to buy insurance coverage. It their income was too low to afford the insurance, they would receive subsidies. Those who could afford to buy insurance coverage but didn't buy it would pay a fine.

The ACA required all insurers to accept all applicants, cover a specific list of conditions and charge the same rates regardless of pre-existing conditions or sex. *To the great credit of ACA, another 20 to 24 million additional persons had coverage by 2016.*

Conservatives criticized the requirement that all eligible people had to buy health insurance. Freedom lovers thought this was unconstitutional, ignoring that all citizens who want to drive a car must buy auto insurance. The requirement was essential if the government was to collect enough money to cover the cost of everyone having healthcare insurance.

Republicans used all their power for seven years to drumbeat that Obamacare was a failure. They focused on healthy, financially secure 25-year-olds who were forced to buy health insurance when they had so many other needs they wanted to satisfy. Republicans refused to recognize that this was necessary to make it possible to insure older and lower income people, something these people would appreciate later in life if they fell into the same lack of funds. Ryan proclaimed: "The idea of Obamacare is … that the people who are healthy pay for the people who are sick," He added. "It's not working, and that's why it's in a death spiral."

Another criticism was that President Obama promised that no one would have to change his or her present insurance or doctor relationship. Yet about 5 percent of the population found that they had to change their health plan. But 80 percent who got health care through their companies did not have to change their health plan.

There were other critics. Rich people had to pay higher taxes to fund the subsidies. Many hospitals and doctors faced lower earnings as the law tightened up on unnecessary care.

How About "Ryancare"? (also called "Trumpcare")

When the Republicans came to power with Donald Trump's election in 2016, GOP House Representative Paul D. Ryan had his opportunity to kill Obamacare with an entirely different plan for healthcare delivery.

Ryan wanted a healthcare system that would provide full choice and individual responsibility for one's healthcare. Citizens would establish healthcare savings plans and build up enough savings to meet their ordinary medical needs. Those who lacked income would get a cash subsidy depending on their age. Older persons would receive a higher cash subsidy than younger people, regardless of income.

Paul Ryan's aim was to convert Medicare into a "voucher" program for citizens currently under age 55. People who are now age 55 and older would continue to buy traditional Medicare insurance. Those who didn't meet the age threshold would be given "premium support" from the government when they attain the retirement eligibility age. They would then be free to buy their own insurance coverage from for-profit insurance companies. They would pay any difference between the voucher amount and premiums charged by insurance companies out of their own pocket.

A lot of federal money would be given as block grants to states to use for healthcare as they saw the need. If block grant money was insufficient, the state would have to come up with the difference. However, most states are in a poor financial condition and are not able to add more money beyond the block grant. So, healthcare quality is likely to be very uneven from state to state.

Ryan's original proposal called for capping annual increases in the premium support. If medical premium costs continued to rise much faster than the overall economy, seniors would need to kick in more of their own money to pay for medical insurance. This would hurt lower- and middle-income seniors, Ryan modified his proposal to allow for increases in the premium support amount that would track increases in total premium costs.

Supporters of Ryancare can cut their own costs in a number of ways:

1. Restrict eligibility by raising the retirement age
2. Make participants pay more by increasing premiums,

copayments or deductibles.

3. Reduce demand for medical care by encouraging preventive care (with no deductible or copayment on these services)
4. Pay less to hospitals, physicians and other medical providers by reducing reimbursement rates
5. Provide incentives to medical providers to improve efficiency
6. Reduce or eliminate unnecessary costs by restricting malpractice awards, reducing fraud and encouraging the use of electronic records

Ryan's plan is to turn free enterprise loose to pull all the other levers, while limiting government involvement in Medicare. The plan assumes that people would make informed, economically smart choices among a variety of distinct medical plans. The invisible hand of capitalism would then reward innovative medical insurance providers and punish inefficient providers that don't meet Americans' needs.

Ryan assumes that there will be real competition among insurance companies and that consumers will make informed choices about their medical plan. In most geographic areas, there are only handful of insurance companies that offer medical insurance plans. There isn't the kind of intense market competition that relentlessly drives down costs and rewards innovation.

And how can we assume that consumers can make really informed decisions about something as complicated as health insurance? Consumers make awful tradeoffs between spending and saving with a bias toward spending. They invest in fly-by-night stock market tips. They acquire poor health by deciding to smoke, abuse alcohol, take hard drugs, eat sugar, fat and salt-loaded foods. They buy more expensive cars than they can pay for if a recession occurs. How can we be sure that they will make smart decisions on their medical plan coverage?

Ryancare claims that it will make $5.1 trillion in cuts to help bring the government's cost into the black by 2024. The budget legislation promises to serve more as an election-year political and policy statement by House Republicans than a realistic attempt to engage Obama and Democrats in any serious effort to further cut the deficit.

Free enterprise works well to efficiently deliver most goods and services. It is *not* the best system for delivering adequate healthcare. To place Medicare, Medicaid and Social Security in the hands of private enterprise where the aim is to reduce costs and increase investor return, our people are at their mercy. Remember that the first priority of for-profit executives is to their shareholders, not to their customers.

Negative Reactions to the Ryan Plan

The Ryan Plan, called the American Healthcare Plan, calls for $880 million in cuts to Medicaid alone, and it raids $117 billion from Medicare—cutting nearly $1 trillion from both programs that will be used for a massive tax break for the wealthy! This is a case where the poor will be subsidizing the rich.

The Ryan Plan attracted an outpouring of criticism and disparagement. People accused the Republicans as turning their back on the middle and the poorer class. The plan was disparaged by the American Medical Association (AMA), American Hospital Association (AHA), and the American Association of Retired People (AARP), each pointing out the weaknesses that they saw.

The AARP estimates "that the bill's changes to current law's tax credits could increase premium costs for a 55-year old earning $25,000 by more than $2,300 a year. For a 64-year old earning $25,000 that increase rises to more than $4,400 a year, and more than $5,800 for a 64-year old earning $15,000." "[I]t appears that the effort to restructure the Medicaid program will have the effect of making significant reductions in a program that provides services to our most vulnerable populations, and already pays providers significantly less than the cost of providing care." The Republican plan would weaken Medicare and largely benefit the young and rich at the expense of the old and poor.

Several smaller or specialty trade associations have also expressed deep concerns with Ryancare, including the American Academy of Pediatrics, the American Psychiatric Association, and the Federation of American Hospitals. Surprisingly, Powerful conservative groups such as Heritage Action, Freedom Works and Club for Growth have all denounced the Republican legislation.

The Democrats charged that the Ryancare would cause at least 11 million people to lose health coverage, cause premium co-pay and deductible increases, deplete the Medicare trust fund, and transfer wealth to the richest. It would decrease the number of health insured people and do nothing to get the millions of uninsured to get health insurance.

Already 13 Republican Senators are on record as having deep reservations about gutting the Affordable Care Act and enacting Ryancare in its place.

Even former vice presidential nominee Sarah Palin wrote on her Facebook page that Ryan's budget "is a joke." She said that the block grant program managed by the states, could drive millions of people from the program, including those in nursing homes and children from low-income households.

Ryancare made two classic mistakes. They cut out the support needed by lower-income older people, the very people who voted for Trump, who now wants to hand rich people a big tax cut. It would repeal the $158 billion levy on investment income by people in top brackets, Second, they dramatically overreached by going after not just Obamacare but Medicaid, setting up a huge clash with the hospital industry, the medical industry, the AARP and various governors.

All said, Ryan's plan would force Americans to pay more for less coverage - cut 24 MILLION Americans off of their healthcare plan by 2026 - and defund Planned Parenthood.

What about Single-Payer Healthcare?

We believe that ALL people should have the right to healthcare, that it is not just a privilege, and that good-quality healthcare is not just for the rich.

Single-payer healthcare involves the state, rather than private insurers, paying for healthcare costs. The state can contract for healthcare services from private organizations or can own and employ healthcare resources and personnel. In some single-payer systems, consumers may have the option of contracting for private health insurance. Canada and Taiwan have pure single-payer systems while countries such as Australia, France, Spain, and the United Kingdom have hybrid single-payer/private insurance systems.

In a single-payer system, the government provides all health insurance and collects all medical and insurance fees. The insurance is extended to all citizens and legal residents. The aim is *universal healthcare*. The system typically bears a name such as the United Kingdom's National Health Service, Australia's Medicare, Canada's Medicare, and Taiwan's National Health Insurance.

The fund can be managed by the government directly or by a publicly owned and regulated agency. The government may employ doctors and own and run hospitals (United Kingdom). Or the government may purchase healthcare services from outside organizations (Canada).

We will describe the single payer system in Canada, because Canada is physically close and close in values to those of U.S. citizens. Canada provides free medical services through private entities. The government sets federal standards to assure quality of care. The individual's health remains confidential between a person and his or her physician. In each Canadian province, each doctor submits the insurance claim against the provincial insurer. The person who gets healthcare does not get involved in billing and reclaim.

The Canadian government keeps advertising at a minimum. Costs are paid through funding from income taxes. There are no deductibles on basic health care and co-pays are kept extremely low. Provinces issue a health card to each individual who enrolls and everyone receives the same level of care. There is no variety of plans because all essential basic care is covered, including maternity and infertility problems. Dental and vision care may or may not be covered depending on the Province. Some provinces provide private supplemental plans for patients who desire private rooms if hospitalized. Cosmetic surgery and some elective surgery are generally not covered. These can be paid out-of-pocket or through private insurers. One's health coverage is not affected by loss or change of jobs, as long as premiums are up to date. There are no lifetime limits or exclusions for pre-existing conditions.

Canadians chose their family physician (called a general practitioner or GP). If the person wants to see a specialist, the GP will make a referral. The median wait time to see a specialist physician is a month. The median wait time for diagnostic services such as MRI and CAT scans is two weeks. The median wait time for surgery is four weeks.

Pharmaceutical medications are covered by public funds for the elderly or indigent, or through employment-based private insurance. The Canadian government negotiates drug prices with suppliers to control costs.

Physician incomes in Canada rose initially after the single payer system was implemented. A reduction in physician salaries followed, many fearing this would be a long-term result of government-run healthcare. However, by the beginning of the 21st century, medical professionals were again among Canada's top earners.

The main thing to notice is that Canada's healthcare cost to its GDP is 11 percent whereas the U.S. cost is 17 percent of the GDP.

Past Efforts to Bring a Single-payer Healthcare System into the U.S.

Several proposals have been made for introducing a single- payer healthcare system in the U.S. or in several individual States. The most recent is the United States National Health Care Act, (popularly known as "Medicare for All"). Representative John Conyers (D-MI) every year since 2002 has introduced an act for a single-payer system. All medical care would be paid for by the Government of the United States, ending the need for private health insurance and premiums, and probably recasting private insurance companies as providing purely supplemental coverage, to be used when non-essential care is sought. But neither his bill or any others succeeded in getting more than 20 percent congressional co-sponsorship.

Several arguments are presented to favor a single-payer healthcare system. More people will see a physician more frequently who might spot lingering or unrecognized medical problems. For example, catching cancer in Stage 1 is much better than catching it in Stage 3 when it involves so much more hospitalization and pain. Preventative healthcare will save expensive dollars later. Consumers and employers would both face lower administrative costs. Good healthcare will be more uniformly available throughout the land.

Experts see much saving realized through preventive care and the elimination of insurance company overhead and marketing costs and hospital billing costs. A 2008 analysis of a single-payer plan estimated immediate savings at $350 billion per year. Another study estimated savings of $570 billion a year.

The Congressional Budget Office (CBO) has scored on a few occasions the cost of a single-payer health care system. Each time the estimate concluded that a single-payer system would cost less than any other system through its savings in administrative costs.

There have been several single-payer state referendums and bills from state legislatures. Bills have been proposed in Vermont, California, Colorado, Hawaii, Illinois, Massachusetts, Minnesota, Montana, New York, and Oregon. All have failed, with the exception of Vermont which canceled its plan in December 2014 for single-payer health care, citing costs and tax increases as too high to implement.

The Veterans Administration healthcare system is a pure form of single-payer system because it is "owned, operated and financed by government." Researchers of the RAND Corporation reported that the quality of care received by Veterans Administration patients scored significantly higher overall than did comparable metrics for patients currently using United States Medicare.

American citizens have been polled on whether they would favor a single-payer healthcare system like the one in Canada. The polls varied in their findings, much depending on the time of the poll and the wording of the question. The response is different when citizens are asked whether they favor a stronger Medicare system vs. a government-run medical system. There is general support for a "national healthcare plan" but there are also many people who are satisfied with their present healthcare plan.

Among advocates of a single-payer healthcare system are

Physicians for a National Health Program, the American Medical Student Association, Healthcare-NOW! and the California Nurses Association. The Annals of Internal Medicine in 2007 found that 59% of physicians "supported legislation to establish national health insurance" while 9% were neutral on the topic, and 32% opposed it.

What are the major criticisms leveled against a single-payer healthcare system?

They are:
- Many Americans don't want to expand the size of

government and they distrust government.

- Many fear that universal coverage will cost too much and raise taxes too much.
- Many fear that waiting times for diagnosis, treatment and surgery will increase too much and they prefer the present system.
- Many Americans, especially younger citizens, don't want to pay higher taxes for something that won't currently benefit them.
- Many Americans fear that others will use the system more than necessary and cause longer wait times and additional cost and end up ordering more medications than necessary.
- Many Americans worry about dealing with a government monopoly that sets all the standards and that can arbitrarily cut certain medical services to save money.
- Physicians fear that single-payer healthcare will limit their discretion when treating patients, decrease physician salaries, and leave less money to cover more services, thereby reducing, the quality of treatment.

Singapore's Single-Payer System that Costs Less

We must recognize that there are many versions of single payer healthcare systems. We examined the Canada version but it pays to examine how Singapore has designed it single-payer e system. It manages to keep cost down and yet protect Singapore citizens from losing their savings in case they are hit by a major-medical problem.

The Singapore Plan guarantees coverage only for expensive medical events, those events that can eat up the family's savings and lead them into bankruptcy. It is less necessary to provide coverage for more everyday medical expenses. Let market forces cover the latter. Singaporeans pay for much of their own health care out of their own pockets. The major insurance program covers only long-term illnesses and prolonged hospitalizations. Singaporeans experience excellent healthcare costing just 5 percent of their GNP whereas European countries spend around 10 percent and the U.S. spends 17 percent.

The Singapore Plan does not call upon Singapore citizens to set up a health savings account. Their Medisave program requires a *mandatory* health-savings account called MediShield to which employers contribute as well. The government maintains a safety net called Medifund for patients who can't cover their bills, specifically older and poorer citizens. Singapore manages to minimize public spending and third-party payments and maximizes public awareness of what different treatments cost. Everyone is insured for catastrophic events. And the government funds health savings accounts for the working class and poor.

(Based on several public sources. *The Huffington Post* published my article on March 25, 2017).

56. HOW CAN WE MARKET PEACE?

At a dinner in Jeddah, Saudi Arabia, in October 2010, the young son of a prominent Saudi Arabian family took me aside and posed a question. "Dr. Kotler, you have marketed many products and ideas. You have run many marketing campaigns for causes. You are well-known for your work in social marketing and social responsibility. I wonder why you have not run a marketing campaign to bring more peace into the world. I hope that you will do that next."

Why don't we have a real peace movement in the world? We know that there are many peace groups trying to carry on the cause of peace. Every year the Nobel Foundation in Oslo, Norway awards a Peace prize to an outstanding individual whose life and actions serve as a heroic message about peace. Past winners include Barack Obama, Al Gore, and Muhammad Yunis.

Another group is the Oslo Business and Peace Foundation. On May 6, 2015, I gave a talk on how the "sustainability" movement could contribute to a more peaceful world. Over 1,000 persons attend their convention each year.

At the October 2014 World Marketing Summit in Tokyo, I was visited by Governor Yuzaki, the governor of Hiroshima prefecture who invited me to help organize a Peace conference in Hiroshima that would take place in October 2016. The Hiroshima World Peace Conference finally took place on October 14-15, 2016. Governor Yuzaki gave opening remarks and I gave the keynote address. Several sessions were developed with experts speaking at each session.

Here are the topics:

- Session 1: Disarmament Status and What Worked
- Session 2: How NGO's and Government Use Marketing for Peace Advocacy

- Session 3: How Marketing Tools should be Used for Peace-building

- Session 4: Businesses that Build Soft Power and Contribute to Peace

- Session 5: The Young Global Leaders of the World Economic Forum

- Session 6: Business' Peace-building Work for the Poor

- Session 7: Hiroshima as Global Peace Hub

The fact is that there are dozens of organizations working for peace. The United Nations itself was set up to build a peaceful world and put an end to future wars. One could go to Wikipedia and look up the category called Peace Organizations and find a very long list, including such organizations as American Peace Society, Asia-Pacific Peace Research Association, Bertrand Russel Peace Foundation, Buddhist Peace Fellowship, Catholic Association for International Peace, Economists for Peace and Security, German Peace Society, Global Peace Institute for Women, International Peace Institute, and Nonviolence International.

One of the problems preventing a serious and impactful peace movement is exactly the number of separate organizations striving to promote peace. One hopes that these organizations will talk to each other, form larger coalitions, and combine their resources and messages to achieve a strong media presence and impact.

But marketing Peace calls for more than a pointed and continuous communication campaign. It calls for a fundamental change in the distribution of the world's assets and resources! Peace won't come as long as only two billion of the world's current population live middle class lives and five billion struggle to avoid hunger and disease. Peace won't come when so much of the world's wealth, capital and income are in the hands of so few families scattered around the globe.

Peace won't come as long as there are so many different belief and value systems that clash with each other. Each major religion is a belief system. Each ethnic community has developed its own belief system. Each economic class has fashioned a different belief system. Every group lives to defend its own belief system and many strive to impose its belief system on others.

The deep question is how can two groups with competing beliefs and values and resources have a dialogue that would move them toward recognizing their common humanity. How can the Democrats and Republicans work together to produce legislation that makes more Americans better off? How can the Palestinians and Israel find a solution that is a win-win for both? Does conflict resolution theory contain enough insights and processes to help bring conflicting groups into peaceful settlements? I invite more of us to grapple with these challenges.

57. WHAT WOULD MAKE AMERICA GREAT AGAIN?

I have long been a student of country studies. In 1997, I published *Marketing of Nations: A Strategic Approach to Building National Wealth*. One of my co-authors, Somkid Jatusripitak, is now Deputy Prime Minister of Thailand. Our book sought to identify how nations could improve their economic performance and raise their standard of living among other nations.

This is an important question. Citizens have deep feelings about their nation's standing and aspirations. Americans profoundly believe that their country is the best country in the world. People in many countries view their country more favorably that outsiders do.

America's greatness was recently challenged by Donald Trump who asserted that the U.S. had lost its greatness. His campaign slogan was "Make America Great Again." He claimed that only he and his party could restore the country's greatness. This raises the question: How can we define where a country ranks in its "greatness?"

All of us are defined by the nation in which we grew up and its strengths, values and reputation. But today, the citizens of many countries are unhappy and they would readily emigrate. People want to leave Syria and flee some other countries to get into Europe, especially Germany or get into the United States. For years, many Mexicans and Cubans have risked their lives to enter the United States which now has over 11 million illegal residents. Most immigrants are simply trying to improve their lives.

Nations that rank high as a "best nation" or "good nation" will need a strong and thoughtful immigration policy. The U.S., U.K., and Germany rank high as countries where many people would like to live. These countries have to define who they will accept. Japan has chosen to exclude most people from other nations in order to preserve its Japanese character. If the U.S. starts excluding certain groups – such as Muslims, Latin Americans, and Africans — from emigrating to the U.S., it will move away from its multicultural "melting pot" "rainbow" image which gained respect from around the world.

Recent research can help us understand what makes a nation "great." Two studies have been published in 2016 that take a contrasting view of how to define a nation's "greatness." One study, called the Best Countries study, conducted at the Wharton School of Business, ranks 60 countries according to their present and future economic performance and brand image appeal.[i] The other 2016 study, called the Good Country Index, conducted by Simon Anholt of the U.K., ranks countries according to how much they care about helping the whole world become a better living human community.[ii] A country such as the United States has been ranked very differently in the two studies, fourth in one case and twentieth in the other. Let's look at the two studies and see how they differed in defining and measuring "greatness."

The Best Countries Study

The "best countries" study was jointly sponsored by the U.S. News & World Report, WPPs BAV Consulting and the University of Pennsylvania's Wharton School of Business. Professor David Reibstein of the Wharton Business School took a leadership role.

The researchers examined 60 nations and gathered data on 65 factors including such factors as sustainability, entrepreneurship, economic influence, adventure, and cultural influence. More than 16,200 business leaders, informed elites and general citizens became involved in supplying data and their views.

The researchers sought to determine where each country stood in economic performance and brand image appeal. They used sophisticated analytical tools to determine a ranking for the 60 countries. As a result, the study ranked the 10 best countries to be, in order: 1. Germany, 2. Canada, 3. United Kingdom, 4. United States. 5. Sweden, 6. Australia, 7. Japan, 8. France, 9. Netherlands, and 10. Denmark.

The Best Countries researchers went further and used the data to rank countries on 24 decision issues, such as which countries rank highest for starting a career, starting a business, investing in, for education, for raising kids, or for comfortable retirement. For example, the three best countries for raising kids, in order, are Sweden, Denmark, and Canada. The three best countries for comfortable retirement are Costa Rica, Ireland, and Canada.

In a recent article, Professor Reibstein pointed out that the best way for a country to improve its overall best country rank is by identifying its weak areas and improving them. [iii] He identified the indices where the U.S. was weak and said this is where the U.S. political parties must focus their efforts.

The Good Country Index

In 2014, Simon Anholt published a Good Country Index, which was updated again in 2016. Instead of ranking a country by its perceived economic performance and brand image appeal, this study ranks countries by the extent that they contribute to the common good, relative to their size. He knows that large countries may contribute more dollars to good causes than small countries but he corrects this by size. If the U.S. and Canada each gave 1% to a good cause, Canada is giving proportionately more of their GDP and its contribution to a good world is higher.

He asks if the country primarily focuses on serving the interests of their own businesses and citizens, or is the country actively working for all of humanity and the whole planet? He is asking whether the country is a net creditor to mankind, or a burden on the planet, or something in between.

Instead of using 65 factors as in the Best Countries study, Anholt uses 35 datasets and he has grouped them into seven categories: 1. Science and Technology, 2. Culture, 3. International Peace and Security, 4.

World Order, 5. Planet & Climate, 6, Prosperity & Equality, and 7. Health and Well-Being.

Simon Anholt believes that countries aren't unconnected islands; they're all part of one system. If it fails, we all fail. He started the Good Country research hoping to change how leaders run their countries. The Good Country isn't an organization, an NGO, a charity or a company. It's an idea: an idea that needs to spread. He goes on to say: "Anybody can launch a Good Country project, start a Good Country Party, teach a Good Country course, write a Good Country book, make a Good Country speech, start a Good University, a Good School, a Good Company, a Good Village or even a Good Family."

Where the Best Countries study only ranked 60 countries, Simon Anholt' study ranked 163 countries. Here are the 10 top countries in the Good Country Index, in order: 1. Sweden, 2. Denmark, 3. Netherlands, 4. United Kingdom, 5. Switzerland, 6. Germany, 7. Finland, 8. France, 9. Austria, and 10. Canada.

Some Observations in Comparing the Countries in the Two Studies

The first thing to notice is that 7 of the 10 top countries are in both the Best Countries study and the Good Country Index. They are: Germany, Canada, United Kingdom, Sweden, France, Netherlands, and Denmark. These are the countries that we should admire. They not only rank high on economic performance and brand image appeal but they also care about other countries and the planet. They are good world citizens. These countries can serve as role models for other countries to emulate.

The second thing to notice is that several major nations who should be caring about other countries and the planet don't stand as high as we would expect. These are countries have the resources to be caring but not the behavior. They are: Australia (18), Japan (19) and the U.S. (20).

The third thing to notice is that there are other major countries whose "Goodness" is quite low. They are: Brazil (47), India (61), Mexico (62), China (64), and Russia (78). We can say of these countries that they are very self-involved, have tough internal problems and a deficiency of resources.

The last thing is the poor standing on "Goodness" of other countries in the news: Saudi Arabia (89), Pakistan (111), and Iran (130).

Conclusion

We have to acknowledge that in classifying countries as being "Best" or "Good," we are operating at a high level of generalization. A country is a complex entity with a special history, containing many different cities, and carrying on many different activities. It is too easy to stereotype countries using a few observations.

At the same time, both of these studies relied on a huge amount of country data that were analyzed as carefully as possible by the respective research groups. Both research groups stand ready to make their methodologies known and examined. They expect some countries to be upset with their ranking who may want further analysis if not revision.

All said, I believe that both studies are pioneering new methods of viewing countries and ranking their contributions. As these studies become better known, we can hope that more countries will work hard to imagine policies and actions to improve their standing as a Best Country and a Good Country.

All this would be for the good.

[i] www.usnews.com/news/best-countries

[ii] www.economicvoice.com/simon-anholt-launches-the-good-country-party

[iii] http://www.usnews.com/topics/author/david-reibstein

58. LEARN FROM THE MANY MARKETING ASSOCIATIONS

Marketing cannot grow and thrive without external marketing associations.

American Marketing Association (AMA)

The oldest and most important external marketing association is the American Marketing Association (AMA). Formed in 1937, today the AMA has 30,000 members, 76 professional chapters and 250 collegiate chapters across the U.S. The AMA publishes the *Journal of Marketing, Journal of Marketing Research, Journal of Public Policy & Marketing, Journal of International Marketing, and Marketing News*. The AMA manages conferences, trainings, and virtual events catering to marketers, researchers, and academicians in all stages of their careers.

I benefitted greatly from my activities with the AMA. Each year I looked forward to attending the Summer AMA Academic Conference to meet newly minted marketing academics and hear talks from leading senior marketers. I would pass one publisher's table after another to examine the latest textbooks and see how my books are doing. I joined my Kellogg faculty members to interview new candidates. Three of us would meet a candidate and ask questions to determine whether to invite the candidate to give a talk to our marketing faculty and Ph.D. students.

For a time, I served on the AMA Board of Directors and I became familiar with their operations and issues. I was particularly interested in the AMA's efforts to help foreign marketing associations get started.

In 2014, the AMA appointed a new director, Russ Klein. Russ came in with excellent ideas. He helped select a new headquarters for the AMA in downtown Chicago. He invested heavily in improving the AMA's website. He has promoted the AMA Digital Marketing Certification program. He wants the AMA to work closely with the marketing associations found in many other countries.

Academy of Marketing Science

The Academy of Marketing Science is a non-profit, international, scholarly, professional organization dedicated to promoting high standards in the creation and dissemination of marketing knowledge and practice. Beginning in 1971, the Academy grew into a substantial regional association. In 1972, the Academy established the Journal of the Academy of Marketing Science (JAMS). Today, JAMS is widely acknowledged as a premier marketing research journal. The Academy is run by a staff and a Board of Governors, with elections held on a biennial basis.

Presently the Academy of Marketing Science offers a wide range of services, including a series of conferences and special interest programs and symposia, a refereed scholarly journal, a quarterly member newsletter, and conference proceedings. The Academy holds biennial world marketing congresses in many world locations.

Marketing Science Institute

The Marketing Science Institute (MSI), founded in 1967, is dedicated to bridging the gap between marketing theory and business practice. It is set up as a corporate-membership-based organization with marketing executives from 60+ leading companies and an expansive network of marketing academics from top business schools all over the world.

The corporate fees support academic research on topics of importance to business performance. Every two years, MSI asks its Board of Trustees to set priorities for the research that will guide MSI activities for the next few years. MSI disseminates the findings through conferences, workshops, webinars, publications, and online content. MSI's Working Paper Series includes more than one thousand working papers.

The Marketing Journal

In 2016, I became the advisor to the *The Marketing Journal* an online resource. *The Marketing Journal* brings together business executives, marketing thought-leaders, professionals, and practitioners, to:

- Learn about next practices in marketing and branding
- Interview thought-leaders, executives and CMOs on the future of marketing
- Examine and understand the specific factors that contribute to improving the effectiveness of marketing strategy and execution
- Develop recommendations for creating and sustaining an innovative marketing discipline within your organization
- Foster discussion of lessons learned
- Analyze and comment on industry-shaping news
- Create a framework for measuring new marketing performance criteria
- Nurture a worldwide community of marketing professionals

In its short history, The Marketing Journal has published many insightful articles and has developed quite a following.

CMO.com

One of the best ways to learn about marketing practices is to hear from Chief Marketing Officers (CMOs). The CMO.com team issues weekly newsletters containing the thoughts, writings and experiences of CMOs in dealing with different power groups and competitors in the new digital world. CMOs are eager to learn from each other how to justify a high budget request, allocate the funds to the best opportunities, and be able to present management with reliable metrics of the impact of different marketing expenditures.

Asian Marketing Associations

Asia is actively developing its own marketing associations. My friend Hermawan Kartajaya founded many year ago the Asia Marketing Federation (AMF). Today it has 16 country members. It is actively considering launching the World Marketing Community (WMC) to bring about more interaction and knowledge exchange between all the marketing associations in North and South America, Europe, Asia and other areas.

In Conclusion

I have personally benefitted from working with all of these associations that generate new marketing knowledge and disseminate their findings around the world to improve marketing practice. As new themes arise – digital marketing, marketing automation, neuroscience, artificial intelligence, virtual reality, new social media – these marketing associations are quick to examine and critiqued these new areas and disseminate their findings across the world.

59. CHRISTIAN SARKAR, BRAND ACTIVISM, ART, AND POLITICS

I had the good fortune in 2016 to work with three acquaintances – Christian Sarkar, Mark Blessington, and Karl Hellman – on trying to start blogs on economics and democracy. All four of us were caught up in the political election where 17 Republicans were vying for the Presidency. We spent many Sundays conferencing on the phone about the candidates.

Half of our phone talk was on Donald Trump's bizarre performances and that he certainly would not be the chosen Republican candidate.

Boy, were we wrong!

We registered a new website **www.fixcapitalism.com** to carry the best articles we could find on fixing 14 different problems of capitalism. Today this site carries many articles including a number from Mark Blessington and myself. Fixcapitalism.com is enjoying a growing fan base.

Christian Sarkar

Christian Sarkar and I continued conversing on the phone. Christian and I registered **www.democracyindecline.com**. This was followed a few months later by launching *The Marketing Journal* to meet our interests in the New Marketing.

Christian is a gifted artist and knows a large number of other artists. I invited Christian to visit Nancy and me in our winter home in Longboat Key, Florida.

He not only dropped in but he also presented one of his recent paintings to me. It was called "Confronting Capitalism."

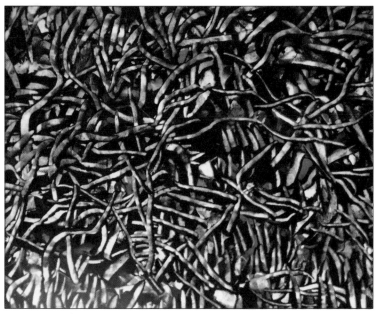

"Confronting Capitalism" by Christian Sarkar, acrylic on canvas

Christian is gifted in another way. He not only knows the digital world; he creates new ways to use digital tools. He knows how to place stories in our media to get maximum reach. He built his own software that maps out the online ecosystem surrounding any person, institution or object. This helps him engage online with the right people at the right time.

Christian has helped me place a number of short articles on *Huffington Post* and elsewhere. See Current Affairs Articles (2016-2017) following the list of published articles toward the end of the book.

Christian and I share a passion for social justice. Recently, we published an article called "Finally, Brand Activism." We were urging brands to go beyond mainly talking about a product's superior characteristics. "Our toothpaste is better than yours in (fill in) "whitening teeth," "preventing cavities," "creating a better breath."

But this type of positioning is no longer enough to win in highly competitive markets. Just consider marketing to millennials. Millennials live in a world filled with constant problems – air and water pollution, crime, drugs, job insecurity. Many millennials would like brands to show some caring not only of them but of their communities. The candy company Mars developed a film showing how it sources its beans from Africa and makes investments to raise education levels in different communities.

Coca Cola, one of the world's longest lasting brands, keeps its momentum going by its "positivity." "We lift people up. We thrill them. We inspire them. And we leave them refreshed. All through our history, we…use our voice to make a significant, positive difference in the world."

Unilever wants each of its brands to establish "thought leadership" on some issue. It wants not only to sell its Lifebuoy branded soap but to also sell "personal hygiene." Unilever developed a sweeping handwashing education program in poorer countries that changed the behavior of millions of citizens in these countries.

Howard Schultz, CEO of Starbucks, wants Starbucks to take responsibility for disposing of the millions of cups carrying its coffee. Starbucks endorses the "green revolution" and makes positive contributions to climate protection. Starbucks runs "My Starbuck Idea" welcoming its customers to send ideas to Starbucks to improve Starbucks' customers' experience.

Frito-Lay wants its consumers to help determine the company's offerings. It runs an annual "Do Us a Flavor" campaign hoping to use crowdsourcing to get new ideas for flavors.

Patagonia is proud of its conservation ethics. Patagonia wants you to use and reuse your clothing items and eventually give it away to someone else who can use it.

The Body Shop was one of the first companies to broadcast its ethical values and beliefs. Its founder and CEO, Anita Roddick, not only wanted to make really fine skincare lotions but also care for "animal rights," "civil rights," "fair trade," and "environmental protection." Many Body Shop clients said they were mainly interested in her products but many more approved of her consumer activism and often gathered to march together for some cause.

What Should Your Company Do with Brand Activism?

Here are the questions that you should ask.

- What kinds and how many consumers are likely to care about the cause you chose?
- Will consumers believe that the company authentically and passionately believes in this cause?
- Will the cost of implementing this cause require the company to raise its prices? Will the company's clients be paid a little more for a brand with this cause?

The $300 House Project

A few years ago, Christian began an online experiment called the $300 House Project. The main idea was to challenge businesses, institutions and individuals to come up with new ideas for the housing for the poor. I am an adviser to this project.

The goal was to design, build, and deploy a simple dwelling that keeps a family safe from the weather, allows them to sleep at night, and gives them a little bit of dignity. If we can give the poor a chance to live safely and build an inclusive ecosystem of services around them which includes, clean water, sanitation, health services, family planning, education, and micro enterprise, maybe we can start reducing the disease of poverty. By helping create this ecosystem, we believe companies can make money while providing services needed by the poor at an affordable cost.

Christian enlisted the help of all who would participate – from the *Harvard Business Review* to jovoto.com to create an online challenge to rethink what it means to design a radically affordable house.

Moladi.net – one of the participants in the $300 House Project – was recognized by the World Economic Forum in 2017. Learn more about the project at **www.300house.com**.

60. THE FUTURE OF MARKETING (AN INTERVIEW WITH PHILIP KOTLER)

Philip Kotler is the "father of modern marketing." He is the S.C. Johnson & Son Distinguished Professor of International Marketing at the Kellogg School of Management at Northwestern University. He was voted the first Leader in Marketing Thought by the American Marketing Association and named The Founder of Modern Marketing Management in the Handbook of Management Thinking. Professor Kotler holds major awards including the American Marketing Association's (AMA) Distinguished Marketing Educator Award and Distinguished Educator Award from The Academy of Marketing Science. The Sales and Marketing Executives International (SMEI) named him Marketer of the Year and the American Marketing Association described him as "the most influential marketer of all time." He is in the Thinkers50 Hall of Fame, and is featured as a "guru" in the Economist.

Phil, you're called the "father of marketing"…

Actually, marketing has several fathers of marketing.

Marketing has been around for over 100 years. We could mention many marketing luminaries who had a great impact on our marketing theory and practice.

I have been labeled the "father of modern marketing." This is the result of two things. My marketing textbooks have been used around the world for the last 50 years. I published *Marketing Management* in 1967 and it is now in its 15th edition. I have also written about 50 other marketing books and over 150 scholarly articles.

If I am the "Father of Modern Marketing," I would call **Peter Drucker** the "Grandfather of Modern Marketing" for all the brilliant insights and statements that he made about the critical importance of marketing in managing a business.

With over 50 years of experience in the field, what do you see as the biggest challenges for marketers today?

Today marketing is undergoing a true revolution and I am doing everything to keep up with it. Contrast the old marketing with the new marketing. The old marketing was all about mass marketing. Companies such as Coca Cola or McDonalds needed to sell their brand everywhere and to everyone. The answer was to develop mass advertising and mass distribution.

Mass advertising started with print ads, then radio ads, and finally TV commercials, along with many promotions such as "2 for 1," "today only discounts," "rebates," "lay away plans," and so on. Companies sought to distribute their products in every conceivable venue and obtain top shelf space. Consumers had little product information except for the ads they saw and their friends' word-of-mouth. Major competitors saw the key to their success as resting on better messages and copy and spending more than their competitors.

Marketing today is going through a digital revolution. The Internet has made it possible for consumers to look up a great deal of information about a company, its products, its social responsibility, and the ratings of its products. Consumers can go on Facebook and exchange product and brand experiences and opinions. Every consumer can learn the prices of competing brands and their quality ranking and features. As a result, consumers are now in full control of the buying process. A consumer can be in a store ready to buy a certain product but pause to check on their smart phone whether a better price can be found elsewhere, leading the consumer to negotiate for a better price or leave. All companies now see the smart phone as the consumer's critical companion in making buying decisions. "**Mobile marketing**" is the hottest subject. Companies are now viewed as **participants in ecosystems and platforms**.

Our companies today collect vast personal information on individual consumers. This is the **Age of Big Data**. Companies have hired mathematicians to shovel through this data to find insights and to know the likes of individual customers. Companies are developing new tools and metrics to guide their moment-to-moment decision making. They are using the **Internet-of-Things** and **Artificial Intelligence (AI)** to carry on some automatic marketing initiatives and responses.

Any manager or student who studies only the old marketing will be no match against digital marketers. I expect the average age of professional marketers to get lower as companies recruit young digital natives. Marketing is changing in another way. The old marketers thought that consumers knew what they liked and even why they liked it. Consumers would make conscious decisions and share their opinions and likes in surveys and focus groups. We are now recognizing the power of **unconscious factors shaping their purchase decisions**. Consumers are influenced by deeper frames of mind and metaphors that they are less conscious of. Marketers are using new methods to search out unconscious forces and frames of reference and turning these findings into **storytelling** and **narratives** to click in at deeper levels of consumer motivation.

How is marketing automation and Big Data changing marketing? What are the new competencies that companies must master? What does the future hold for the CMO?

In 1993, Don Pepper and Martha Rogers wrote a book called the *One to One Future: Building Relationships One Customer at a Time* in which they argued that companies need to know more not just about market segments but also about individual customers. The digital revolution hadn't started yet but now we have the tools to implement the One to One Future. Almost every customer transaction is conducted by charging a credit card. A supermarket can look up the products and brands that any individual customer has purchased. The British supermarket operator Tesco even sets up events to invite new mothers or wine-drinkers or some other group to gather and hear a valued talk on a subject of interest to these groups, all made possible by their transaction data.

Companies are hiring digital marketers and giving them a small budget to use with different digital tools to promote more sales. If the initial results are strong, the company will increase its digital budget. I've seen predictions that say in 2016, the average firm will allocate 30% of their marketing budget to online, and this rate is expected to grow to 35% by 2019.

Digital marketing can eventually go to 50% if it creates good results. But it is important to maintain strong traditional TV advertising – despite the "cord- cutting" phenomenon – because it provides the best platform for building the overall image of the brand. The company's chief marketing officer (CMO) has to balance the company's spending between traditional and digital marketing and to take advantage of synergies between the two. CMOs are recognizing the growing importance of content marketing which does not directly promote the brand but feeds into promoting a stronger engagement between the customer and the brand. The real challenge is to develop good metrics to help the company know which marketing activities and investments are generating a good investment return.

How do sales and marketing work together in the digital age? Is alignment easier or more of a challenge?

In theory, marketing and sales people should be the best of friends. They are both dedicated to increasing the sales and profits of the company. The marketing people set the broad strategy and the specific incentives to drive the sales people to carry out their activities in the most effective way. Unfortunately, issues arise that lead one group to criticize the other.

Sales people often say that marketing failed to produce ads that work with their customers and indeed that their customers may never have seen these ads. Sales people might complain that the sales targets set by marketing are unrealistically high and that marketing set an unrealistically high price on the product. Sales people might complain that marketers don't really understand customers and the difficulty of selling to them. Marketers have their complaints too, that many sales people don't know how to sell the price ("sales people always want a lower price"), that sales people go after small sales opportunities rather than larger one that take more time and patience to pursue.

Any company living with these two unhappy groups that don't respect each other will fail. A good consultant could come in, help the groups lay out the issues, and participate with each other to improve their marketing and sales activities.

I covered the solutions in my co-authored article in the *Harvard Business Review* entitled "Ending the War Between Sales and Marketing" (HBR, July 2006).

What are companies doing differently to innovate? Are there some marketing innovations that you feel could change the way the industry works?

Most companies prefer to operate the same way from year to year but this attitude can be fatal in such a rapidly changing world. We need to recognize that people get tired of old products and seek new products and experiences. Companies need to constantly refresh their product and service mix.

They can innovate in a number of ways:

• Quickly copy the successful products of their competitors and introduce some difference.
• Inspire everyone in the company to see innovation as a key to the company's success. Encourage innovations in products, services, marketing, finance, accounting and so on.
• Conduct customer interviews to develop a fresh list of new product and service ideas.
• Work with a small set of prime customers to co-create new product and service ideas.
• Develop a *crowdsourcing* project to stimulate customers to come up with new ideas.

- Examine *Kickstarter* for new ideas that others are developing that might interest this company.

As for marketing innovations, there is a whole history of promotional tools to stimulate more buying, such as rebates, layaway plans, frequent buyer discounts, and so on. Marketing innovations are occurring in the area of understanding better how consumers think and decide. *Neural scanning* is now used by many companies to capture and measure customer responses to controlled print and video stimuli. The *Zaltman Metaphor Elicitation Technique* (ZMET) is giving us deeper insight into the customer's unconscious mind and images that are triggered by product situations and experiences.

We are seeing new marketing metrics for tracking brand strength and returns on marketing investment. The marketing field today is ripe with new marketing innovations to improve the performance of professional marketers.

What about CSR? Do you see companies focusing on sustainability and ethics as a business strength? As someone who coined the phrase "social marketing," how do you see companies responding?

Companies need to see themselves as more than a profit producing machine. Companies have a big impact on their customers, employees, distributors, suppliers, investors and communities. Companies that operate with a more holistic picture of their stakeholders, not just their shareholders, and that seek to satisfy all of their stakeholders, will outperform companies that only squeeze all of their costs to maximize their short run profits. I would argue that low paying companies will have low motivated employees, distributors and suppliers and perform more poorly for their shareholders.

I wrote a number of books to stress the importance of companies adopting a corporate social responsibility mindset:

• Philip Kotler and Nancy R. Lee, *Corporate Social Responsibility: Doing the Most Good for Your Company and Your Cause*, Wiley, 2005.

• Philip Kotler and Nancy Lee, *Social Marketing: Influencing Behaviors for Good*, Sage, 2008, 5th edition.

• Adam Lindgreen, Philip Kotler, Joelle Vanhamme and Francoise Maon, *A Stakeholder Approach to Corporate Social Responsibility: Pressures, Conflicts and Reconciliation*, London, UK, Gower, 2012.

• Philip Kotler, David Hessekiel, and Nancy R. Lee, *Good Works! Marketing and Corporate Initiatives that Build a Better World...and the Bottom Line*, Wiley, 2013.

The country of Indonesia has made you a brand ambassador. But in many ways, you have been an ambassador for marketing – Western marketing – for many decades.

During the past 40 years, I did as much marketing teaching in other countries as I did at the Kellogg School of Management of Northwestern University. My favorite countries where I have lectured several times include Italy, Sweden, Russia, Great Britain, Indonesia, Taiwan, Thailand, South Korea, India, Japan, and China. I have many lifelong friends in these countries and I follow the course of each country's business, political and cultural evolution. In Indonesia I work closely with Hermawan Kartajaya who runs the very capable Mark Plus company. Hermawan and I have written 6 books together with *Marketing 3.0* being one of the world's best-selling marketing books.

Together we developed the first *marketing museum* in the world. It is situated in the beautiful island of Bali in Indonesia and draws many visitors who want to see the best in the world's products, advertisements, and innovations. The Indonesian government asked me to consider acting as a brand ambassador for Indonesia to share positive impressions with others that I have about the Indonesia's economic and social progress. This is a non-pecuniary relationship and I gladly accepted.

What message do you have for emerging markets like China and India?

I would stress the following:

• Let their markets be as free as possible for entrepreneurs to start a business and for existing companies to conduct their business. Keep regulations to a minimum. Too often, regulations become a corrupting tool requiring payoffs to regulators to perform something that is prohibited.

• Identify those industries in which that country is especially gifted. China has become the *world's factory* as a result of its low-cost labor and its ability to copy and master modern production techniques. India, while not as good at production, is superb at becoming the *world's office* because of its low cost professional trained labor and facility with the English language.

• The government should play a lead role in identifying which additional industries to initiate with an early capital investment in a public-private ownership arrangement.

• The country should encourage foreign capital to invest in the country and earn good returns. If the country only relies on its own resources to grow important industries, the country will improve much more slowly.

Your latest book – *Confronting Capitalism* – was quite a shift from the more traditional fare we've been accustomed to as marketers. What made you write that book?

Although most of my writing and teaching have centered on marketing, I always approached marketing as an economist hoping to help firms maximize their long run sales and profits. I received my Master's degree in economics at the University of Chicago from Milton Friedman, the Nobel Prize economist, who advocated free competitive markets with little or no regulation except to prevent monopolies or collusion. I received my Ph.D. in economics at M.I.T. from two other

Nobel Prize economists, Paul Samuelson and Robert Solow, who turned me on to Keynesian economics.

I mention this because my latest book, *Confronting Capitalism*, is my returning to the economist in me who is interested in assessing the performance of Capitalism itself. I came to the conclusion that **marketing is an essential ingredient in Capitalism**. People have very limited incomes. Marketers compete to sell their goods to people who may need to borrow money to buy a car, home, furniture and other expensive goods. Marketing has been practiced as the art of getting people to part with their money and borrow more than might be wise. If marketers are not good at their marketing, many goods will fail to sell, many jobs will be cut, and many businesses will close down. Effective marketing is essential to keep a Capitalist economy going.

My book *Confronting Capitalism* carries **the idea that Capitalism is in danger of destroying itself** by limiting its great benefits to too few people. Most workers have not had an increase in their real wages since 1973 while the 1% has continued to grow richer and richer. Our growing productivity and profits has not "trickled down" and led to "all boats rising."

In *Confronting Capitalism*, I examined **14 problems** that modern Capitalism must address so that more citizens share in our growing GDP. In fact, our GDP would grow faster if more money got into the hands of our working and middle income classes.

A small group of friends and I started a site called **fixcapitalism.com** where we feature provocative articles on how to *make Capitalism work better* for more people. I invite your readers to join us. We also have a channel on *Huffington Post*.

You've written over 60 books. I have to ask: what's the next book about? What else are you working on?

My last book was *Democracy in Decline: Rebuilding its Future*. Just as I identified 14 shortcomings in Capitalism hurting its performance, I have identified 12 shortcomings in our modern Democracy blocking it from serving our citizens well.

Our two systems, Capitalism and Democracy, have an interesting impact on each other. Capitalism is a system flush with money that goes into lobbying in the interests of business and into electing candidates who favor the interests of the rich.

Capitalism is affecting our Democracy by using wealth to determine who gets elected to Congress and whose interests they will primarily represent. We badly need *to shorten our election period*, now 3 1/2 years from the first candidate announcing that he or she is seeking to be the next President to November 8, when the final ballots are cast. We must find *another way to finance candidates* who seek to run for President.

Today's candidates are all backed by billionaires with an interest in preserving and expanding their capital and wealth.

You have made a distinction between companies that care about their social obligations and companies that don't. Why is this such a big deal? Economists used to say that the only responsibility of business is to make a profit. Many companies still believe that. What do you say to that?

The idea of brand activism is not really a new one. In our book, *Corporate Social Responsibility*, we interviewed 45 companies. We asked each company: "Do you give money to charity? Have you adopted a favorite cause? Why did you choose that cause? Do you monitor whether the money has helped the cause? Do you know whether your company's reputation improved as a result?"

Our book shows the findings.

Consumers who are interested in buying from caring companies will have a better sense of whether the caring is real or just window-dressing.

But what is now critical is to understand is that the landscape has changed.

Millennials led the way, but now most customers have high expectations for brands. We live in a world filled with constant problems – air pollution, bad drinking water, crimes, income inequality.

The brands that show real concern not just for profits but for the communities they serve, and the world we live in are the ones that are coming to the forefront.

A caring company must make its activities visible to its customers. It needs to show its values and commitments early, and that it cares about its people, cities, communities, and the planet.

If you present the evidence, customers will reward you.

More and more customers are become aware of their voting power in the market place and that they favor buying from caring companies.

And when you add social media to the mix, there is "instant activism."

What do you think of the recent scuffle between Kraft Heinz and Unilever?

That is exactly the issue. We are fighting a battle, as Bill George says, for the Soul of Capitalism.

As George explains, you have Unilever CEO Paul Polman championing sustainable growth in earnings to raise long-term shareholder value. On the other side, you have KHC's Bernardo Vieira Hees and its Brazilian owner 3G Capital. They want to maximize short-term earnings to increase near-term valuation.

Of course, the outcry was loud, and 3G withdrew its offer just 50 hours after it was made.

I agree with George when he says that the *larger issue at stake here is not just the fate of a single company, but the fate of capitalism itself.*

Is it really that bleak? What can businesses do to understand their place in society?

We have a disconnect. Businesses that think they exist independent of society are not going to last. Perhaps it is the fault of our MBA education and perhaps it is the fault of our business culture that still emphasizes "maximizing shareholder value."

Even **Jack Welch** is now reversing his philosophy. In his now infamous interview with the *Financial Times* he tells us – "On the face of it, shareholder value is the dumbest idea in the world. Shareholder value is a result, not a strategy… your main constituencies are your employees, your customers and your products. Managers and investors should not set share price increases as their overarching goal. … Short-term profits should be allied with an increase in the long-term value of a company."

Where did this idea of "maximizing shareholder value" come from?

I think it was Roger Martin who said that this mess begins with Michael Jensen and Dean William Meckling of the Simon School of Business at the University of Rochester. They published "Theory of the Firm: Managerial Behavior, Agency Costs and Ownership Structure" in the *Journal of Financial Economics*. That was in 1976.

The article was intellectually and philosophically incorrect. It basically said that shareholders are the owner of the business, while the executives are agents who are hired by the principals to work on their behalf. Jensen and Meckling argued that the goal of a company should be to maximize the return to shareholders.

And that was the biggest scam in business. Now anything goes under the mantra of "maximizing shareholder value."

What do you mean?

Well, let's reference Peter Drucker. He tells us that the only valid purpose of a firm is to create a customer. I am convinced that the polarization in society, the stark rise in income inequality and the staggering rise in the levels of CEO pay are directly related.

I agree with Bill George when he says that unconstrained capitalism focusing on short-term gains can cause great harm to employees, communities and the greater needs of society.

And it is precisely because of this that we have the rise of populism around the world.

Our titans of industry are shooting themselves in the foot by not comprehending the existential threat populism holds for the future of their businesses.

But isn't this really about price? Don't customers deserve the best and lowest prices?

That is again a misapplication of the philosophy that low prices are the end-all.

Do we really want low-prices that are the result of exploitation, slave labor, or environmental degradation on the other side of the globe? The true cost of low prices is that the cost is borne by society – to its detriment.

Globalization has brought many changes, and as we are learning now, not all of them were good. The feelings of powerlessness and frustration in a world dominated by wealthy elites has led to the resurgence of nationalism, protectionism, and growing threats of war and violence.

Our business leaders forgot their history.

Let's discuss the concept of Demarketing. How does that play into all of this?

We have built this unsustainable world on the backs of consumer debt.

The question is how do we get people to use a scarce resource more carefully.

We started thinking about this in our 1971 article called *Demarketing, Yes, Demarketing.*

The 4Ps (product, price, place, promotion) provide solutions:

First, we design products that will use less water, such as by designing more efficient showerheads. Second, we raise the price of water to discourage consumption. Third, we make less water available in certain channels. Fourth, we use promotion to make people more ashamed of wasting water.

The demarketing idea is very generic. We just reverse the direction of the 4 Ps.

Make the product less necessary, more expensive, less available, and more shameful. Companies like Patagonia will sell you a jacket that lasts a lifetime. They'll even repair it for you. This is good sense. It should be a best practice for the future of product development.

Does the conflict also arise out of the power structure within organizations? How many CEOs were promoted from sales, where they are responsible for "maximizing revenue"?

If you look at a study done by *Harvard Business Review* on the *Best Performing CEOs*, we learn that there are so many reasons for leaders to focus on the short term: slow growth, shareholder activism, political turmoil—to name just a few. Yet the study highlights the CEOs that still manage to focus on the long term and deliver strong performance over many years. Prior to 2015, the rankings were based *purely on financial returns*; by that measure Jeff Bezos of Amazon led the pack for three years running.

What's interesting is that when *HBR* started including ratings of companies' environmental, social, and governance (ESG) performance as a variable, there was a big shift in ranking.

There's a profound discussion led by Adi Ignatius on this – with Novo Nordisk CEO Lars Rebien Sørensen, WPP CEO Martin Sorrell, and Inditex CEO Pablo Isla – the three top ranked CEOs based on paying attention to their ESG performance.

So how should businesses change? How can they become more caring and still balance profit-making with the future?

Perhaps the best explanation of this comes from **Ratan Tata** who tells us that:

Profits are like happiness in that they are a byproduct of other things. Happiness, for example, can stem from having a strong sense of purpose, meaningful work and deep relationships. Those who focus obsessively on their own happiness are usually narcissists — and end up miserable. Similarly, companies need a purpose that transcends making money; they need sustainability strategies that recognize that you can make money by doing good things rather than the other way around.

Marketers need to lead the way, working with their CEOs to nurture the future. The $64,000 question is: How do we create and nurture markets, communities, and the future of society?

If folks are interested, I encourage them to visit **fixcapitalism.com**.

Thanks so much for your time. You have inspired so many of us over the past 50 years!

INTERVIEW by ***Christian Sarkar***

Six Epilogues

Epilogue 1. Do I ever relax?

Many friends say they view me as a writing machine. How else could I have written over 60 books? My answer is that I gave up watching TV sports events. Many people spend their leisure time watching baseball, football, hockey, soccer and other endless sports events. I enjoy them too. I just enjoy producing more than consuming.

I do acknowledge the importance of a healthy body and mind. I played tennis for over 50 years. My only regret is that I didn't hire a tennis trainer. I played a good game but I could have learned to play a better game. I enjoyed biking but never did much with it. I now look enviously on my friend Gary Massel who at the age of 60 took up serious biking. He bought a $15,000 bike and rides alone or with groups for 20 or 30 miles at a time. Another friend, Michael Lyon, goes to Europe and bikes in new locations each time. He ended up writing an excellent book on the best bike trails in Europe. I regret not taking biking more seriously.

I want to thank James Ward for helping my academic life run smoothly, and Steve Schewe and Deborah Leslie for helping me keep my body fit.

James Ward

James Ward has been my indispensable Kellogg staff assistant for nearly the last 20 years. He has helped me print my work assignments, order marketing cases, magazines and journal subscriptions, arrange foreign and domestic flights, find missing books and notes, and manage my mail and phone calls. James is the most wonderful caring person. I can leave the country and know that James will take care of everything.

James Ward, my indispensable Kellogg staff assistant

Steve Schewe

I never did much exercising until age 70. I have a home in Longboat Key, Florida and on an impulse, I walked into a gym and met one of the trainers, Steve Schewe. I enjoyed the first session and I decided to sign up for a Monday-Thursday one-hour training each week. Steve has been training people like me for over 40 years. Steve started in Los Angeles. He showed me a photo taken when he was 12 years old sitting next to a tall 14 year old, none other than Arnold Schwarzenegger, later the governor of California. I was hoping for an introduction to Schwarzenegger but Steve said that he lost contact with him.

Steve Schewe, gifted trainer and nutritionist, Sarasota, Florida

I look forward to each training session with Steve. Our sessions now take place in the gym in my condominium in Florida. Steve left the training group and he prefers to do in-home training. As I pump iron, he shares a few new jokes and we chat about the crazy election politics and also how to market his business. He does a super job of self-marketing, putting out a news blog, planting his business cards in various condominium gyms, and attracting a newspaper interview from time to time. I enjoy his Facebook page where he shares exercise and nutritional ideas. Steve is extremely knowledgeable about human anatomy and about nutritional health. His first question each session is: "What did you eat yesterday." I confess to eating too many sweets and carbohydrates and failing to drink enough water. So, he operates on my conscience and I find myself eating a little more wisely each time.

Steve introduced me to an unusual form of exercise. Suddenly I was a boxer. Steve wears a special boxing glove and I use a pair of regular boxing gloves. Then he trains me on how to jab, swing a cross cut, then an upper cut. After 5 minutes of punching away, I feel ready to engage in a real boxing match. At this point, however, we take off our gloves and catch our breath. Steve has offered to train me to earn a black belt, but at this point I am happy to return to muscle building and stretching exercises and treadmill aerobics.

Deborah Leslie

Every Tuesday and Friday I schedule one hour massages with a wonderful body therapist and trainer, Deborah Leslie. Debbie is a born athlete who entered triathlon contests where athletes compete by going through three endurance disciplines, swimming, cycling, and running. Debbie also occasionally enters a long swimming contest such as a 12-mile swim off the coast of Key West.

For her professional life, Debbie trained to be a massage therapist. Debbie is able to put me in a mental state where I completely let go of all thought. I end up feeling that I am floating. I rise feeling totally refreshed. Debbie also leads Nancy and me in wonderful yoga positions and stretches. For over a half-hour, we follow Debbie in bending, standing on one leg, stretching into a warrior position, along with a sequence of 10 other postures and exercises. Debbie has turned out to be a wonderful friend to Nancy and me.

Deborah Leslie, massage therapist and trainer

Epilogue 2. Thanks to Great Friends and Mentors

One's life is shaped by one's family, early friends and schooling, the times, and chance circumstances. I owe so much to my parents Betty and Maurice Kotler and to my two brothers, Milton and Neil Kotler. I owe so much to my lovely wife Nancy. Life is enriched by social friends of which Nancy and I have been blessed with many.

Certain people come into one's life at different times and they have a major impact on that person's career and future. Some of my university professors have greatly influenced me, such as Milton Friedman, Paul Samuelson, Robert Solow, and David Riesman. I owe a great deal to the following circumstantial shapers of my life: Don Jacobs (USA), Dipak Jain (USA), Sidney Levy (USA), Gerald Zaltman (USA), Gary Armstrong (USA), Kevin Keller (USA), Steven High (USA), John Caslione (USA), Irving Rein (USA), Mohan Sawhney (USA), Bala Balachandran (USA), Joanne Bernstein (USA), Hiroko Osaka (USA), Robert Wolcott (USA), Howard Tullman (USA), Nancy Lee (USA), Christian Sarkar (USA), Werner Erhard (USA), Fahim Kibria (Canada), Pietro Guido (Italy), Christer Engleus (Sweden), Heribert Meffert (Germany), Waldemar Pfoertsch (Germany), Richard Straub (Austria), Fernando Trias de Bes (Spain), Jose Salibi Neto (Brazil), Ned Roberto (Philippines), Walter Vieira (India), Hermawan Kartajaya (Indonesia), Xavier López Ancona (Mexico), Somkid Jatusripitak (Thailand), Suvit Maesincee (Thailand), Hooi Den Hua (Singapore), and "Tiger" Caohu (China). I mentioned most of these special people in earlier stories. They are in the best position to know why I thank them personally in this book.

Epilogue 3. Thanks to Nikkei in Japan

This book exists thanks to Nikkei. They invited me to write 30 columns about my life that led to the writing My Adventures in Marketing.

Thanks to Mr. Tanaka at Nikkei and Mr. Goa at the Japan Marketing Association, and my former student Mitsu Shibata. I was so carried away with the assignment that I ended up writing 57 columns.

Mr. Goa, Tanaka, Philip Kotler, Mitsu Shibata

I send my best wishes to the people of Japan. I know that Japan will reach a turnaround point in its trajectory and will show renewed energy and power to advance its place among the world's strongest economies.

Epilogue 4. A friend's letter

Sometimes a friend grasps better what another person's life is about than the person himself. I received this recent birthday greeting from a wise friend:

Phil,

No one we know has discovered a way of finding joy in life and pleasure in people as you do. You also seem to live in a universe of adventures:

- *In widening the boundaries of your field*
- *In bringing coherence to the large questions of our times*
- *In tackling projects "easily" that leave us breathless by their boldness and scope.*

To us, having you for a treasured friend is the very best of all.

Epilogue 5. Family

Jessica's Family: Upper level: Dan and Jessica Stahl.
Lower level: Dante, Sapphire, Shaina

Amy's Family: Jordan, Amy, Dan, Ellie, Jamie, and Abby

Melissa's Family: Steve, Melissa, Sam, and Olivia

Epilogue 6. To Nancy, my love and closest friend, who has had the greatest influence on my life and happiness.

Philip and Nancy Kotler

Philip and Nancy Kotler

Philip and Nancy Kotler

Publications

Philip Kotler

S.C. Johnson & Son Distinguished Professor of International Marketing, Kellogg School of Management, Northwestern University

BOOKS

1. Philip Kotler, *Marketing Management: Analysis, Planning, and Control*, Prentice-Hall, 1967. (Now in the 15th edition). Kevin Lane Keller joined as in 2006.

2. Philip Kotler, Gerald Zaltman, and Ira Kaufman, *Creating Social Change*, Holt, Rinehart, and Winston, 1972.

3. Philip Kotler, *Marketing Decision Making: A Model-Building Approach*, Prentice-Hall, 1972.

4. Philip Kotler, Harold Guetzkow, and Randall L. Schultz, *Simulation in Social Administrative Science: Overviews and Case-Examples*, Prentice-Hall, 1972.

5. Philip Kotler, *Strategic Marketing for Nonprofit Organizations*, Prentice-Hall, 1975. (Now in its 7th edition). Alan Andreasen joined as in 1986.

6. Philip Kotler, *Principles of Marketing*, Prentice-Hall, 1980. (Now in its 16th edition). Gary Armstrong joined as in 1989.

7. Philip Kotler and Gary Lilien, *Marketing Models*, Harper & Row, 1983. Revised in 1992 and published by Prentice-Hall with the addition of K. Sridhar Moorthy as third author.)

8. Philip Kotler, *Marketing Essentials*, (later changed to Marketing-An Introduction), Prentice-Hall 1984. Now in the 10th edition.* Gary Armstrong joined in 1990.

9. Philip Kotler, *Marketing Professional Services*, Prentice-Hall, 1984, 2002. Paul N. Bloom in the first edition and Tom Hayes joined us in the second edition.

10. Philip Kotler and Karen Fox, *Strategic Marketing for Educational Institutions*, Prentice-Hall 1985, 1995.

11. Philip Kotler, Liam Fahey, and Somkid Jatusripitak, *The New Competition: What Theory Z Didn't Tell You About – Marketing*, Prentice-Hall, 1985.

12. Philip Kotler and Roberta N. Clarke, *Marketing for Health Care Organizations*, Prentice-Hall, 1987.

13. Irving Rein, Philip Kotler, and Marty Stoller, *High Visibility: The Making and Marketing of Professionals into Celebrities*, Dodd, Mead, & Co., 1987, 1998, 2006.

14. Philip Kotler and Eduardo Roberto, *Social Marketing: Strategies for Changing Public Behavior*, The Free Press, 1989.

15. Philip Kotler, Norman Shawchuck, Bruce Wrenn, and Gustave Rath, *Marketing for Congregations: Choosing to Serve People More Effectively*, Abingdon Press, 1992. (Revised in 2009 as *Building Strong Congregations*).

16. Philip Kotler, Irving Rein, and Donald Haider, *Marketing Places: Attracting Investment, Industry, and Tourism to Cities, States, and Nations*, The Free Press, 1993.

17. Philip Kotler, John Bowen, and James Makens, *Marketing for Hospitality and Tourism*, Prentice-Hall, 1996. (Now in the 6th edition.)

18. Philip Kotler, Gary Armstrong, and Veronica Wong, *Principles of Marketing - European Edition*, Prentice-Hall Europe, 1996. (Now in the 4th edition).

19. Philip Kotler, Somkid Jatusripitak, and Suvit Maesincee, *The Marketing of*

Nations: A Strategic Approach to Building National Wealth, The Free Press, 1997.

20. Philip Kotler and Joanne Scheff, *Standing Room Only: Strategies for Marketing the Performing Arts,* Harvard Business School Press, 1997.

21. Neil Kotler and Philip Kotler, *Museum Strategy and Marketing: Designing Missions, Building Audiences, Generating Revenue and Resources,* Jossey Bass, 1998, 2008.

22. Philip Kotler, *Kotler on Marketing: How to Create, Win, and Dominate Markets*, The Free Press, 1999.

23. Philip Kotler, Swee Hoon Ang, Siew Meng Leong, and Chin Tiong Tan, *Marketing Management-An Asian Perspective*, Prentice-Hall, 1999, 2006.

24. Philip Kotler, Irving Rein, Donald Haider, and Christer Asplund, *Marketing Places Europe*, Financial Times, 1999.

25. Philip Kotler and Hermawan Kartajaya, *Repositioning Asia: From Bubble to Sustainable Economy*, Wiley, 2000.

26. Philip Kotler, Michael Hamlin, Irving Rein, and Donald Haider, *Marketing Asian Places: Attracting Investment, Industry, and Tourism to Cities, States, and Nations*, Wiley, 2001.

27. Philip Kotler, *A Framework for Marketing Management*, Prentice-Hall, 2001 (Now in the 5th edition).

28. Philip Kotler, Dipak Jain, and Suvit Maesincee, *Marketing Moves: A New Approach to Profits, Growth, and Renewal,* Harvard Business School, 2002.

29. Philip Kotler, Nancy Lee and Eduardo Roberto, *Social Marketing: Improving the Quality of Life*, The Free Press, 2002. (5th edition with title, Social Marketing: Influencing Behaviors for Good, Sage, 2008).

30. Philip Kotler, *Marketing Insights from A to Z: 80 Concepts Every Manager Needs to Know*, Wiley, 2003.

31. Francoise Simon and Philip Kotler, *Global Biobrands: Taking Biotechnology to Market*, The Free Press, 2003.

32. Philip Kotler, Hermawan Kartajaya, Hooi Den Hua, and Sandra Liu, *Rethinking Marketing: Sustainable Marketing Enterprise in Asia,* Prentice-Hall, 2003.

33. Philip Kotler and Fernando Trias de Bes, *Lateral Marketing: A New Approach to Finding Product, Market, and Marketing Mix Ideas*, Wiley, 2003.

34. Philip Kotler, Ten Deadly Marketing Sins: Signs and Solutions, Wiley, 2004.

35. Philip Kotler, Hermawan Kartajaya, and David Young, *Attracting Investors: A Marketing Approach to Finding Funds for Your Business*, Wiley, 2004.

36. Philip Kotler and Nancy R. Lee, *Corporate Social Responsibility: Doing the Most Good for Your Company and Your Cause*, Wiley, 2005.

37. Philip Kotler, *According to Kotler: The World's Foremost Authority on Marketing Answers All Your Questions*, AMACOM, 2005.

38. Philip Kotler and Waldemar Pfoertsch, *B2B Brand Management*, Springer, 2006.

39. Philip Kotler, David Gertner, Irving Rein, and Donald Haider, *Marketing Places, Latin America*, Makron and Paidos, 2006.

40. Irving Rein, Philip Kotler, and Ben Shields, *The Elusive Fan: Reinventing Sports in a Crowded Marketplace*, McGraw-Hill, 2006.

41. Philip Kotler and Nancy R. Lee, *Marketing in the Public Sector: A Roadmap for Improved Performance*, Wharton School Publishing, 2006.

42. Philip Kotler, Hermawan Kartajaya, and Hooi Den Hua, *Think ASEAN: Rethinking Marketing Toward ASEAN Community* 2015, McGraw-Hill, 2007.

43. Philip Kotler, Joel Shalowitz, and Robert Stevens, *Strategic Marketing for Health*

Care Organization: Building a Customer Driven Health Care System, Jossey-Bass, 2008.

44. Philip Kotler and John A. Caslione, *Chaotics: The Business of Managing and Marketing in the Age of Turbulence* (New York: AMACOM, Spring 2009).

45. Philip Kotler and Nancy R. Lee, *Up and Out of Poverty: The Social Marketing Solution* (Philadelphia: Wharton School Publishing, Spring 2009). (A winner in the 800-CEO-Read Business Book Awards for 2009).

46. Hong Cheng, Philip Kotler and Nancy R. Lee, *Social Marketing for Public Health: Global Trends and Success Stories,* Sudbury, Ma. Jones and Bartlett, 2011.

47. Philip Kotler, Hermawan Kartajaya, and Iwan Setiawan, *Marketing 3.0: From Products to Customers to the Human Spirit* (Wiley, 2010).

48. Bruce Wrenn, Philip Kotler, and Norman Shawchuck, *Building Strong Congregations,* Autumn House Publishing, 2010.

49. Philip Kotler and Waldermar Pfoertsch, *Ingredient Branding: Making the Invisible Visible,* Springer 2011.

50. Philip Kotler, Roland Berger, and Nils Bickhoff, *The Quintessence of Strategic Management,* Springer, 2010.

51. Doug McKenzie-Mohr, Nancy R. Lee, P. Wesley Schultz, and Philip Kotler, *Social Marketing to Protect the Environment: What Works.* Sage 2012.

52. Fernando Trias de Bes and Philip Kotler, *Winning at Innovation: The A to F Model.* Palgrave, 2012.

53. Philip Kotler, David Hessekiel, and Nancy R. Lee, *Good Works! Marketing and Corporate Initiatives that Build a Better World...and the Bottom Line,* Wiley, 2013. (Voted 4th best marketing book of the year by Expert Marketing Magazine EMM)

54. Adam Lindgreen, Philip Kotler, Joelle Vanhamme and Francoise Maon, *A Stakeholder Approach to Corporate Social Responsibility: Pressures, Conflicts and Reconciliation,* London, UK, Gower, 2012.

55. Philip Kotler and Milton Kotler, *Market Your Way to Growth: Eight Ways to Win,* Wiley, 2013.

56. Philip Kotler, Kevin Keller, Salah S. Hassan, Imad B. Baalbaki, and Hamed M. Shamma, *Marketing Management (Arab World Edition),* Pearson Higher Education, 2012.

57. Philip and Milton Kotler, *Winning Global Markets: How Businesses Invest and Prosper in the World's High Growth Cities,* Wiley 2015. (Voted #3 of the 20 top marketing books in 2015.

58. Philip Kotler, *Confronting Capitalism: Real Solutions for a Troubled Economic System,* AMACOM, 2015.

59. Philip Kotler, Hermawan Kartajaya and Hooi Den Hua, *Think ASEAN: Rethinking Marketing Toward ASEAN Community* 2015, McGraw-Hill, 2007.

60. Philip Kotler, Marian Dingena, and Waldemar Pfoertsch, *Transformational Sales,* Springer 2016.

61. Philip Kotler, *Democracy in Decline: Rebuilding its Future,* Sage 2016 (July).

62. Philip Kotler, Hermawan Kartajaya, and Hooi Den Huan, *Marketing for Competitiveness: Asia to the World. Into Digital Consumers,* World Scientific Publishing Co., 2017

63. Philip Kotler, Hermawan Kartajaya, and Iwan Setiawan, *Marketing 4.0: Moving from Traditional to Digital,* Wiley, 2017.

64. Svend Hollensen, Philip Kotler, and Marc Oliver Opresnik, *Social Media Marketing: A Practitioner's Guide,* Amazon Direct Publishing, 2017.

65. Philip Kotler, My Adventures in Marketing, Amazon, 2017.

JOURNAL ARTICLES

1.   Philip Kotler, "Elements in a Theory of Growth Stock Valuation," Financial Analysts Journal, May-June, 1962, pp. 3-10. (Winner of the 1962 Graham and Dodd Award for best article of the year in the Financial Analysts Journal.).

2.   Philip Kotler. "The Use of Mathematical Models in Marketing," Journal of Marketing, October 1963, Vol. 27. Issue 4, pp. 31-41.

3.   Philip Kotler, "Marketing Mix Decisions for New Products," Journal of Marketing Research, February 1964, Vol. 1, Issue 1, pp. 43-49.

4.   Philip Kotler, "Toward an Explicit Model for Media Selection," Journal of Advertising Research, March 1964, Vol. 4, No. 1, pp. 34-41. (Winner of the 1964 MacLaren Advertising Research Award and the 1964 Media/Scope Merit Award.)

5.   Philip Kotler, "Quantitative Analysis in Marketing Research," in Reflections on Progress in Marketing, ed. L. George Smith, (Chicago: American Marketing Association, 1965), pp. 651-663.

6.   Philip Kotler, "The Competitive Marketing Simulator - A New Management Tool," California Management Review, Spring 1965, pp. 49-60. (Winner of the McKinsey Award for the second-best article for the year 1964-65 and winner of the 1964 Merit Award of the Chicago Chapter of the American Marketing Association.)

7.   Philip Kotler, "Phasing Out Weak Products," Harvard Business Review, March-April 1965, Vol. 43, Issue 2, pp. 107-118.

8.   Philip Kotler, "Behavioral Models for Analyzing Buyers," Journal of Marketing, October 1965, Vol.29, Issue 4, pp. 37-45.

9.   Philip Kotler, "Competitive Strategies for New Product Marketing Over the Life Cycle," Management Science, December 1965, Vol. 12, No. 4, pp. 104-119.

10.   Philip Kotler, "Diagnosing the Marketing Takeover," Harvard Business Review, November-December 1965, Vol. 43, Issue 6, pp. 70-72.

11.   Philip Kotler, "Profits and the Marketing Concept," Synopsis, Journal of the Belgian National Productivity Center, December 1965, pp. 1-16.

12.   Philip Kotler, "Evaluating Competitive Marketing Strategies through Computer Simulation," in Marketing and Economic Growth, ed. Peter D. Bennett, (Chicago: American Marketing Association, 1966), pp. 338-352.

13.   Philip Kotler, "Computerized Media Selection: Some Notes on the State of the Art," Occasional Papers in Advertising, (Applications of the Sciences in Marketing Management, Special Editor C. H. Sandage) Vol. 1, No. 1, January 1966, pp. 45-52. (Babson Park, MA: American Academy of Advertising, The Babson Institute). (Winner of a Silver Award in the 1965 Thomson Media Research Award Program.)

14.   Philip Kotler, "A Guide to Long-Range Product-Market Planning," Synopsis, Journal of the Belgian National Productivity Center, July-August 1966, pp. 13-24.

15.   "New Mathematics for Marketing Planning," in New Ideas for Successful Marketing, ed. John S. Wright and Jack L. Goldstucker, (Chicago: American Marketing Association, 1966), pp. 507-528.

16. Philip Kotler, "A Design for the Firm's Marketing Nerve Center," Business Horizons, Fall 1966, Vol. 9, Issue 3, pp. 63-74.

17. Philip Kotler, "Operations Research in Marketing," Harvard Business Review, January-February 1967, Vol. 45, Issue 1 pp. 3-188.

18. Philip Kotler, "Computer Simulation in the Analysis of New-Product Decisions," in Applications of the Sciences in Marketing Management, ed. Frank M. Bass, Charles W. King and Edgar A. Pessemier, (NY: John Wiley & Sons, 1968), pp. 281-331.

19. Philip Kotler, "Decision Processes in the Marketing Organization," in Systems: Research and Applications for Marketing, Ed. Daniel Slate and Robert Ferber, (Urbana, IL: University of Illinois, Bureau of Economic and Business Research, 1968), pp. 57-70.

20. Philip Kotler, "Mathematical Models of Individual Buyer Behavior," Behavioral Science, July 1968, Vol. 13, No. 4, pp. 274-287.

21. Philip Kotler, "Marketing Education in the 1970s," in Changing Marketing Systems: Consumer, Corporate, and Government Interface, Ed. Reed Moyer, (Chicago, IL: American Marketing Association, 1969.)

22. Philip Kotler, "Some Needed Extensions in the Theory of Marketing Programming," Proceedings of the 1968 Fall Conference of the American Marketing Association (Chicago, IL: American Marketing Association, 1969.)

23. Philip Kotler and Sidney J. Levy, "Broadening the Concept of Marketing," Journal of Marketing, January 1969, Vol. 33, Issue 1, pp.10-15. (Winner of the 1969 Alpha Kappa Psi Foundation Award for the best 1969 paper in the Journal of Marketing.)

24. Philip Kotler, "Coping with the Complexities of Marketing," The Conference Board Record, January 1969, Vol. 1, Number 1, pp. 53-59.

25. Philip Kotler, "The Future of the Computer in Marketing," Journal of Marketing, January 1970, Vol. 34, Issue 1, pp. 11-14.

26. Sidney J. Levy and Philip Kotler, "Beyond Marketing: The Furthering Concept," California Management Review, Winter 1969, Vol. 12, No. 2, pp. 67-73.

27. Philip Kotler and Randall L. Schultz, "Marketing Simulations: Review and Prospects," Journal of Business of the University of Chicago, July 1970, Vol. 43, No. 3, pp. 237-295.

28. Philip Kotler, "Corporate Models: Better Marketing Plans," Harvard Business Review, July-August 1970, Vol. 48, Issue 4, pp. 135-149.

29. Philip Kotler, "A Guide to Gathering Expert Estimates: The Treatment of Unscientific Data," Business Horizons, October 1970, Vol. 13, Issue 5, pp. 79-87.

30. Philip Kotler, "The Elements of Social Action," American Behavioral Scientist, May-June 1971, Vol. 14, Issue 5, pp. 691-717.

31. Philip Kotler and Gerald Zaltman, "Social Marketing: An Approach to Planned Social Change," Journal of Marketing, July 1971, Vol. 35, Issue 3, pp. 3-12. (Winner of the 1971 Alpha Kappa Psi Foundation Award for the best 1971 article in the Journal of Marketing.)

32. Philip Kotler, "Metamarketing: The Furthering of Organizations, Persons, Places, and Causes," Marketing Forum, July-August 1971, pp. 13-23.

33. Philip Kotler and Sidney J. Levy, "Demarketing, Yes, Demarketing," Harvard Business Review, November-December 1971, Vol. 49, Issue, 6, pp. 74-80.

34. Philip Kotler, "A Generic Concept of Marketing," Journal of Marketing, April 1972, Vol. 36, Issue 2, pp. 46-54. (Winner of the 1972 Alpha Kappa Psi Foundation Award for the best 1972 article in the Journal of Marketing.)

35. Philip Kotler, "What Consumerism Means to Marketers," Harvard Business Review, May-June 1972, Vol. 50, Issue 3, pp. 48-57.

36. Philip Kotler and Sidney J. Levy, "Buying is Marketing, Too!" Journal of Marketing, January 1973, Vol. 37, Issue 1, pp. 54-59.

37. Philip Kotler, Fred C. Allvine, and Paul N. Bloom, "It's Time to Cut Down on Advertising Waste," Business and Society Review, Winter 1972-73, Number 4, pp. 9-18.

38. Philip Kotler, "Atmospherics as a Marketing Tool," Journal of Retailing, Winter 1973-74, Vol. 49, Issue 4, pp. 48-64.

39. Philip Kotler and Bernard Dubois, "Education Problems and Marketing," in Marketing Analysis For Societal Problems, ed. Jagdish N. Sheth and Peter L. Wright, (Urbana, IL.: Bureau of Business and Economic Research, 1974), pp. 186-206.

40. Philip Kotler, "The Major Tasks of Marketing Management," Journal of Marketing, October 1973, Vol. 37, Issue 4, pp. 42-49.

41. Philip Kotler, "Marketing During Periods of Shortage," Journal of Marketing, July 1974, Vol. 38, Issue 3, pp. 20-29.

42. Philip Kotler, "Advertising in the Nonprofit Sector," in Advertising and Society, ed. Yale Brozen, (NY: New York University Press, 1974), pp. 169-189.

43. Paul N. Bloom and Philip Kotler, "Strategies for High Market-Share Companies," Harvard Business Review, November-December 1975, Vol. 53, Issue 6, pp. 63-72.

44. Philip Kotler and Michael Murray, "Third Sector Management - The Role of Marketing," Public Administration Review, September-October 1975, Vol. 35, Issue 5, pp. 467-472. (Part winner of the Dimock Award, awarded to articles judged to present the most "innovative solutions for the 70s.")

45. Philip Kotler and V. Balachandran, "Strategic Remarketing: The Preferred Response to Shortages and Inflation," Sloan Management Review, Fall 1975, Vol. 17, Issue 1, pp. 1-17.

46. Philip Kotler and Gerald Zaltman, "Targeting Prospects for a New Product," Journal of Advertising Research, Feb 1976, Vol. 16, Issue 1, pp. 7-20.

47. Philip Kotler and Richard A. Connor, Jr., "Marketing Professional Services," Journal of Marketing, January 1977, Vol. 41, Issue 1, pp. 71-76.

48. Philip Kotler, "Applying Marketing Theory to College Admissions," in A Role for Marketing in College Admissions, by the College Entrance Examination Board, pp. 54-72, (NY: College Entrance Board, 1976).

49. Philip Kotler, William Gregor, and William Rodgers, "The Marketing Audit Comes of Age," Sloan Management Review, Winter 1977, Vol. 18, Issue 2, pp. 25-43.

50. Philip Kotler, "From Sales Obsession to Marketing Effectiveness," Harvard Business Review, November-December 1977, Vol. 55, Issue 6, pp. 67-75.

51. Philip Kotler, "Marketing's Drive to Maturity," in Changing Marketing Strategies in a New Economy, ed. Jules Backman and John A. Czepiel, (Indianapolis: Bobbs-Merrill Education Publishing, 1977), pp. 43-64.

52. Philip Kotler and Lenore Borzak, "The Market for Personal Growth Services," in Advances in Consumer Research, ed. H. Keith Hunt, Vol. 5, (Ann Arbor, MI: Association for Consumer Research, 1978), pp. 290-294.

53. Philip Kotler, "Axioms for Societal Marketing," in New Frontiers for Marketing, ed. George Fisk, Johan Arndt, and Kjell Gronhaug, 1978.

54. Philip Kotler, "Marketing," in Handbook of Operations Research, Chapter 3, Section 1, Vol. 2 (NY: Van Nostrand Reinhold Company, 1978).

55. Philip Kotler, "Harvesting Strategies for Weak Products," Business Horizons, August 1978, Vol. 21, Issue 4, pp. 15-22.

56. Philip Kotler and William Mindak, "Marketing and Public Relations: Should They Be Partners or Rivals?" Journal of Marketing, October 1978, Vol. 42, Issue 4, pp. 13-20.

57. Philip Kotler, "Educational Packagers: A Modest Proposal," The Futurist, August 1978, Vol. 12, No. 4, pp. 239-242.

58. Philip Kotler, "A Critical Assessment of Marketing Theory and Practice," in Diffusing Marketing Theory and Research: The Contributions of Bauer, Green, Kotler and Levitt, ed. Alan R. Andreasen and David M. Gardner, (Champaign, IL: The University of Illinois Press, 1978).

59. Philip Kotler, "Strategies for Introducing Marketing into Nonprofit Organizations," Journal of Marketing, January 1979, Vol. 43, Issue 1, pp. 37-44.

60. Philip Kotler, "The Future Marketing Manager," in Proceedings of the American Marketing Association, ed. Betsy Gelb, 1978.

61. Philip Kotler, "Market Challenger Strategies," in Handbook of Business Planning and Budgeting for Executives with Profit Responsibility, ed. Thomas S. Dudick and Robert V. Gorski. (NY: Van Nostrand Reinhold, 1980) pp. 66-70.

62. Arthur Sterngold and Philip Kotler, "A Marketing Approach to Energy Conservation," in The Conserver Society, ed. Karl Henion II and Thomas Kinnear, (Chicago, IL: American Marketing Association, 1979), pp. 193-207.

63. Karen F.A. Fox and Philip Kotler, "The Marketing of Social Causes: The First 10 Years," Journal of Marketing, Fall 1980, Vol. 44, No. 4, pp. 24-33.

64. Philip Kotler and Patrick E. Murphy, "Strategic Planning for Higher Education," Journal of Higher Education, September-October 1981, Vol. 52, No. 5, pp. 470-489.

65. Philip Kotler and Ravi Singh (Achrol), "Marketing Warfare in the 1980s," Journal of Business Strategy, Winter 1981, Vol. 1, Issue 3, pp. 30-41.

66. Philip Kotler and Neil Kotler, "Business Marketing for Political Candidates," Campaigns and Elections, Summer 1981, pp. 24-33.

67. Karen F.A. Fox and Philip Kotler, "Reducing Cigarette Smoking: An Opportunity for Social Marketing?" Journal of Health Care Marketing, Winter 1980-81, Vol. 1, Issue 1 pp. 8-17.

68. Philip Kotler and Liam Fahey, "The World's Champion Marketers: The Japanese," Journal of Business Strategy, Summer 1982, Vol. 3, Issue 1, page 3-13.

69. Philip Kotler and Leslie A. Goldgehn, "Marketing: A Definition for Community Colleges," in New Directions for Community Colleges: Marketing the Program, ed. William and Marybelle Keim, (San Francisco: Jossey-Bass Inc., 1981).

70. Philip Kotler, ""Dream" Vacations: The Booming Market for Designed Experiences," The Futurist, October 1984, Vol. 18, Issue 5, pp. 7-13.

71. Philip Kotler and G. Alexander Rath, "Design: A Powerful But Neglected Strategic Tool," Journal of Business Strategy, Fall 1984, Vol. 5, Issue 2 pp. 16-21.

72. Somkid Jatusripitak, Liam Fahey, and Philip Kotler, "Strategic Global Marketing: Lessons from the Japanese," Columbia Journal of World Business, Spring 1985, Vol. 20, Issue 1, pp. 47-53.

73. Philip Kotler and Murali K. Mantrala, "Flawed Products: Consumer Responses and Marketer Strategies," Journal of Consumer Marketing, Summer 1985, Vol. 2, No. 3, pp. 27-36.

74. Philip Kotler and Liam Fahey, "Japanese Strategic Marketing: An Overview," in Strategic Marketing and Management, ed. Howard Thomas and David Gardner (NY: John Wiley & Sons, Inc., 1985), pp. 441-451.

75. Karen F.A. Fox and Philip Kotler, "Strategic Marketing for New Programs," Selections (The Magazine of the Graduate Management Admissions Council), Autumn 1984, pp. 15-22.

76. Philip Kotler and Karen F.A. Fox, "The Marketing Planning Process," Journal of Higher Education Management, Summer/Fall 1985, pp. 33-55.

77. Philip Kotler, "Megamarketing," Harvard Business Review, March/April 1986, Vol. 64, Issue 2, pp. 117-124.

78. Philip Kotler, "Prosumers: A New Type of Consumer," The Futurist, September/October 1986, Vol. 20, Issue 5, pp. 24-28.

79. Philip Kotler, "How to Set the Hospital's Marketing Budget," Journal of Health Care Marketing, March 1986, Vol. 6, No. 1 pp. 7-12.

80. Philip Kotler and Roberta E. Clark, "Creating the Responsive Organization," Healthcare Forum, May/June 1986, pp. 26-32.

81. Philip Kotler, "Idea Management," AWH Healthcare Forum, March/April 1986, pp. 45-48.

82. Philip Kotler, "Global Standardization - Courting Danger," Journal of Consumer Marketing, Spring 1986, Vol. 3, No. 2, pp. 13-15.

83. Philip Kotler, "Global Marketing Strategies," in Protectionism: Can American Business Overcome It, ed. Douglas Lamont (Indianapolis, In: Books Craft, Inc., 1986).

84. Philip Kotler, "Meeting the New Competition from Japan and the Far East," Journal of Global Marketing.

85. Philip Kotler, "Semiotics of Person and Nation Marketing," in Marketing and Semiotics, ed. by Jean Umiker-Sebeok, (Berlin; Paris: Mouton de Gruyer, 1987) pp. 3-12.

86. Philip Kotler, "The Convenience Store: Past Developments and Future Prospects," in Historical Perspectives in Marketing: Essays in honor of Stanley C. Hollander, ed. Terrence Nevett and Ronald A. Fullerton (Lexington, MA: Lexington Books, 1988), pp. 163-175.

87. Philip Kotler, "Humanistic Marketing: Beyond the Marketing Concept," in Philosophical and Radical Thought in Marketing, ed. A. Fuat Firat, Nikhilesh. Dholakia, and Richard P. Bagozzi, (Lexington, MA: Lexington Books, 1987), pp. 271-288.

88. Philip Kotler, "Broadening the Concept of Marketing Still Further: The Megamarketing Concept," in Contemporary Views on Marketing Practice, ed. Gary L. Frazier, and Jagdish N. Sheth. (Lexington, MA: Lexington Books, 1987), pp. 3-18.

89. Philip Kotler, "The Potential Contributions of Marketing Thinking to Economic Development," in Marketing and Development: Toward Broader Dimensions (Research in Marketing, Supplement 4), ed. Erdoğan Kumcu and A. Fuat Firat (Greenwich, Conn. JAI Press Inc., 1988), pp. 1-10.

90. Philip Kotler and Nikhilesh Dholakia, "Ending Global Stagnation: Linking the Fortunes of the Industrial and Developing Countries," Business in the Contemporary World, Spring 1989, pp. 86-97.

91. Philip Kotler, "From Mass Marketing to Mass Customization," Planning Review, September-October 1989, Vol. 17, No. 5, pp. 10-13.

92. Howard Barich and Philip Kotler, "A Framework for Marketing Image Management," Sloan Management Review, Winter 1991, Vol. 32, No. 2, pp. 94-104.

93. Philip Kotler, "Globalization - Realities and Strategies," Die Unternehmung, February 1990, pp. 79-99.

94. Philip Kotler and Paul J. Stonich, "Turbo-Marketing Through Time Compression," Journal of Business Strategy, September/October 1991, Vol. 5, Issue 5, pp. 24-29.

95. Philip Kotler, "It's Time for Total Marketing," Business Week Advance Briefs, Vol. 2, September 1992 pp. 1-21.

96. Philip Kotler, "Marketing's New Paradigm: What's Really Happening Out There," Planning Review (a Publication of the Planning Forum), Conference Special Issue, September-October 1992, Vol. 20, No. 5, pp. 50-52.

97. Philip Kotler and Bruce Wrenn, "The Marketing of Parochial School Modeled as an Exchange Process," Journal of Research on Christian Education, Spring 1993, pp. 119-134.

98. Bruce Wrenn, Norman Shawchuck, Philip Kotler, and Gustave Rath, "What Does It Mean for Pastors to Adopt Market Orientation?" Journal of Ministry Marketing, and Management, Summer 1995, Vol. 1, No. 1, pp. 5-23.

99. Philip Kotler, Donald Haider, and Irving Rein, "There's No Place Like Our Place! The Marketing of Cities, Religions, and Nations," The Futurist, November-December 1993, Vol. 27, No. 6, pp. 14-21.

100. Philip Kotler, Bruce Wrenn, Norman Shawchuck, and Gus Rath, "Can (Should) Religion Be Marketed?" Quarterly Review, Summer 1994, pp. 117-134.

101. Philip Kotler and Alan Andreasen, "Strategic Marketing for Non-Profit Organizations," in Companion Encyclopedia of Marketing, ed. Michael J. Baker, (London: Routledge, 1995), pp. 930-950.

102. William H. Rodgers, Gerard A. Osborne, and Philip Kotler, "Auditing the Marketing Function," in AMA Management Handbook, ed. John J. Hampton, (3rd edition) (N.Y.: AMACOM, 1994).

103. Philip Kotler, "Reconceptualizing Marketing: An Interview with Philip Kotler," European Management Journal, December 1994, Vol. 12, No. 4, pp. 353-361.

104. Philip Kotler, "Marketing and Merchandising," Encyclopedia Britannica, 1995, pp. 495-508.

105. Philip Kotler, "From Mass Marketing to Self-Marketing," in Markt-und Menschenorientierte Unternehmensführung, ed. Bruno Staffelbach and Hans Peter Wehrli, (Essays in honor of Krulis-Randa, University of Zurich, 1996).

106. Joanne Scheff and Philip Kotler, "How the Arts Can Prosper through Strategic Collaborations," Harvard Business Review, January-February, 1996, Vol. 74, Issue 1, pp. 52-62.

107. Joanne Scheff and Philip Kotler, "Crisis in the Arts: The Marketing Response," California Management Review, Fall 1996, Vol. 39, No. 1, pp. 28-52.

108. Philip Kotler, "Mapping the Future Marketplace," in Rethinking the Future: Rethinking Business, Principles, Competition, Control & Complexity, Leadership, Markets, and the World, ed. Rowan Gibson, (London: Nicholas Brealey Publishing, 1997), pp. 196-210.

109. Philip Kotler, "Competitiveness and Civic Character," in The Organization of the Future, ed. Frances Hesselbein, Marshall Goldsmith, and Richard Beckhard (San Francisco: Jossey-Bass, 1997), pp. 151-58.

110. Philip Kotler and Alan R. Andreasen, "Not-for-Profit Marketing," International Encyclopedia of Business and Management, ed. Malcolm Warner. (London: Thompson Publishing, 1996), pp. 3696-3707.

111. Philip Kotler, "Role of the Marketing Department in the Organization of the Future," in Marktorientierte Unternehmensführung: Reflexionen, Denkanstöße, Perspektiven (Frankfurt: Germany, Gabler, 1997), pp. 491-496.

112. Philip Kotler, "Managing Direct and Online Marketing," in Handbuch Database Marketing, ed. Jörg Link, Dieter Brändli, Christian Schleuning, and Roger E. Kehl. IM Fachverlag, Auflage, 1997, pp. 492-511.

113. Philip Kotler and Bernard Dubois, "Le Marketing Direct Interactif: Marketing du 21 ème Siècle?" Revue Francaise de Marketing, No. 164, 1997/4, pp. 43-58.

114. Philip Kotler and Neil Kotler, "Political Marketing—Generating Effective Candidates, Campaigns, and Causes," in Handbook of Political Marketing, ed. Bruce Newman. Sage, 1999, pp. 3-18.

115. Philip Kotler, "The Marketing of Leadership," Leader to Leader, Winter 1999, pp. 22-27.

116. Philip Kotler, "Boards Should Tune in to Corporate Marketing Programs," Directorship, July/August 1999, Vol. 25, (7), pp. 12-13 and 19.

117. Ravi S. Achrol and Philip Kotler, "Marketing in the Network Economy," Journal of Marketing, Special Issue 1999, Vol. 63, (4) pp.146-163.

118. Nirmalya Kumar, Lisa Sheer, and Philip Kotler, "From Market Driven to Market Driving," European Management Journal, April 2000, Vol. 18, No. 2, pp. 129-142.

119. Mohanbir Sawhney and Philip Kotler, "Marketing in the Age of Information Democracy," in Kellogg on Marketing, ed. Dawn Iacobucci. Wiley, 2000, Chapter 13, pp. 386-408.

120. Swee Hoon Ang, Siew Meng Leong, and Philip Kotler, "The Asian Apocalypse: Crisis Marketing for Consumers and Businesses," Long Range Planning, February 2000, Vol. 33, (1), pp. 97-119.

121. Philip Kotler, Dipak Jain, and Suvit Maesincee, "Nine Major Shifts in the New Economy," in Electronic Customer Relationship Management, ed. Andreas Eggert and Georg Fassott. Schäffer-Poeschel, 2001, pp. 15-26.

122. Philip Kotler and Hermawan Kartajaya, "Only the Sustainable Succeed: Lessons from Asian Survivors," Nanyang Business Review, Vol. 1, Number 1, 2002.

123. Neil Kotler and Philip Kotler, "Can Museums Be All Things to All People? Missions, Goals, and Marketing's Role," Museum Management and Curatorship, Vol. 18, No. 3, 2000, pp. 271-287.

124. Philip Kotler and David Gertner, "Country as Brand, Product and Beyond: A Place Marketing and Brand Management Perspective," Journal of Brand Management, April 2002, Vol. 9, (4/5), pp. 249-261.

125. Philip Kotler and Robert Spekman, "The Marketing Consultant," in Handbook of Management Consulting: The Contemporary Consultant, Insights from World Experts, ed. Larry E. Greiner and Flemming Poulfelt. South-Western College Publishing, 2004.

126. Philip Kotler and Nancy Lee, "Best of Breed," Stanford Social Innovation Review, Vol. 1, No. 4, Spring 2004, pp. 14-23.

127. Philip Kotler, "Wrestling with Ethics: Is Marketing Ethics an Oxymoron?" Marketing Management, November-December 2004, Vol. 13, (6), pp. 30-35.

128. David Gertner and Philip Kotler, "How Can a Place Correct a Negative Image," Place Branding, January 2005, Vol. 1, No 1, pp. 50-57.

129. Philip Kotler, "A Three-Part Plan for Upgrading Your Marketing Department for New Challenges," Strategy and Leadership, Vol. 32, No. 5, 2004, pp. 4-9.

130. Philip Kotler, "The Role Played by the Broadening of Marketing Movement in the History of Marketing Thought," Journal of Public Policy and Marketing, May 2005, Vol. 24, (1), pp.114-116.

131. Ravi S. Achrol and Philip Kotler, "The Service-Dominant Logic for Marketing: A Critique," in The Service-Dominant Logic of Marketing: Dialog, Debate, and Directions, ed. Robert F. Lusch and Stephen L. Vargo. M.E. Sharpe, 2006.

132. Philip Kotler, "Ethical Lapses of Marketers," in Does Marketing Need Reform, ed. Jagdish N. Sheth and Rajendra S. Sisodia. M.E. Sharpe, 2006, pp. 153-157.

133. Kevin Lane Keller and Philip Kotler, "Holistic Marketing: A Broad, Integrated Perspective to Marketing Management," in Does Marketing Need Reform, ed. Jagdish N. Sheth and Rajendra S. Sisodia. M.E. Sharpe, 2006, pp. 300-05.

134. Philip Kotler, "Alphabet Soup," Marketing Management, 2006, Vol. 15, (2), p. 51.

135. Philip Kotler, Neil Rackham, and Suj Krishnaswamy, "Ending the War Between Sales and Marketing," Harvard Business Review, July 2006, Vol. 84, (7/8), pp. 68-78.

136. Philip Kotler, Ned Roberto, and Tony Leisner, "Alleviating Poverty: A Macro/Micro Marketing Perspective," Journal of Macromarketing, December 2006, Vol. 26, No. 2, pp. 233-39.

137. Philip Kotler and John C. Westman, "What CEO's Need to Know and Do About Marketing," Leader to Leader Journal, No.42, Fall 2006.

138. Philip Kotler and Nancy R. Lee, "Marketing in the Public Sector: The Final Frontier," The Public Manager, Spring 2007, Vol. 36, (1), pp. 12-17.

139. Philip Kotler and Waldemar Pfoertsch, "Being Known or Being One of Many: The Need for Brand Management for Business-to-Business (B2B) Companies," The Journal of Business & Industrial Marketing, 2007, Vol. 22, No. 6, pp. 357-362.

140. Philip Kotler, "Marketing: The Unappreciated Work Horse," Market Leader, Quarter 2, 2009, pp. 2-4.

141. Philip Kotler, Rob Wolcott, and Suj Chandrasekhar, "Masters of Value and Possibility: Optimizing the Marketing and Research & Development Relationship, Business Insight," *Sloan Management Review.*

142. Robert Shaw and Philip Kotler, "Rethinking the Chain: Make Marketing Leaner, Faster and Better," Marketing Management, July-August 2009, pp.18-23.

143. Philip Kotler and John Caslione, "How Marketers Can Respond to Recession and Turbulence," Journal of Consumer Behavior, Vol 8- Summer 2009, pp. 187-191.

144. Nancy R. Lee and Philip Kotler, "Ending Poverty: "What's Social Marketing Got to Do With It?" SMQ, Winter 2009, pp. 134-40.

145. Robert Shaw and Philip Kotler, "Rethinking the Chain: Leaner, Faster and Better Marketing," Market Leader, Quarter 1, 2010.

146. Kevin Lane Keller and Philip Kotler, "Branding in B2B Firms," in Business to Business Marketing Handbook, eds. Gary L. Lilien and Rajdeep Grewal, Edward Elgar Publishing, forthcoming.

147. Philip Kotler and David Gertner, "A Place Marketing and Brand Management Perspective Revisited," in Nigel Morgan and Annette Prichard's Destination Brands: Managing Place Reputation, 3rd ed., Elsevier, 2011.

148. R. Craig Lefebvre and Philip Kotler, "Design Theory, Demarketing, and Behavioral Economics: Fostering Interdisciplinary Growth in Social Marketing," in Hastings and Bryants, The SAGE Handbook of Social Marketing, 2012.

149. Philip Kotler and Ravi Achrol, " The Frontiers of the Marketing Paradigm in the Third Millenium," Journal of the Academy of Marketing Science (JAMS), ...2012

150. Philip Kotler, "Philip Kotler's Contributions to Marketing Theory and Practice", for volume 8 of Review of Marketing Research: "Special Issue – Marketing Legends".

151. Philip Kotler, "Re-Inventing Marketing to Manage the Environmental Imperative," Journal of Marketing, July 2011 volume 75, pp. 132-135.

152. Philip Kotler, Bobby J. Calder, Edward C. Malthouse and Peter J. Korsten "How Chief Marketing Officers Rate Their Influence," M.I.T. Sloan Management Review, October?

153. Philip and Milton Kotler, "The Global Economy of Cities," Cambridge Review, 2013.

154. Philip Kotler, "What the Presidential Candidates Are Failing to Address About CEO Pay," Fortune Insider, November 11, 2015.

155. Ravi Achrol and Philip Kotler, "Marketing's Last Frontier: The Poor," International Society of Markets and Development (ISMD), Vol.1, No.1, 2016

FOR MORE INFORMATION on PHILIP KOTLER

Visit
www.philkotler.com
www.pkotler.org
www.fixcapitalism.com
www.democracyindecline.com

CURRENT AFFAIRS: SHORT ARTICLES (2016-2017)

- Are Capitalism and Democracy Compatible?
- Are CEOs Overpaid?
- Are We Facing a Jobless World?
- Are We Kissing Democracy Goodbye? (with Christian Sarkar)
- Brand Activism, the Next Stage of Branding
- Can a Company Prosper with More Democracy?
- Can Marketing Improve Capitalism?
- Can You Trust a Socialist to be President?
- Democracy in Decline. An Interview with Philip Kotler
- Do We Really Want Democracy?
- 5 Serious Problems With the Current Election
- Is Trump a Great Business Leader?
- It's Time for a Single-Play Healthcare System
- Killing the Truth: How Trump's Attack on the Free Press Endangers Democracy
- Kulturkampf: Trump's War on the Arts
- Lobbying. The Scourge of Good Government
- Needed. A New Set of Income Tax Brackets
- Our Democracy is Spinning into Rapid Decline
- Social Democracy. The Case for It
- The "Terrorist" in the White House
- The Future of Brand America. Lessons from the Super Bowl and Beyond
- The Robots are Coming. Will America be Able to Produce Enough Jobs?
- Trump Tries to Shut Off Free Speech
- Trump's Plan to Turn America into a Third World Country
- United Airline's Stupidity
- When the Wheels Fall Off Our Democracy

For more info:

www.philkotler.com or www.fixcapitalism.com

'The theory of maximising shareholder value has done great harm to businesses'

He is 81 and still going strong. His *Marketing Management*, the textbook for scholars, is now in its thirteenth edition and still remains an essential read for anyone who hopes to get an MBA degree. He's often called the 'father of marketing' — something he regards as a compliment, while at the same time ceding the title of the 'grandfather of marketing' to management thinker Peter Drucker. Meet **Philip Kotler**, the S C Johnson & Son Distinguished Professor of International Marketing at Northwestern University's Kellogg Graduate School of Management in Chicago, and, in the words of Management Centre Europe, "the world's foremost expert on the strategic practice of marketing." In this freewheeling interview with **Vivek Kaul**, Kotler discusses all things marketing and then some

Philip Kotler

> **6** Smart companies must focus on their stakeholders first — customers, employees, suppliers and distributors — and make sure that these stakeholders are all rewarded appropriately and that they work together as a winning team. Satisfying the stakeholders is the best way to maximise the long-run profitability of the company

> **6** Companies that operate on the triple bottomline — people, planet and profits — will outperform those who only pursue profit

ITC rides non-cigarette segments for fast growth

DNA Correspondent

The L&T boss who wasn't

90%的行銷
在廣告播出前就要完成

科特勒是現代行銷學的集大成者，
被譽為「現代行銷學之父」。

他的《行銷管理》一書，
多年來一直被奉為行銷的聖經。
而他提出行銷人是一種專業，
甚至當今企業經營
該由行銷切入主導的觀念，
更常常引起許多的討論。

在本刊此次越洋採訪中，
科特勒談到他最核心的行銷概念，
也提出台灣應該進行國家品牌行銷。

採訪整理 孫秀惠

297